The Best of

I.F. STONE

ALSO BY I. F. STONE

The Court Disposes (1937)

Business as Usual (1941)

Underground to Palestine (1946)

This is Israel (1948)

*The Hidden History of the
Korean War, 1950–1951* (1952, 1988)

The Truman Era, 1945–1952 (1953, 1988)

In a Time of Torment, 1961–1967 (1967)

The Haunted Fifties (1969)

Polemics and Prophecies, 1967–1970 (1970)

The Killings at Kent State (1971)

The I.F. Stone's Weekly Reader (1973)

The Trial of Socrates (1988)

The War Years, 1939–1945 (1988)

The Best of

I. F. STONE

I. F. STONE

Edited by
KARL WEBER

Introduction by
PETER OSNOS

PublicAffairs
New York

Published in the United States by PublicAffairs™, a member of the Perseus Books Group.

All rights reserved.

Printed in the United States of America.

No part of this book may be reproduced in any manner whatsoever without written permission except in the case of brief quotations embodied in critical articles and reviews. For information, address PublicAffairs, 250 West 57TH Street, Suite 1321, New York, NY 10107. PublicAffairs books are available at special discounts for bulk purchases in the U.S. by corporations, institutions, and other organizations. For more information, please contact the Special Markets Department at the Perseus Books Group, 11 Cambridge Center, Cambridge, MA 02142, call (617) 252–5298, or email special.markets@perseusbooks.com.

BOOK DESIGN BY JEFF WILLIAMS

A CIP Catalog Record for this book is available from the Library of Congress

1-58648-463-X

First Edition
10 9 8 7 6 5 4 3 2 1

CONTENTS

3. TWILIGHT STRUGGLE

4. THE WALL BETWEEN BLACK AND WHITE

INTRODUCTION

by Peter Osnos

In late summer 1965, as I. F. Stone scrambled to find a replacement for an assistant who had landed a job at *The New Republic*, he took me to lunch at a restaurant in Washington, D.C.'s small Chinatown. We had, as I recall, fish with ginger, wrapped in paper and dipped in boiling water. I was twenty-one and working for the *Providence Journal* in one of their local bureaus. Stone offered me $100 per week and said I would earn every penny. I stayed until the following summer, got a raise to $110 and an education in journalism (or what Izzy would have called "being a newspaperman") worth millions.

This was a particularly good period, personally and professionally, for Stone and his four-page *I. F. Stone's Weekly*. After years of being so hard-of-hearing that he had to wear an elaborate headset with antenna, making him look like a bespectacled Martian, Izzy's ears had been repaired by a doctor (Cohen was his name) who had performed the same operation on Chairman Mao. Many people would still talk to him as though he was deaf, especially on the phone, so speaking and listening habits of years duration were being relearned. Even news gathering was different. Izzy was especially well known for poring through transcripts and finding nuggets other reporters would miss. Now he could actually hear what was being said at events like press conferences. Izzy was naturally gregarious and excited to be part of any and all conversations. But he needed to also retain his relentless pursuit of news,

hidden in the recesses of papers and documents other reporters largely ignored. His restored ears were both a thrill and a distraction.

The political tenor of the time was also working to his benefit. In the
first half of the 1960s, the youthful idealism of the Kennedy years, as expressed in such ways as the Peace Corps, the Freedom Riders, and sit-ins,
was evolving into what soon became the campus-based anti–Vietnam War
and civil rights movements. This also coincided with the emergence of what
was known as the New Left. The Old Left of the 1930s, '40s, and '50s was
exhausted by the alliances and battles of that era: the Popular Fronts, for example; the Nazi-Soviet pact of 1939 and the Anglo-Soviet-U.S. partnership
of World War II's later years; the sour loyalty tests of the Cold War and Mc-
Carthyism; the Soviet invasion of Hungary in 1956. Six months before the
Hungarian upheaval, Izzy visited Moscow and wrote what turned into one
of his most famous citations: "I feel like a swimmer under water who must
rise to the surface or his lungs will burst. Whatever the consequences, I have
to say what I really feel after seeing the Soviet Union and carefully studying
the statements of its leading officials. *This is not a good society and it is not
led by honest men.*"

History's view of the Kremlin has hardened considerably over the years,
but at the time, only a decade after the Allies had defeated the Nazis, to
break with Moscow in this way was a radical move—all the more so because
Stone did not veer sharply to the anti-Communist right as so many other
apostates of that era did. He held to his convictions about free expression,
human rights, and the dangers of using anti-communism as justification for
war in countries with nationalist aspirations—Vietnam, for instance. These
positions made Izzy especially attractive to the New Left, whose manifestos,
like the Students for a Democratic Society's Port Huron statement of 1962,
rejected Communist orthodoxies but argued for profound social change at
home and around the world. Izzy was already decades older than the students and civil rights leaders like Martin Luther King, Jr. But his writing
was so vigorous, fresh, and clever that he appealed to this new generation
with humor as well as insight. He was older and wiser, yet still able to identify with the instincts of the young.

In a 1969 piece called "In Defense of the Campus Rebels," Izzy wrote,
"My boyhood idol was the saintly anarchist Kropotkin. I looked down on

college degrees and felt that a man should do only what was sincere and true and without thought of mundane advancement. This provided lofty reasons for not doing homework. I majored in philosophy with the vague thought of teaching it, but though I revered two of my professors, I disliked the smell of a college faculty. I dropped out in my third year to go back to newspaper work. Those were the '20s and I was a pre-depression radical. So I might be described I suppose as a premature New Leftist, though I never had the urge to burn anything down. . . ." Then, after affirming his own objections to the intolerance and violence pursued by some in the antiwar and civil rights movements, he concluded, "I feel about the rebels as Erasmus did about Luther. Erasmus helped inspire the Reformation but was repelled by the man who brought it to fruition. . . . I feel that the New Left and the black revolutionaries are doing God's work, too, in refusing any longer to submit to evil, and challenging society to reform or crush them."

Izzy entertained his readers and forced them to examine their beliefs. This refusal to be doctrinaire and his exuberance (despite the sometimes intimidating erudition that went with it) was a vast asset to his expanding circle of readers. The *Weekly*'s circulation climbed from 5,000 in 1953 to 70,000 when he ended it in 1971 and shifted his main writing to *The New York Review of Books*. He was treasured by his friends, like Bernard Fall, the great Washington-based French-born expert on Vietnam, whom Izzy admired for his knowledge and his *savoir faire* (Fall was killed by a mine in Vietnam in 1967), and Richard Dudman, the dapper and daring Washington correspondent of the *St. Louis Post-Dispatch*, who had run-ins with both the Khmer Rouge and the Viet Cong. But it was a major challenge to be his assistant.

I was expected to have read thoroughly by 7:30 A.M. *The Washington Post, The New York Times,* and several other out-of-town newspapers (though, mercifully, not *Le Monde*, the Paris paper that Izzy seemed to most admire). In the course of my day, I would swing by the Capitol and the State Department to collect handouts, read the wire services, attend hearings and press conferences, and generally cover the beat that extended, as did Izzy's interests, very widely. He liked to say "there is a great story hanging from every tree," but to me it seemed that there were a great many trees. Stone's home and office was at 5618 Nebraska Avenue in northwest Washington. I worked in the basement, maintained the enormous clip file, and was summoned upstairs by buzzer. The kitchen was on the way and Izzy's wife, Esther, who as circulation manager was the *Weekly*'s only other employee, kept a supply of peanut butter and other snacks in the fridge that maintained my stamina as the day wore on. In the evening, I digested the *Congressional Record* and other formidable official publications in search of revelations. Izzy also encouraged me to write my own pieces and gave me a fistful of bylines, an honor rarely accorded an apprentice.

Izzy would take the finished *Weekly* to his printer, McDonald and Eudy, on Wednesdays and then celebrate with dinner out and a movie. Sometimes Izzy and Esther went dancing, which they both adored, and for years, their summer routine included traveling across the Atlantic on oceanliners because they especially enjoyed the nightly *dansants*. By Sunday morning, Izzy was in full stride again on the next week's issue and so, therefore, was I. In retrospect, I recognize the enormous benefits and experience I derived from my year with Izzy, but at the time the long-term gains were obscured by the torrential work load and the fact that I was too busy to satisfy a growing urge to kick up my own heels a bit.

Someday when I go through the papers I have stored in various trunks and boxes, I hope to find the letter Izzy sent me after I left the *Weekly*. I was working in London as the assistant editor on *The Washington Post*'s news service and writing occasionally for the paper as a stringer. (This position, for all its obvious virtues, actually paid less than the *Weekly* did, $80 a week). The message of the letter was that having endured my tenure as an assistant, I was now eligible for friendship. And that is what happened.

Over the next thirty-three years until he died on June 18, 1989, Izzy and I were very good friends. Once in the late 1960s, I had a book review in the *Post* of a new work by Herbert Marcuse, a dense, philosophical tract by a much-admired German émigré icon of the New Left. Stone told the *Post* operator to tell me that Marcuse was calling and then, in his distinctive high-pitched voice, tried to impersonate a German accent. When I challenged the caller's identity, he feigned outrage that I would critique him in the newspaper and then defy him on the phone. I was, among other things, very flattered that Izzy had noticed the piece. Over the next decade as I worked abroad for *The Washington Post* in Vietnam and Moscow, Izzy would take me to lunch whenever I was in town, often at a favorite restaurant called the Piccadilly on Upper Connecticut Avenue. He was very careful about his weight, but insisted that I order and eat the desert trifle—which he would not.

One of our last sustained encounters was around his eightieth birthday in 1989. I had the idea of renting Town Hall and having a celebratory evening in his honor. I had approached several of Izzy's other admirers, including the publishers of *The Nation* magazine, *The New York Review,* and Pantheon Books at Random House, and raised the cost of renting the venue. I called to tell him the news and get some dates.

"You sure are a pistol, Pete," he said, "I never should have let you go." But then he pointed out that one of his principal sources of income at that time was public speaking so that rather than a "charity" event, he would prefer the occasion be observed at a place where admission would be charged and he could receive the proceeds. The evening was eventually held at the New School. The moderator was *Nation* Editor-in-Chief Victor Navasky and it was a sell-out. When Stone died in 1989, Esther and Izzy's two sons, Jeremy and Christopher, and their daughter, Celia, asked me to organize the memorials in Washington and New York. We selected the Ethical Society auditorium on Central Park West and the Friends Meeting House in Washington. Izzy was a Jew, of course, but his religion was humanism, even though he did invoke God, as in the piece quoted above. The cover of the program for the memorials was a syndicated cartoon by Pat Oliphant. It is St. Peter at the Pearly Gates on the phone, talking to a higher authority, with Stone, holding a pencil and notebook standing by. St. Peter is saying, "Yes, that I. F. Stone, Sir. He says he doesn't want to come in—he'd rather hang around out here, and keep things honest."

The New York event was on a warm day and the air conditioning at the Ethical Society was barely functioning. Many in the crowd were fanning themselves and one woman ostentatiously took out a battery-powered fan to cool off. Sensing the mood and as the presider, I took off my jacket and said, "Sorry about the temperature, but I'm sure that on an occasion such as this, Izzy would prefer that we were all a little uncomfortable." Thinking about that comment now, I'd go even further. I. F. Stone liked people, especially, and particularly his readers, but he did prefer that they were a little uncomfortable as they wrestled with the eternal nature of certain problems in contemporary life. Reading this collection, so well edited by Karl Weber,

I see that we are still coping with the same issues today as we did fifty years ago, when *I. F. Stone's Weekly* was launched: nuclear weapons, religious and ethnic fundamentalism, racial bias, and the instinctively repressive and/or dissembling nature of so many governments. A first-rate biography of Izzy being published this fall by Myra MacPherson is called *All Governments Lie*. The rest of the quote is, "But disaster lies in wait for those countries whose officials smoke the same hashish they give out." In the Vietnam era, Izzy parsed government statements to reveal the reality of what was happening in the war. He would be equally robust today in unraveling the justifications and, subsequently, rationalizations for the Bush administration's forays into Iraq and Afghanistan.

What makes this collection of *The Best of I. F. Stone* valuable is that it seems so relevant to our times. Some aspects of language have changed: calling oneself a "newspaperman" seems quaint in today's media-driven, gender-neutral world, but otherwise, Stone's wisdom, informing his perceptions and framing his arguments, reads with spectacular currency. One small measure of Izzy's lasting influence can be found in a quintessential twenty-first century exercise. If you type in "I. F. Stone" on Google, you come up with 237,000 items. That is an impressive amount for what Izzy described in 1963 as a "four-page miniature journal of news and opinion," a publication long gone, but clearly not forgotten.

PETER OSNOS

June 2006

EDITOR'S NOTE

The 65 essays in this book have been drawn primarily from the archives of *I. F. Stone's Weekly,* the one-man newsletter founded by Stone in 1953 and maintained by him until 1971. Additional contents have been selected from *The Nation,* where Stone was Washington editor from 1940 to 1946, and *The New York Review of Books.*

I chose the essays with several criteria in mind. First, I wanted to convey the full breadth of Stone's journalistic talent, which embraced not only the investigative work for which he is most famous but also spot reporting, travel narratives, personality profiles, policy analysis, philosophical ruminations, and satire. Second, I tried to select pieces that accurately reflected Stone's primary social and political concerns, and the themes to which he returned throughout his career. Third, I favored stories with special contemporary relevance, as with the essays on the Cold War and Vietnam that shed light on the mindset underlying today's "war on terror." Finally, and most important, I chose pieces that I liked—articles that embodied the unique blend of factual precision, historical depth, unpretentious learning, mordant wit, and passion for justice that make I. F. Stone such an important and treasured figure in the history of American journalism.

The essays are divided into seven thematic parts: "Worth the Risk," which focuses on freedom of speech, conscience, and the press; "A Good War—But For What?" which highlights some of the best of Stone's reporting on World War II; "Twilight Struggle," on the Cold War; "The Wall Between Black and White," on civil rights and race relations; "A Promised Land?" on the fate of the Jews, Palestine, and the Arab/Israeli conflict; "A

War Made of Lies," on Vietnam; and "Heroes and Others," which contains profiles of some of the public figures Stone admired or deplored. A Prologue introduces Stone and his method in his own words, and an Epilogue offers a final comment on the century whose history he covered.

I hope that admirers of I. F. Stone will enjoy reading this selection from his work as much as I've enjoyed immersing myself in his writings. I hope, too, that this volume will serve to introduce Stone's journalism to a new generation of readers in an era when his integrity, energy, and intelligence are greatly needed and sorely missed.

KARL WEBER
Chappaqua, New York
April 2006

Prologue: A Word About Myself

This essay, which appeared as the introduction to *The Haunted Fifties,* one of several now out-of-print collections of I. F. Stone's writings, vividly sketches Stone's journalistic background, the circumstances of the *Weekly's* founding, and the editorial philosophy that sustained it. The self-portrait it presents is typically paradoxical: the crusading journalist with the soul of an esthete (lovingly designing the *Weekly* with its "beautiful type face, Garamond"); the socialist scourge of big business who pays his bills "promptly, like a solid bourgeois"; the political gadfly, thoroughly skeptical of America's self-proclaimed virtues, who treasures our "tradition of a free press" right down to the impartially administered second-class mailing privilege that made the *Weekly* possible. Stone even has a good word for the arch-conservative Robert R. McCormick, owner of the *Chicago Tribune,* on the ground that, unlike most American newspapermen, "he stood for something." It's a fair introduction to Stone's work and character. The message: Prepare to be surprised.

.   .   .

July 1963

I AM, I SUPPOSE, AN ANACHRONISM. In this age of corporation men, I am an independent capitalist, the owner of my own enterprise, subject to neither mortgager or broker, factor or patron. In an age when young men, setting out on a career of journalism, must find their niche in some huge newspaper or magazine combine, I am a wholly independent newspaperman, standing alone, without organizational or party backing, beholden to no one but my good readers. I am even one up on Benjamin Franklin—I do not accept advertising.

The pieces collected in this volume are from a four-page miniature journal of news and opinion, on which I have been a one man editorial staff, from proofreader to publisher. This independence, like all else, has its price—the audience. My newspaper reaches a relative handful, but the five thousand readers with whom I started have grown to more than twenty thousand in ten years. I have been in the black every one of those ten years and paid off the loans which helped me begin, without having had to appeal to my readers or to wealthy friends to keep going. I pay my bills promptly, like a solid bourgeois, though in the eyes of many in the cold-war Washington where I operate I am regarded, I am sure, as a dangerous and subversive fellow.

Once before, a newspaperman successfully attempted this same experiment in independence. My predecessor was a distinguished foreign correspondent and crusading liberal journalist, George Seldes. His four-page paper, *In Fact,* published much that was brushed under the rug by the conventional press. But Mr. Seldes had the advantage of publishing in a kind of Popular Front in the late '30s and the early '40s when there were powerfully organized left-wing unions and organizations ready to take bulk subscriptions to a maverick publication (though the dangers in such support were demonstrated when it was withdrawn from Seldes after he backed Tito in his fight with Stalin). I, on the other hand, had the disadvantage of starting my paper in January 1953, when McCarthy and McCarthyism were in the ascendant. That very month the unscrupulous Wisconsan had become chairman for the first time of the Senate Committee which he used to terrorize the left of center, the Eisenhower Administration and even his own Senate colleagues. There could not have been a less propitious time to launch a radical paper, fighting the witch hunt and the cold war. In these essays collected from its pages one may savor again the full flavor of those haunted years.

I HAVE BEEN A NEWSPAPERMAN all my life. In the small town where I grew up, I published a paper at fourteen, worked for a country weekly and then as correspondent for a nearby city daily. I did this from my sophomore year in high school through college, until I quit in my junior year. I was a philosophy major and at one time thought of teaching philosophy, but the atmosphere of a college faculty repelled me. While going to college I was working ten hours afternoon and night doing combination rewrite and copy desk on the *Philadelphia Inquirer,* so I was already an experienced newspaperman making $40 a week—big pay in 1928. I have done everything on a newspaper except run a linotype machine.

I had become a radical in the '20s while in my teens, mostly through reading Jack London, Herbert Spencer, Kropotkin, and Marx. I became a member of the Socialist Party and was elected to the New Jersey State Committee of the Socialist Party before I was old enough to vote. I did publicity for Norman Thomas in the 1928 campaign while a reporter on a small city daily, but soon drifted away from left-wing politics because of the sectarianism of the left. Moreover, I felt that party affiliation was incompatible with independent journalism, and I wanted to be free to help the unjustly treated, to defend everyone's civil liberty and to work for social reform without concern for leftist infighting.

I was fortunate in my employers. I rarely, if ever, felt compelled to compromise with my conscience; even as an anonymous editorial writer I never had to write something I thought untrue. I worked for a succession of newspaper people I remember with affection: J. David Stern and his editor Harry T. Saylor on the *Camden Courier-Post*, the *Philadelphia Record*, and the *New York Post*; Freda Kirchwey of *The Nation*; Ralph Ingersoll and the late John P. Lewis of the newspaper *PM*; the late Bartley Crum and his editor Joseph Barnes of the short-lived *New York Star*; and Ted O. Thackrey of the *New York Post* and the *New York Daily Compass*. Working for them was a wonderfully rewarding experience and I learned much from all of them. From 1932 to 1939 I was an editorial writer on the *Philadelphia Record* and the *New York Post*, then strongly pro-New Deal papers. In 1940 I came to Washington as Washington Editor of *The Nation* and have been here ever since, working as reporter and columnist for *PM*, the *New York Star*, the *New York Post* (for a short interval) and the *New York Compass*. When the *Compass* closed in November 1952 and no congenial job seemed likely to open up, I decided to launch a four-page weekly newsletter of my own.

I succeeded because it was what might be called a piggy-back launching. I had available the mailing lists of *PM*, the *Star*, the *Compass*, and of people who had bought my books. For a remarkably small investment, in two advance mailings, I was able to get five thousand subscribers at $5 each. I was my own biggest investor, but several friends helped me with loans and gifts. The existence of these highly selective mailing lists made it possible to reach what would otherwise appear to be needles in a haystack—a scattered tiny minority of liberals and radicals unafraid in McCarthy's heyday to support, and go on the mailing lists of, a new radical publication from Washington. I am deeply grateful to them.

It speaks well for the tradition of a free press in our country that even in the heyday of McCarthy it was possible for me to obtain my second-class mail permit without trouble. I had then been working in Washington for 12 years as correspondent for a succession of liberal and radical papers. I had supported Henry Wallace in 1948. I had fought for the civil liberties of Communists, and was for peace and coexistence with the Soviet Union. I had fought the loyalty purge, the FBI, the House Un-American Activities Committee, and McCarran as well as McCarthy. I had written the first magazine article against the Smith Act, when it was first used against the Trotskyites in 1940. There was nothing to the left of me but the *Daily Worker*.

Yet I was able to get second-class mail privilege without a single political question. As George Seldes had before me, I encountered old-fashioned civil service courtesy and political impartiality in the post office, and the second-class mail privilege when I started was my bread and butter. The difference between the second-class rate and the cheapest third-class rate was the equivalent of my salary.

MY IDEA WAS TO MAKE the *Weekly* radical in viewpoint but conservative in format. I picked a beautiful type face, Garamond, for my main body type, and eschewed sensational headlines. I made no claim to inside stuff—obviously a radical reporter in those days had few pipelines into the government. I tried to give information which could be documented so the reader could check it for himself. I tried to dig the truth out of hearings, official transcripts and government documents, and to be as accurate as possible. I also sought to give the *Weekly* a personal flavor, to add humor, wit and good writing to the *Weekly* report. I felt that if one were able enough and had sufficient vision one could distill meaning, truth and even beauty from the swiftly flowing debris of the week's news. I sought in political reporting what Galsworthy in another context called "the significant trifle"—the bit of dialogue, the overlooked fact, the buried observation which illuminated the realities of the situation. These I often used in "boxes" to lighten up the otherwise solid pages of typography unrelieved either by picture or advertising. I tried in every issue to provide fact and opinion not available elsewhere in the press.

In the worst days of the witch hunt and cold war, I felt like a guerilla warrior, swooping down in surprise attack on a stuffy bureaucracy where it least expected independent inquiry. The reporter assigned to specific beats like the State Department or the Pentagon for a wire service or a big daily newspaper soon finds himself a captive. State and Pentagon have large press relations forces whose job it is to herd the press and shape the news. There are many ways to punish a reporter who gets out of line; if a big story breaks at 3 A.M., the press office may neglect to notify him while his rivals get the story. There are as many ways to flatter and take a reporter into camp—private off-the-record dinners with high officials, entertainment at the service clubs. Reporters tend to be absorbed by the bureaucracies they cover; they take on the habits, attitudes and even accents of the military or the diplomatic corps. Should a reporter resist the pressure, there are many ways to get rid of him. If his publisher is not particularly astute or independent, a little private talk, a hint that the reporter seems irresponsible—even a bit radical—"sometimes one could even mistake him for a Marxist"—will do the job of getting him replaced with a more malleable man.

But a reporter covering the whole capital on his own—particularly if he is his own employer—is immune from these pressures. Washington is full of news—if one story is denied him he can always get another. The bureaucracies put out so much that they cannot help letting the truth slip from time to time. The town is open. One can always ask questions, as one can see from one of my "coups"—forcing the Atomic Energy Commission to admit that its first underground test was detected not 200 miles away—as it claimed—but 2600 miles away. This is the story of how I got that story—one example of what independent news gathering can be like.

The first underground test was held in the fall of 1957. The *New York Times* report from the test site in Nevada next morning said the results seemed to confirm the expectations of the experts: that it would not be detected more than 200 miles away. But the Times itself carried "shirttails" from Toronto, Rome and Tokyo saying that the shot had been detected there. Since the experts (viz. Dr. Edward Teller and his entourage at

Livermore Laboratory, all opposed to a nuclear test ban agreement) were trying to prove that underground tests could not be detected at a distance, these reports from Toronto, Rome and Tokyo piqued my curiosity. I did not have the resources to check them by cable, so I filed the story away for future use.

Next spring, Stassen, then Eisenhower's chief disarmament negotiator, testified before the Humphrey Disarmament Sub-committee of the Senate that a network of stations a thousand kilometers (or 580 miles apart) could police a nuclear test ban agreement and detect any underground tests. Two days after his testimony the AEC issued its first official report on the Nevada explosion for publication the following Monday. This said that the Nevada underground explosion had not been detected more than 200 miles away. The effect was to undercut Stassen's testimony. If the Nevada blast could not be detected more than 200 miles away then a network of stations 580 miles apart would not be able to police an agreement. I recalled the *New York Times* report of the previous fall, dug it out of a basement file and telephoned the AEC press office. I asked how the AEC reconciled its statement in the report about to be released that the blast was not detected more than 200 miles away with the reports from Rome, Tokyo and Toronto the morning after that it had registered on seismographs there. The answer was that they didn't know but would try to find out.

In the meantime I decided to find me a seismologist. By telephoning around I learned there was a seismology branch in the Coast and Geodetic Survey, where I duly found a seismologist and asked him whether it was true that Tokyo, Rome and Toronto had detected the Nevada underground blast. He said that he did not believe the claims of these three foreign stations but he showed me a list of some 20 U.S. stations which he said had certainly detected it. One of these was 2600 miles north of the test site in Fairbanks, Alaska, another was 1200 miles east in Fayetteville, Arkansas. I copied the names and distances down. When he asked why I was so interested, I said the AEC was about to release a report for the following Monday claiming that the explosion was not detected more than 200 miles away. When he heard the AEC angle, he became less communicative. I had hardly got back to my office when the phone rang; it was the AEC press relations man. He said "We just heard from Coast and Geodetic. There must be some mistake. We'll reach Nevada by teletype in the morning and let you know." When the Joint Committee on Atomic Energy later investigated the incident, the AEC claimed it was an "inadvertent" error. No agency in Washington—not even State Department or Pentagon—has a worse record than the AEC for these little "errors."

No BUREAUCRACY LIKES an independent newspaperman. Whether capitalist or communist, democratic or authoritarian, every regime does its best to color and control the flow of news in its favor. There *is* a difference here and I'm grateful for it. I could not operate in Moscow as I do in Washington. There is still freedom of fundamental dissent here, if only on the edges and in small publications.

The fault I find with most American newspapers is not the absence of dissent. It is the absence of news. With a dozen or so honorable exceptions, most American newspapers carry very little news. Their main concern is advertising. The main interest of our society is merchandising. All the so-called communications industries are primarily concerned not with communications, but with selling. This is obvious on television and radio but it is only a little less obvious in the newspapers. Most owners of newspapers are businessmen, not newspapermen. The news is something which fills the spaces left over by the advertisers. The average publisher is not only hostile to dissenting opinion, he is suspicious of *any* opinion likely to antagonize any reader or consumer. The late Colonel McCormick, in his *Chicago Tribune*, ran a paper about as different as possible from mine in outlook. But I admired him. He stood for something, he was a newspaperman, he gave the *Tribune* personality and character. Most U.S. papers stand for nothing. They carry prefabricated news, prefabricated opinion, and prefabricated cartoons. There are only a handful of American papers worth reading—*The New York Times, The St. Louis Post-Dispatch, The Washington Post, The Washington Star, The Baltimore Sun, The Christian Science Monitor*—these are *news* papers in the real sense of the term. But even here opinion is often timid; the cold war and the arms race are little questioned though these papers do speak up from time to time on civil liberty. There are only a few maverick daily papers left like the *York* (Pennsylvania) *Gazette and Daily* and the *Madison* (Wisconsin) *Capital Times*. All this makes it easy for a one-man four-page Washington paper to find news the others ignore, and of course opinion they would rarely express.

For me, being a newspaperman has always seemed a cross between Galahad and William Randolph Hearst, a perpetual crusade. When the workers of Csespel and the 1956 Hungarian Revolution put a free press among their demands, I was thrilled. What Jefferson symbolized for me was being rediscovered in a socialist society as a necessity for good government.

I believe that no society is good and can be healthy without freedom for dissent and for creative independence. I have found among the new Soviet youth kindred spirits in this regard and I watch their struggle for freedom against bureaucracy with deepest sympathy. I am sorry, when discussing our free press with them, to admit that our press is often almost as conformist as theirs. But I am happy that in my own small way I have been able to demonstrate that independence is possible, that a wholly free radical journalist can survive in our society. In the darkest days of McCarthy, when I often was made to feel a pariah, I was heartened by the thought that I was preserving and carrying forward the best in America's traditions, that in my humble way I stood in a line that reached back to Jefferson. These are the origins and the preconceptions, the hopes and the aspirations, from which sprang the pieces that follow.

Part One

WORTH THE RISK

Free Speech Is Worth the Risk

The impetus for this piece was the decision in *Terminiello v. Chicago*, a now largely-forgotten free speech case centered on an inflammatory, right-wing speech given in a Chicago auditorium by Arthur Terminiello. When disturbances erupted between the crowd in the hall and the larger crowd of protestors outside (including the smashing of windows and the tossing of stink-bombs), Terminiello was arrested under a local breach-of-the-peace ordinance. Here Stone, consistent with his devotion to freedom of expression, praises the five-to-four Supreme Court decision that overturned Terminiello's conviction—despite the obvious contempt he felt for both the message and the messenger.

.   .   .

May 18, 1949

IN PRINCIPLE, THE MAJORITY and the minority of the United States Supreme Court were separated by a mere hair's breadth in deciding the successful appeal of the Jew-baiting suspended priest, Terminiello, against a $100 fine for breach of the peace.

The majority left untouched an earlier decision which permits local authorities to punish when hatemongers use so-called "fighting words"—derisive racial or religious epithets likely to precipitate a rumpus. The minority agreed that free speech protects advocacy of "fascism or communism" and allows speakers to "go far" in expressing sentiments hostile to Jews, Negroes, Catholics, or other minority groups.

It was in deciding where the line shall be drawn between the permitted and the prohibited in this area that the Court nicely illustrated Mr. Justice Holmes' astringent dictum, "General propositions do not decide concrete cases."

The majority, through Justice Douglas, reversed Terminiello's conviction on the ground that the Illinois trial judge went too far in ruling that "breach of the peace" was broad enough to allow the prosecution of any speech which "stirs the public to anger . . . dispute . . . unrest."

The decision is given unusual interest because Justice Jackson, with his experience at the Nuremberg trials fresh in mind, protested bitterly for the minority that "if the court does not temper its doctrinaire logic with a little practical wisdom, it will convert the Constitutional Bill of Rights into a suicide pact."

In the Terminiello case, as in most questions of law, the Court had to choose between two dangers. Justice Jackson and the minority are impressed with the danger that fascist or revolutionary movements may utilize the basic freedoms of the Constitution to destroy it. Chief Justice Vinson, though dissenting, did not take a position on the merits. But Justices Jackson, Burton, and Frankfurter obviously prefer the risk of some infringement on basic liberties to the risk of permitting antidemocratic movements to get out of hand. The majority, Justices Douglas, Black, Murphy, Rutledge, and Reed, are more fearful of the risk that officials will abuse this power and limit the open discussion which is the foundation of a free society.

Justice Jackson's distillations from German experience do not impress me; they embody commonly current misconceptions. The German people did not succumb to Hitlerism because there was too much freedom in their laws but because there was too little freedom in their hearts. The Weimar Republic could be energetic enough in dealing with the Left. There as elsewhere it was demonstrated that it is the Left rather than the Right which ultimately bears the impact of these shoddy rationalizations about turning the Bill of Rights into a suicide pact. This is the panic of faltering spirits.

The choice the Court had to make was difficult because the dangers either way are real enough. But you cannot have freedom without the risk of its abuse. The men who wrote the Bill of Rights were willing to take their chances on freedom. This willingness to take risk, whether in theology, science, or monetary investment, is the prime characteristic of the whole period of human history which encompasses the Reformation, capitalism, and rationalism in one great burst of human energy. The world has seen any number of closed systems, from the ancient Roman Catholic to the modern Communist, which sought to eliminate risk by relying on revelation of one kind or another, and on this basis justified inquisition and purge. But everything we know from the past teaches us that suppression in the long run provides an illusory security, and this is why, though a socialist, I am also a libertarian.

Almost every generation in American history has had to face what appeared to be a menace of so frightening an order as to justify the limitation of basic liberties—the Francophiles in the days of the Alien and Sedition Laws, the abolitionists, the anarchists, the Socialists in the days of Debs; fascists, anti-Semites, and Communists in our own time. Each for various people seemed to provide compelling arguments for suppression, but we managed to get through before and will, I hope, again without abandoning basic freedoms. To do so would be to create for ourselves the very conditions we fear.

I am, I suppose, exactly what Terminiello in his harangues meant by an "atheistic, communistic, zionistic Jew." I would not demean myself or my people by denying him the right to say it. I do not hold the liberties I enjoy as an American in so little esteem that I am prepared to run from them like a rabbit because someone else uses them to say what I suppose ought to disturb me deeply. It does not disturb me.

I do not think the danger from fascist ideas on the Right can be met by imprisonment any more than can the danger from revolutionary ideas on the Left. All history testifies to the contrary. The judges of the minority who would have permitted some measure of suppression in my protection are not men whose championship I care to have. In too many recent cases I have seen how current anti-Red hysteria has kept them from doing the humane, the just and rightful thing.

I learned in Israel what men here once learned at Lexington—not to scare easily. If there is a growth of unemployment and mass misery, it will be exploited by the Right as well as the Left, and anti-Semitism will grow like any other fungus on the muck of despair. This gutter paranoia can only be prevented by fighting the conditions in which it can breed, and for that fight we need more and not less freedom of discussion, even though it be at the price of a few Terminiellos.

Quis Custodiet Custodem?

In January 1953, as Dwight D. Eisenhower prepared to take office, Senator Joseph McCarthy of Wisconsin was just beginning his reign of fear in Washington. Having been named chairman of the Senate's Government Operations Committee as well as of its Permanent Investigations Subcommittee, he was preparing to use his subpoena powers to terrorize thousands of suspected Communists and other "subversives." I. F. Stone was among the first to recognize the danger to American liberties posed by McCarthy. In this early dispatch, he traces some of the senator's financial history, suggesting the dubious character of the nation's self-proclaimed watchdog.

· · ·

January 17, 1953

THE ROMANS HAD A SAYING, *"Quis custodiet custodem?"*—Who will watch the watchman? The wry question applies patly to the case of Joe McCarthy. The Senator who is now the chairman of the Senate's key watchdog committee is the Senator who most needs watching. The report made on McCarthy by the Senate subcommittee on privileges and elections is a monument to the ineptitude of gentlemen in dealing with a brawler who pays no attention to the rules, Queensberry or otherwise. The report, spottily covered in the nation's newspapers despite a very full account sent out (to its credit) by the Associated Press, is the first official full-length portrait of the most brazen operator to appear in the United States Senate since the days of Huey Long.

The new document is the third Senate report which has found McCarthy mixed up in funny business on which action by law enforcement agencies has been asked. A subcommittee of the Senate Armed Services Committee reporting in October, 1949, called for investigation by the Justice and Defense Departments into the campaign to save the Malmédy slayers. McCarthy figured in this as an advocate of strict Anglo-Saxon due process for the SS men who killed 350 unarmed American prisoners and 150 Belgian civilians in the Battle of the Bulge. Nothing happened. The Rules Committee in August, 1951, suggested state and federal inquiry into the financial irregularities and defamatory tactics of the campaign in which McCarthy helped defeat Millard Tydings for re-election to the Senate the year before. Again nothing happened. It is now the honor of the Senate, not McCarthy, which is going down for the third time.

McCarthy cannot complain that he got less than the due process due him. Six times the subcommittee invited him to appear and rebut the charges bravely made by former Senator Benton, six times McCarthy failed to show up. The subcommittee lacked the nerve to subpoena him.

The picture drawn by the new report is of a man who cannot resist speculation on margin. His activities in and out of the market since 1942 are those of a born gambler. A series of financial difficulties were eased by some odd transactions of which the $10,000 he received from Lustron for a housing pamphlet is the best known. Newly brought to light in this report is the $20,000 note signed for McCarthy by the Washington representative of Pepsi-Cola at a time when the Senator's bank account in Wisconsin was overextended. Pepsi-Cola was then lobbying for decontrol of sugar and McCarthy was chairman of a Senate subcommittee—on sugar!

McCarthy's financial accounts are hectic. From January 1, 1948, to November 12, 1952, he deposited $172,000 in one Washington bank; his administrative assistant and alter ego, Ray Kiermas, deposited $96,000. Of these amounts almost $60,000 deposited by McCarthy and almost $45,000 deposited by Kiermas "has not been identified as to source." The Senator's most successful speculation was his flier in anticommunism. Contributions flowed in after his famous attack on the State Department, February 9, 1950. In the months which followed more than $20,000 was deposited by him in a special account used for donations to help him fight communism. "However," the report says dryly, "no connection could be established between many of the disbursements from this account and any possible anti-Communist campaign." In one case traced by the committee, McCarthy deposited a $10,000 loan to fight communism in a special account, and then withdrew it three weeks later to pass on to a friend for a speculation in soybeans.

Outgoing Democrats and incoming Republicans will live equally to re-
gret that they did not cut McCarthy down to size when they had the
chance. With his congenital cheek and the enormous powers conferred
upon him by his key Senate chairmanship, McCarthy promises to become
Eisenhower's chief headache. McCarthy is in a position to smear any government official who fails to do his bidding. With much daring and few
scruples, McCarthy can make himself the most powerful single figure in
Congress and terrorize the new Administration. All those mumblings and
rumblings about how Communists are "already infiltrating" the Republicans are indicative.

Einstein, Oxnam, and the Inquisition

By mid-1953, the distinguished scientist Albert Einstein had become alarmed over the rising power of Joseph McCarthy and was actively seeking an opportunity to voice a protest against it. The opportunity came when a New York City schoolteacher named William Frauenglass wrote to Einstein after having been fired for refusing to disclose his political beliefs before the Senate. Einstein's reply made headlines: "Every intellectual who is called before the committees ought to refuse to testify. . . . If enough people are ready to take this grave step, they will be successful. If not, then the intellectuals deserve nothing better than the slavery which is intended for them." Stone contrasts Einstein's stance with what he viewed as the equivocal response offered by G. Bromley Oxnam, a liberal Methodist Bishop also facing scrutiny by the Senate.

.   .   .

June 20, 1953

THE BACKGROUND AGAINST WHICH Einstein has issued his call for civil disobedience of the witch hunters is encouraging. There are signs of a growing revulsion against congressional inquisition. McCarthy has had the guidance of Father Edmund A. Walsh at Washington's ancient Jesuit university, Georgetown. But at its sister institution in the capital, Catholic University, the principal address at the commencement exercises last week was devoted to warning the graduates against the hysteria fomented by congressional investigating committees. The Archbishop of Washington, the Most Reverend Patrick A. O'Boyle, presided and "some politicians" were criticized for their readiness to "seize upon any issue, real or spurious, to boost their fame and publicity."

There were similar warnings from as unexpected a source at Radcliffe. There the commencement speaker was Senator Stuart Symington, a businessman and a right-wing Democrat from Missouri, himself a member of the Senate Government Operations Committee over which McCarthy presides. Symington has distinguished himself on the committee in the past by asking witnesses some remarkably inane questions about whether they believe in God. Just what their private theological opinions had to do with government operations, the committee's field of authority, has never been explained. But at Radcliffe, Symington executed a quick metamorphosis and turned up as a liberal to warn that the recklessness of the Red hunters could easily turn into "a new reign of terror." Symington's sudden conversion on the road to Cambridge, Massachusetts, was gratifying, though important chiefly as a weather indicator. Symington wants to be President, and is prepared to move left or right with the prevailing winds. Eisenhower's own gratifying remarks at Dartmouth will help turn those winds against the witch hunt.

In this ripening situation, with public opinion slowly being aroused, Einstein's proposal for civil disobedience of the congressional inquisitors has the merit of getting down to rock-bottom. What McCarthy, Jenner and Velde are doing is wrong. It is therefore wrong to submit to them. They are poisoning the air of America and making people in all walks of life fearful of expressing opinions which may be a little "controversial." It is in this way that they are beginning to impose thought control.

The First Amendment says Congress "shall make no law respecting an establishment of religion." This means that it can establish no standard of orthodoxy. Can it inquire into beliefs it may not regulate? There are many Catholics and not a few Protestants who believe that heterodox opinions on certain fundamental religious dogmas create a political danger for the state by leading directly to "subversive" political views. But this connection of political danger with theological error is hardly new. The Pilgrim Fathers fled from just such inquisition in the England of their time and the provision against an Established Church was intended to prevent the development of similar practices here.

A characteristic of the American system is the denial of absolute powers to the government or any of its coordinate branches. No one would argue that Congress may pass a law taking a man's property without compensation or his life without trial. But the notion has grown up that the congressional power of investigation, unlike all other governmental powers, is

virtually unlimited. The recent Rumely decision was only the latest in a series of Supreme Court opinions which have held to the contrary, though
the court has yet to apply the same protection to the privacy of men's minds
that it has in the past to the privacy of their moneyed accounts.

The witch hunt abuses of our time find their support in two fallacies
which have nothing to do with the legitimate exercise of the congressional
power of investigation. One is that while Congress has no power to regulate
opinion it has a right to expose, disgrace and pillory holders of opinions it
regards as dangerous, subversive, heretical or un-American. The other is
that which permits a committee of Congress to act as a roving grand jury
for the discovery and punishment of individual crimes.

A section of the Fifth Amendment to which amazingly little attention
has been paid in the current controversy over congressional investigation
says, "No person shall be held to answer for a capital or otherwise infamous
crime, unless on a presentment or indictment of a grand jury." The purpose
was to protect accused persons from having to stand the shame of public
accusation and the expense of trial until a grand jury in secret session had
determined that there was enough substance in any charge to warrant publicity and trial.

Ever since Martin Dies and John Rankin these congressional committees
have announced their determination to act as a peculiar new type of "grand
jury," operating in public and more than content to leave the stigma of serious crime by hit-or-miss questioning of the sort that has been well termed a
"fishing expedition." Congressman Keating referred to this type of abuse in
a thoughtful speech last month to the San Francisco Bar Association. Keating said that an area which "should be scrupulously avoided" by congressional committees "is the domain of law enforcement officers and the
criminal courts." Keating pointed out that "Only in the case of impeach-
ment does Congress have the right to determine whether a particular individual has committed a specific crime against society." None of the
procedural reform proposals now in Congress would prevent investigating
committees from acting as quasi grand juries or as pillories for holders of
unpopular opinions.

The *New York Times,* objecting to civil disobedience of the witch hunters,
says, "Two wrongs never did add up to one right." The old chestnut, in this

sense, is quite untrue. Gandhi made two "wrongs" add up to one right by refusing to pay the British salt tax. Long before Gandhi, an earlier generation
of Americans made two wrongs add up to one right by dumping that tea in
Boston harbor rather than pay the British tax upon it. The white folk of the
North who refused to obey the Fugitive Slave Law were adding the "wrong"
of civil disobedience to the wrong of slavery, and these ultimately added up
to the right of emancipation. Even more in point is the fact that our privilege against self-incrimination derives in large part from the civil disobedience of John Lilburne, who refused to testify before Star Chamber in 1637
when accused of importing heretical works from Holland and asked to identify his collaborators. The evil of compulsory testimony from which the Pil-
grims fled to this country was eradicated by his bravery in refusing to testify
at the expense of going to jail for contempt.

The need for such fundamental defiance is illustrated by the objections
advanced against it. "One cannot start," the *New York Times* said, "from the
premise that congressional committees have no right to question teachers
and scientists or to seek out subversives wherever they can find them; what is
profoundly wrong is the way some of them have been exercising it." The fact
is that one cannot start from any *other* premise without making defeat inevitable. To accept ideological interrogation is to make nonconformist views
of any kind hazardous. To permit Congress to seek out something as vague,
undefined and undefinable as "subversion" or "un-Americanism" is to acquiesce in a heresy hunt that must inhibit free discussion in America. One man's
"subversion" is another man's progress; all change subverts the old in preparing the way for the new. "Un-American" is an epithet, not a legal standard.

The *New York Times* says "it is one thing to fight the investigations because of the manner of their procedure and another to oppose the right of
investigation, which has always been one of the fundamentals of our governmental system." Investigations have been fundamental but the kind of
investigations utilized in this witch hunt are something new in American
life. The first congressional committee of this kind was the Hamilton Fish
investigation in 1930, the Red-hunt precursor of the Un-American Activities Committee. The idea that a committee of Congress could interrogate
Americans on their political beliefs is a revolutionary excrescence not a fundamental of American government in the past.

One need only compare Einstein's approach with Bishop Oxnam's to see how right the great physicist is. One cannot at one and the same time object to investigation of the churches by the House Un-American Activities Committee and the Senate Internal Security Subcommittee and at the same time insist on a hearing before them as the good Bishop has done. To ask for a hearing is to acquiesce in the committee's power, to establish a precedent by which other clergymen may be hauled into the pillory. To defend oneself, as the Bishop did in that famous point-by-point rejoinder the *Washington Post* published last April 5, is to cut the ground out from under any principled objection to the inquisition. To plead that one is not "subversive" by the standards of the committee or of that *ex parte* blacklist drawn up by the Attorney General is to accept their right to establish a standard of orthodoxy and heresy in American political and religious thinking.

No one can "clear" himself or defend himself fairly before one of these committees. James Wechsler's experience before McCarthy should be demonstration enough of that. We are not dealing with men anxious to learn the truth or prepared to act honorably. We are dealing with unscrupulous political adventurers using the Red menace as their leverage to power. To try and explain to them that one is not a Communist is as humiliating as it is useless, unless one is prepared to go over completely to their service.

At the same time these committees regard the invocation of the Fifth Amendment with equanimity. To invoke the Fifth is to brand oneself in the eyes of the public as guilty of any offense implied by the dirty questions these committees put. Those who plead the Fifth in most cases lose their jobs and reputations. This satisfies the committees, for their purpose is nothing less than an ideological purge of radicals and liberals from all positions of influence in American life and the demonstration to others that nonconformity is dangerous.

Great faiths can only be preserved by men willing to live by them. Faith in free society requires similar testament if it is to survive. Einstein knows fascism at first hand. History confirms his statement that "if enough people are ready to take this grave step" of defiance "they will be successful" but that if not, "the intellectuals of this country deserve nothing better than the slavery which is intended for them."

The path pointed out by Einstein is that taken by the Hollywood Ten and the directors of the Joint Anti-Fascist Refugee Committee, all of whom went to jail for contempt. But tactics that did not succeed at a time when the cold war was begun may fare differently now when it is ebbing away. The Supreme Court did not hear those earlier cases and there has never been final adjudication on two major points of attack against the committees. One is whether they violate the First Amendment by inquiring into beliefs and the other whether they violate the Fifth Amendment by arrogating to themselves the functions of a grand jury. Neither point can be tested until someone dares invite prosecution for contempt.

This is the moment to try. Einstein has lent the world prestige of his name to such an effort. I propose an association of American intellectuals to take the "Einstein pledge" and throw down a fundamental challenge to the establishment of an inquisition in America.

The First Welts on Joe McCarthy

This article offers Stone's appraisal of the start of the famous Army–McCarthy hearings, the Senate investigation that spelled the beginning of the end for McCarthy's anti-Communist witch hunt. McCarthy made a serious tactical error when he accused the U.S. Army of harboring and promoting Communist sympathizers (and of mistreating G. David Schine, a draftee who'd been a member of McCarthy's staff). The charges were so outlandish that President Eisenhower was finally goaded into publicly rebuking McCarthy; the dramatic Senate hearings that followed were televised live from coast to coast, exposing McCarthy's dishonest and bullying personality to a disgusted public.

·   ·   ·

March 15, 1954

BUDS ARE BEGINNING TO APPEAR on the forsythia, and welts on Joe McCarthy. The early arrival of spring and a series of humiliations for our would-be *Führer* have made this a most pleasant week in the capital.

The events of the week are worth savoring. Blunt Charlie Wilson called McCarthy's charges against the Army "tommyrot" and for once Joe had no comeback. Next day came the ignominious announcement that he was dropping that two million dollar suit against former Senator Benton for calling McCarthy a crook and a liar; the lame excuse promised to launch a nationwide "I Believe Benton" movement. Stevenson followed with a speech calculated to impress those decent conservatives who had grown disgusted with the Eisenhower Administration's cowardice in the Zwicker affair.

When McCarthy sought to answer Stevenson, the Republican National Committee turned up in Ike's corner and grabbed the radio and TV time away from him. Nixon was to reply, and McCarthy was out (unless somebody smuggled him into the program in place of Checkers).

While McCarthy fumed and threatened, his own choice for the Federal Communications Commission, Robert E. Lee, ungratefully declared he thought the networks had done enough in making time available to Nixon. Next day a Republican, albeit a liberal Republican, Flanders of Vermont, actually got up on the floor of the Senate and delivered a speech against McCarthy. That same night Ed Murrow telecast a brilliant TV attack on McCarthy.

Under Stevenson's leadership, Eisenhower rallied. At press conference he endorsed the Flanders attack, said he concurred heartily in the decision to have Nixon reply to Stevenson, asserted that he saw no reason why the networks should also give time to McCarthy. Like an escaped prisoner, flexing cramped muscles in freedom, the President also made it clear he had no intention of turning Indo-China into another Korea and even had the temerity to suggest that it might be a good idea to swap butter and other surplus farm commodities with Russia.

The White House conference was no sooner over than Senator Ferguson as chairman of the Senate Republican Policy Committee released a set of suggested rules for Senate investigating committees which are no great shakes at reform but would, if adopted, make it impossible for McCarthy any longer to operate his subcommittee as a one-man show. These may be small enough gains in the fight against McCarthyism, but they were bitter pills for McCarthy to swallow.

So far McCarthy's colleagues on both sides of the aisle have been lying low. When Flanders attacked McCarthy, the Senate was as silent as it was some weeks earlier when Ellender of Louisiana made a lone onslaught and Fulbright of Arkansas cast the sole vote against his appropriation. Only Lehman of New York and John Sherman Cooper, a Republican of Kentucky, rose to congratulate Flanders. Nobody defended McCarthy, but nobody joined in with those helpful interjections which usually mark a Senate speech. When the Democratic caucus met in closed session, the Stevenson speech was ignored. Lyndon Johnson of Texas, the Democratic floor leader, is frightened of McCarthy's Texas backers.

Great issues are rarely resolved by frontal assault; for every abolitionist prepared to challenge slavery as a moral wrong, there were dozens of compromising politicians (including Lincoln) who talked as if the real issue were states rights or the criminal jurisdiction of the federal courts or the right of the people in a new territory to determine their own future. In the fight against the witch-mania in this country and in Europe, there were few enough to defend individual victims but fewer still who were willing to assert publicly that belief in witchcraft was groundless. So today in the fight against "McCarthyism." It is sometimes hard to draw a line of principle between McCarthy and his critics. If there is indeed a monstrous and diabolic conspiracy against world peace and stability, then isn't McCarthy right? If "subversives" are at work like termites here and abroad, are they not likely to be found in the most unlikely places and under the most unlikely disguises? How talk of fair procedure if dealing with a protean and Satanic enemy?

To doubt the power of the devil, to question the existence of witches, is again to read oneself out of respectable society, to brand oneself a heretic, to incur suspicion of being oneself in league with the powers of evil. So all the fighters against McCarthyism are impelled to adopt its premises. This was true even of the Stevenson speech, but was strikingly so of Flanders. The country is in a bad way indeed when as feeble and hysterical a speech is hailed as an attack on McCarthyism. Flanders talked of "a crisis in the age-long warfare between God and the Devil for the souls of men." He spoke of Italy as "ready to fall into Communist hands," of Britain "nibbling at the drugged bait of trade profits." There are passages of sheer fantasy, like this one: "Let us look to the South. In Latin America there are sturdy strong points of freedom. But there are likewise, alas, spreading infections of communism. Whole countries are being taken over. . . ." What "whole countries"? And what "sturdy strong points of freedom"? Flanders pictured the Iron Curtain drawn tight about the United States and Canada, the rest of the world captured "by infiltration and subversion." Flanders told the Senate, "We will be left with no place to trade and no place to go except as we are permitted to trade and to go by the Communist masters of the world."

The center of gravity in American politics has been pushed so far right that such childish nightmares are welcomed as the expression of liberal statesmanship. Nixon becomes a middle-of-the-road spokesman and conservative papers like the *Washington Star* and *New York Times* find themselves classified more and more as parts of the "left-wing press." In this atmosphere the Senate Republican reply to McCarthy's silly "Communist coddling" charges against the Army is to launch a formal investigation of their own through Saltonstall and the Armed Services Committee. This will be the Republican and Army analogue of the Tydings inquiry into the charges against the State Department and will be greeted with the same cry of whitewash by the growing lunatic fringe behind McCarthy.

There are some charges which must be laughed off or brushed off. They cannot be disproved. If a man charges that he saw Eisenhower riding a broomstick over the White House, he will never be convinced to the contrary by sworn evidence that the President was in bed reading a Western at the time. Formal investigations like Saltonstall's merely pander to paranoia and reward demagogy. What if McCarthy were next to attack the President and the Supreme Court? Are they, too, to be investigated? Is America to become a country in which any adventurer flanked by two ex-Communist screwballs will put any institution on the defensive?

McCarthy is personally discomfited, but McCarthyism is still on the march. Acheson fought McCarthy, but preached a more literate variation of the bogeyman theory of history. Eisenhower fights McCarthy, but his Secretary of State in Caracas is pushing hard for a resolution which would spread McCarthyism throughout the hemisphere, pledging joint action for "security" and against "subversion." Nowhere in American politics is there evidence of any important figure (even Stevenson) prepared to talk in sober, mature and realistic terms of the real problems which arise in a real world where national rivalries, mass aspirations and ideas clash as naturally as the waves of the sea. The premises of free society and of liberalism find no one to voice them, yet McCarthyism will not be ended until someone has the nerve to make this kind of fundamental attack upon it.

What are the fundamentals which need to be recognized? The first is that there can be no firm foundation for freedom in this country unless there is real peace. There can be no real peace without a readiness for live-and-let-live, i.e., for coexistence with communism. The fear cannot be extirpated without faith in man and freedom. The world is going "socialist" in one form or another everywhere; communism is merely the extreme form this movement takes when and where blind and backward rulers seek by terror and force to hold back the tide, as the Czar did and as Chiang Kai-shek did.

There must be renewed recognition that societies are kept stable and healthy by reform, not by thought police; this means that there must be free play for so-called "subversive" ideas—every idea "subverts" the old to make way for the new. To shut off "subversion" is to shut off peaceful progress and to invite revolution and war. American society has been healthy in the past because there has been a constant renovating "subversion" of this kind. Had we operated on the bogeyman theory of history, America would have destroyed itself long ago. It will destroy itself now unless and until a few men of stature have the nerve to speak again the traditional language of free society.

The Cost of Anticommunism

Stone uses some pathetically comic moments from the Senate debate on the so-called Flanders resolution censuring Joseph McCarthy as the vehicle for broader and deeper reflections on the malign impact of America's anti-Communist paranoia on the nation and the world. Stone's warning, "We cannot inculcate unreasoning hate and not ultimately be destroyed by it ourselves," may be newly relevant in an era when the "clash of civilizations" and the "war on terror" sometimes seem to place Western "values" in a battle to the death against the billion-plus adherents of one of the world's major religions.

·　　·　　·

August 9, 1954

THERE WAS ONE SCENE, in the final minutes, before the tense galleries, after three days of debate on McCarthy, with tired and impatient senators crying "Vote, vote," that would have entranced the creator of Babbitt. Capehart, that rotund Midwestern businessman, was on the floor in a final plea to table any resolution of censure. "There have been times," Capehart told a Senate which could not have cared less, "when, if I could have gotten hold of him, I think I would have thrown him out. There have been other times when I thought, 'By golly, there is a great guy.'" Capehart was maneuvering into position to agree with both the pro's and the anti's when he got back to Indianapolis.

It was comic, as comic as Welker's assurance that McCarthy must be a good man because he loved Welker's children "and he loves the children of almost every other senator." But amid the burlesque, Capehart's main point faithfully reflected the confusions which haunt Main Street. Capehart declared "out of one corner of our mouths" we say we want billions of dollars to fight communism. We say, "We are going to send your boys all over the world. You may have a third world war." Yet, Capehart continued, "on the other hand" we say, "We do not like McCarthy because he is a little too rough

28

and a little too tough with these so-called Communists." How explain that in South Bend or Little Rock?

This is the heart of the Senate's difficulty. This is why for the sixth time in six years (since the Malmédy inquiry in 1949) the Senate is wearily setting up yet another committee to investigate charges against McCarthy with no more prospect than in the past of a decision. McCarthy is resourceful, unscrupulous and wily, but the Senate is full of politicians as deft and clowns as crafty. They would have brought him down long ago if it were not for the dilemma created by our own demonology. If Communists are some supernatural breed of men, led by diabolic master minds in that distant Kremlin, engaged in a Satanic conspiracy to take over the world and enslave all mankind—and this is the thesis endlessly propounded by American liberals and conservatives alike, echoed night and day by every radio station and in every newspaper, the thesis no American dare any longer challenge without himself becoming suspect—then how fight McCarthy?

If the public mind is to be conditioned for war, if it is being taught to take for granted the destruction of millions of human beings, few of them tainted with this dreadful ideological virus, all of them indeed presumably pleading for us to liberate them, how can we argue that it matters if a few possibly innocent men lose jobs or reputations because of McCarthy? Is not this additional cost too slight, are not the stakes too great? How contend for constitutional niceties while acquiescing in the spread of poisonous attitudes and panicky emotions?

Writ in the skies of the H-bomb era is the warning that mutual destruction is the alternative to coexistence. Until there is a national leadership willing to take a pragmatic view of revolution, a charitable and Christian view of the misery that goes with the great rebirths of mankind, a self-respecting view of the example a free America can set and the constructive leadership an unafraid America can give, we cannot fight the drift to fascism at home and war abroad. We cannot inculcate unreasoning hate and not ultimately be destroyed by it ourselves. We who prate constantly of "atheistic communism" forget that this is what all the great teachers of mankind have taught. There is a retribution that lies in wait for the arrogant and the self-righteous. Where is the man big enough to reach the American people with this message before it is too late?

Incommensurate Equation:
Justice and Security

Wolf Ladejinksy, a Russian-born naturalized citizen, had started his government career in 1935 working at the Department of Agriculture; by the end of the Second World War, he had become the head of the department's Far East division, and from 1950 to 1954 he had been detailed to the State Department. However, on December 16, 1954, Agriculture Secretary Ezra Taft Benson announced that he was denying Ladejinsky a job in his department, considering him a security risk. A departmental security office investigation had concluded that Ladejinsky still had relatives in the Soviet Union, that he had visited them in the late 1930s, and that he had once worked as a translator for a Soviet trade firm. For I. F. Stone, the Ladejinsky case illustrated the inevitable clash between the 1950s "fetish" for security and the American concept of justice enshrined in our constitution.

. . .

January 24, 1955

IN THE GROWING UPROAR over the loyalty-security program, its critics still cling to a comfortable fallacy. They assume that it is possible to reconcile "security" with justice. They speak as if, by some reform of the rules, or better adherence to them, maximum security for the government and fair trial for the individual can evenhandedly be assured. Thus Mr. Walter Lippmann, in criticizing the President's clumsiness in the Ladejinsky case, asserts the citizen's right in such matters "to have the charge tried by due process" without stopping to consider whether due process is possible in such proceedings. How do you try the "charge" that a man once worked for Amtorg or has two sisters in Russia?

If we stop to compare what happens in the trial of a crime with what happens in the trial of a loyalty-security case, we will begin to see that a more fundamental attack on the problem is necessary if the miasma of suspicion is to be dissipated. Here are some of the differences:

1. The matter of proof: A trial deals with something that happened. A loyalty-security hearing deals with something that *might* happen. When a crime has been committed or attempted, objective proof is possible: a body, a cracked safe, a forged check, witnesses, may all be put in evidence.

But when a man is up on loyalty or security charges, nothing has *happened*. The tribunal is not dealing with an act but with future possibilities. It is engaged in an exercise in clairvoyance. It must determine whether a man might commit a crime some time in the future, whether he might steal or sell secrets. There are no ways to prove what a man *might* do. The essence of the loyalty-security procedure is not the trial of a fact but a guess as to future conduct.

2. How any doubt is resolved: In the trial of a crime, even for the most heinous, such as murder or treason, any reasonable doubt is resolved in favor of the accused. As Blackstone phrased the rule, already venerable in his time, "The law holds that it is better that ten guilty persons escape than the one innocent suffer." Law enforcement is thereby made more difficult. But justice to the individual, not the security of society, is the primary concern.

All this is reversed in loyalty-security cases. To bar a man from a job and label him disloyal because in your opinion he might do something bad in the future is by its nature a decision which resolves the doubt in favor of the State and against the individual. "Security" means to take as few chances as possible, even at the expense of injustice to some people who never have committed a crime and never will.

This is vividly illustrated by Fifth Amendment cases. A man summoned before a magistrate and asked whether he had ever committed larceny who thereupon pleaded the Fifth Amendment could not be thrown in jail or even prosecuted. But a worker in the government or at General Electric or Bethlehem Steel who invokes the Fifth Amendment loses his job. No evidence that he ever committed a crime or was ever a radical—the two are equated by now in the public mind—is required. The invocation of his constitutional right is enough to ruin his reputation and his right to work.

Those who defend these standards fall back on a totalitarian logic. David Lawrence protested recently against what he terms a "left-wing drive" to "surround governmental employees with complex procedural safeguards which would supersede the right of the American government to protect its own safety." Mr. Lawrence forgets that much of the Constitution and the common law is devoted to surrounding people of all kinds, including the disreputable, with complex procedural safeguards which supersede the right of government to protect itself. In such restrictions lies the essence of free government.

3. Avoidance: The difference in the two procedures becomes clearer if you ask yourself how you avoid getting into trouble. To avoid arrest and trial for a crime, one has to obey the law. But what does one avoid to keep out of loyalty-security trouble? One has to avoid political activity. Since you never know what organization may some day be regarded as suspect, better join none. Since almost any cause may some day be regarded as subversive, better keep away from all. Since there are now informers everywhere, including the campus, say as little as possible, avoid the discussion of dangerous subjects. Be careful what books you have in your library and what publications you read. These may be held against you. Safety lies in the abnegation of one's rights.

4. Standards: Here, too, the difference becomes sharp. There is little doubt as to what is murder, larceny, or espionage. These are defined in the law books.

But what is "subversion" or "un-Americanism"? The latter is an epithet, the former is a wholly relative term. Much that we take for granted today seemed un-American and subversive a century ago—income taxes for example. Much that existed then would seem "un-American" today—for example, the earlier restriction which limited the right to vote to those citizens who owned property. What one man sees as subversion another man sees as progress.

5. The mode of defense: In a criminal trial, the accused is furnished with a bill of particulars. It informs him that the government will allege that a safe was cracked at such and such an address in such and such a city at such and such a time. The accused may then prove he was elsewhere.

But anything remotely approaching a bill of particulars is rare in loyalty-security cases. The accused is usually asked to rebut vague charges of Communist sympathy or association. The task of the defense is to prove a negative.

Even where particulars are furnished, the outcome is not necessarily conclusive. A man may indeed "clear" himself by proving that he never engaged in liberal or left-wing activity of any kind. But what if he did belong to a radical organization? Does that mean that he is a security risk?

The only espionage case turned up in the whole security program is one which would never be suspected by normal "loyalty" standards. Joseph Petersen had no left-wing connections. A Catholic, graduated from a Catholic school, he never belonged to any organization on the Attorney General's or any similar "list." Whatever this code expert did was for a friendly power, Holland, and for no ideological reasons. He could slip easily through the sieve of customary loyalty standards.

On the other hand a Ladejinsky, for all his demonstrated value as an agricultural expert, could never hope to qualify under them for government employment if he were a new applicant. A man who had once worked for Amtorg, with two sisters in Russia, whose name had been on the mailing list of several "front" organizations during the war would never be freshly hired today. The liberals would never dare defend him. The Ladejinsky case shows the advantage of judging a man by what he *does* when employed, by the record he makes rather than by a system based on paranoid surmise.

6. Witnesses: The difficulty is made the greater by the mode of presenting evidence. In a criminal trial, the accusing witness must be produced in court and subjected to cross-examination. The right to confront one's accuser is fundamental. The government may use informers, as in narcotic or smuggling cases, but it cannot come into court and ask for conviction on undisclosed evidence by undisclosed persons on the ground that to reveal them would endanger its sources of information. The conviction can be obtained only on the basis of whatever evidence and witnesses the government produces in open court.

But in loyalty-security cases nothing is more familiar than the submission of allegations from undisclosed informers. The accused has no chance to confront the accuser. Such confrontations in criminal cases often disclose mistaken identity. Cross-examination may uncover perjury. All these safeguards are absent in loyalty-security cases because here again the security of the state, its secrets and informers, is ranked ahead of justice to the individual.

The anxiety over security reflects its widening impact on our society. As more people are drawn into its orbit, more become aware of its injustices. The government is having trouble; the loyalty program, designed originally to purge the government of liberals and radicals, has ended by making people of all kinds afraid to take government jobs. Something has to be done, and the politicians scent popularity in the issue. But they, like all of us, take the lines of least resistance, and talk only of correcting the "abuses" of the security program.

Few will dare to say it now, but the time is coming when the truth will be recognized, a truth which the Framers of our Constitution wove into the fabric of American government. They saw that there could not be freedom without risk, that no stable society could be built except on a foundation of trust, and that when trust was violated—and only then—a man could be punished. They did not think it was the province of government to police men's minds, or that it had a right to punish them unless they committed some wrongful act. They would have been horrified at our growing system of thought police, of guessing-game "law" about prospective crime, and indeed most of all by our obsession with "security."

An administrative official has a right and duty to judge the reliability of a man he hires. But what is proper and necessary in private administrative judgment is improper when erected into a system of universal surveillance and public defamation of character that chokes off free political discussion in ever wider areas and brands men as "disloyal" or "security risks" on the basis of pseudo-judicial guessing as to whether they might possibly some day commit a crime. The loyalty-security program cannot be reformed. Given peace, it will eventually be abolished.

Freedom of the Press:
A Minority Opinion

Although this essay was written over fifty years ago, its picture of a conformist press, contentedly allowing itself to be "managed" by government spin doctors supplying news with an officially approved slant is all too recognizable. The contrast to I. F. Stone's variety of journalism is provided in the third paragraph from the end, where he remarks that "Washington is in many ways one of the easiest cities in the world to cover. The problem is the abundance of riches." What was—and is—in short supply is a cadre of journalists willing to do the kind of reportorial spadework Stone did and to follow the information fearlessly wherever it leads them.

.   .   .

November 14, 1955

THE MAIN OBSTACLE TO THE CREATION of a well-informed public is its own indifference. In every country with a free press, thoughtful papers which conscientiously try to cover the news lag behind the circulation of those which peddle sex and sensationalism. This is as true in Paris and London as in New York; and if Moscow ever permits a free privately-owned press, *Izvestia* and *Pravda* will fall far behind any paper which prints the latest on that commissar's love nest.

The second obstacle is that most papers are owned by men who are not newspapermen themselves; publishing is a business, not a Jeffersonian passion, and the main object is as much advertising revenue as possible. Thus it happens that between the attitude of the publishers and that of the public, most papers in this country print little news. And this, except for local coverage, is mostly canned, syndicated, and quick-frozen.

The third obstacle is that this has always been and is now more than ever a conformist country; Main Street and Babbitt—and de Tocqueville long before Sinclair Lewis—held a faithful mirror to our true nature. It doesn't take much deviation from Rotary Club norms in the average American community to get oneself set down as queer, radical, and unreliable.

Against this background, it is easy to see why the average Washington correspondent is content to write what he is spoon-fed by the government's press officers. Especially since the press is largely Republican and this is a Republican Administration, there is little market for "exposing" the government. Why dig up a story which the desk back home will spike?

It was this astringent view of our profession and its circumstances which I found lacking in the newspapermen's testimony which opened the investigation launched here by a special House subcommittee on government "information." The most perceptive of the witnesses, and one of our very best reporters, James Reston of the *New York Times,* put his finger on the vital point when he said that worse than suppression was the "managing" of the news by government departments. But the news is "managed" because the reporters and their editors let themselves be managed.

The State Department is an outstanding offender. Very often, for example, newspaper readers get not so much what actually happened at the UN as the "slant" given out in the corridors afterward to the reporters by a State Department attaché.

The private dinner, the special briefing, are all devices for "managing" the news, as are the special organizations of privileged citizens gathered in by State and Defense Departments for those sessions at which highly confidential (and one-sided) information is ladled out to a flattered "elite."

As a reporter who began by covering small towns, where one really has to dig for the news, I can testify that Washington is in many ways one of the easiest cities in the world to cover. The problem is the abundance of riches. It is true that the Government, like every other government in the world, does its best to distort the news in its favor—but that only makes the job more interesting.

Most of my colleagues agree with the Government and write the accepted thing because that is what they believe; they are indeed—with honorable exceptions—as suspicious of the non-conformist as any group in Kiwanis.

Though the first day's witnesses included the best and boldest of the regular press, no one mentioned the recent deportations of radical foreign language editors and of Cedric Belfrage of the *Guardian*. No one mentioned the Communist editors and reporters prosecuted—*for their ideas*—under the Smith Act. No one mentioned the way McCarthy "investigated" James Wechsler. Surely thoughtful men, as aroused as these were over the future of a free press, might have given a moment's consideration to the possible danger in such precedents. Did they feel it would be indiscreet to go beyond respectable limits? That such fundamental principles are best left for orations on Zenger and Lovejoy, both conveniently dead?

The Court Turns Back the Clock

By the time of Joseph McCarthy's death on May 2, 1957, he had been consigned to political impotence and oblivion. In this piece, Stone celebrates a hopeful new mood in Washington, symbolized by a case in which the Supreme Court "turned back the clock"—not in any reactionary sense, but by rejecting the "two decades of carefully nurtured nightmare" of anti-Communist hysteria on which McCarthy and his followers had thrived.

·   ·   ·

May 13, 1957

WHILE THE SENATE LAST WEEK was burying McCarthy, the United States Supreme Court buried McCarthyism. The decisions in the Schware and Konigsberg cases do more than decide that radicals have a right to practice law. The decisions turn their back on an era in which the mere allegation of leftist sympathy or affiliation was enough to put a man outside the pale. A striking example will illustrate how unmistakably the Court has turned back the clock to an earlier and saner period. One of the charges on which the New Mexico Board of Bar Examiners refused to permit Rudolph Schware to take its tests for admission to the bar was his arrest and indictment in 1940 for recruiting volunteers to aid the Loyalists in Spain. The Supreme Court says, "even if it be assumed that the law was violated, it does not seem that such an offense indicated moral turpitude. . . . Many persons in this country actively supported the Spanish Loyalists," and it adds coolly, "In determining whether a person's character is good the nature of the offense which he has committed must be taken into account." This has a positive Rip Van Winkle-ish flavor; it awakens from a twenty-year sleep the forgotten attitudes most thoughtful Americans shared at the time; it expunges two decades of carefully nurtured nightmare.

The words were those of Mr. Justice Black, but no longer speaking in last-ditch isolation for Black and Douglas dissenting. Here he spoke for a majority which included not only Chief Justice Warren and our new (Catholic) Justice, Brennan, but even—*mirabile dictu*—Mr. Justice Burton. Indeed the "right wing" of the Court, Justices Frankfurter, Clark, and Harlan, saw no reason to dispute the majority's judgment in respect to Schware. Their concurring opinion indicates the change in atmosphere as strongly as does the majority decision. The circumstance which they found "controlling" was the fact that the New Mexico Supreme Court, in upholding Schware's exclusion from the bar, laid its main stress on the fact that Schware was admittedly a member of the Communist party from 1932 to 1940. The New Mexico Supreme Court said it felt that "one who has knowingly given his loyalty to such a program and belief for six to seven years during a period of responsible adulthood is a person of questionable character." Even the three Justices on the right find this "so dogmatic an inference as to be wholly unwarranted."

A few years ago, when McCarthy was riding high, it is difficult to imagine the Supreme Court even agreeing to hear the Schware and Konigsberg appeals. The mingled facts and allegations would have made them seem too disreputable to deserve judicial intervention. Beside his past membership in the Communist party and his indictment for recruiting volunteers for Spain, Rudolph Schware had used a false name as a labor organizer, and had been arrested several times for "criminal syndicalism" during the 1934 general strike in California. Normally—or at least by the standards which had become normal during the cold war decade—this would have been regarded as more than sufficient to show bad character and therefore disqualify for admission to the bar. Raphael Konigsberg's record was as bad, if not worse, from this point of view, because his political derelictions were more recent. California's rules require that an applicant for admission to the bar must establish the fact that he is of good moral character and does not advocate violent overthrow of the government. Konigsberg had been identified as a Communist by an informer before the State's own (Tenney) Un-American Activities Committee. He had refused on First Amendment grounds to answer any questions put by the bar examiners as to his political beliefs and associations except to swear that he did not believe in violent overthrow. And he had written a series of editorials during the Korean War for a publication called the *California Eagle* which no one would ever have mistaken for pieces by Walter Lippmann. Indeed the editors of the *Daily Worker* might well have rejected some of them as on the intemperate side.

The selections given in the briefs for the State Bar of California show that Mr. Konigsberg was not slavishly devoted to the cause of understatement. "Not all the criminal gangs in American history put together," he wrote in one editorial, "were as great a danger to our country's welfare as are the generals who today urge that American youth be trained as 'killers.'. . . . None of the murderers have been so sinful as a Dulles who uses religion to champion the anti-Christ. None such a threat to our security as a United States Attorney General who denies us the right to bail and tells brother to spy on brother." Another selection was headed, "The Cesspool" and subheaded "Traitor! Traitor!" It was succinct, if not calm. "Betrayal is in the air," he wrote. "Judges with impunity violate our constitutional rights. . . . Stool pigeons are the new national heroes. . . . The President violates his oath of office by dragging us into war." Another selection said, "To consider loyalty to America as identical with Truman, Dulles & U. S. Steel is, to me, the ultimate in sacrilege. . . . Lynchers of Americans and engineers of the doctrine of guns over butter." Obviously Mr. Konigsberg is not one to use his First Amendment rights sparingly. The horrified bar examiners found these selections not only heretical politically but "morally deficient." His own intrepid attorneys, Edward Mosk and Samuel Rosenwein, must have wondered whether the Justices of the Supreme Court would not hastily pull the bedcovers over their heads after reading these selections and deny Mr. Konigsberg a hearing.

The majority seems to have regarded these brash utterances with a sense of humor that has been lacking here for some time. Indeed Mr. Justice Black exhumes from the record and cites in a footnote, with an almost audible chuckle, an editorial in which Mr. Konigsberg in his machine-gun prose centered his fire on the Supreme Court for refusing to hear the Hollywood Ten and said this made "that high tribunal an integral part of the cold war machine directed against the American people." Mr. Justice Black for the majority finds that these editorials "fairly interpreted only say that certain officials were performing their duty in a manner that, in the opinion of the writer, was injurious to the public. We do not believe that an inference of bad moral character can rationally be drawn from these editorials. . . . Courts are not, and should not be, immune to such criticism. Government censorship can no more be reconciled with our national constitutional standard of freedom of speech and press when done in the guise of determining 'moral character' than if it should be attempted directly." It has been a long time since a majority of the Supreme Court regarded radical utterances with such Hyde Park calm.

The majority, as if celebrating a kind of field day after the long winter of judicial evasion and abnegation, has no time for craftsmanlike legal conservatism. "The State argues," Mr. Justice Black says, "that Konigsberg's refusal to tell the examiners whether he was a member of the Communist party . . . tends to support an inference that he is a member of the Communist party and therefore a person of bad moral character. . . . Obviously the State could not draw unfavorable inferences as to his truthfulness, candor or his moral character in general if his refusal to answer was based on a belief that the United States Constitution prohibited the type of inquiries which the committee was making. On the record before us, it is our judgment that the inferences of bad moral character which the committee attempted to draw from Konigsberg's refusal to answer questions about his political affiliations and opinions are unwarranted." This gives new weight and dignity to claims of First Amendment privilege.

It is always hazardous to draw straight lines from general propositions in current cases to the outcome of other future cases. But it is hard not to be hopeful about a court on which a majority of the members (the newest judge, Whittaker, took no part) regard so astringently views, facts and allegations which until recently would have been damning. The two appellants, Schware and Konigsberg, though men with honorable war and civilian records, would have been crucified by a McCarthy. Liberals, middle-of-the-roaders and conservatives alike on this Court seem prepared to take an adult view of past Communist party membership, and a respectful attitude toward First Amendment claims. They seem prepared at last here, as in other free societies, to untangle the real problems of communism from the hobgoblins of cold war demonology. Whatever that evil and unscrupulous adventurer McCarthy died of, a black sense of failure and public rejection hastened his sodden end. His punier successors are likely to contract similar ailments when they ponder on the *Schware* and *Konigsberg* decisions. It looks as if the witch hunt is drawing to its close.

Boris Pasternak

Boris Pasternak, the Russian poet best known in the West for his novel *Doctor Zhivago,* was announced as the winner of the Nobel Prize for Literature on October 25, 1958. Two days later, Pasternak sent the following telegram to the Swedish Academy: "Immensely thankful, touched, proud, astonished, abashed." However, this was followed four days later by a second telegram: "Considering the meaning this award has been given in the society to which I belong, I must reject this undeserved prize which has been presented to me. Please do not receive my voluntary rejection with displeasure." It was clear that this second message was motivated by Pasternak's fear that he would be stripped of citizenship and barried from the U.S.S.R. if he traveled to Stockholm to accept the prize. The resulting controversy turned a fine writer into a political football, which clearly disturbed I. F. Stone.

.   .   .

November 3, 1958

I READ BORIS PASTERNAK'S *Doctor Zhivago* with joy and admiration. In its sensitive pages one is back in the wonderful world of the nineteenth-century Russian novelists. He is a fine writer, and a brave man; there are passages which, read against the background of Soviet realities, are of a sublime courage.

But I find myself more and more annoyed by the chorus of Pasternak's admirers in this country. I do not remember that *Life* magazine, which glorifies Pasternak, ever showed itself any different from the *Pravda-Kommunist* crowd in dealing with our own Pasternaks. I do not recall that *Life* defended Howard Fast for receiving the Stalin award or deplored the venomous political hostility which drove Charlie Chaplin and more recently Paul Robeson into exile.

Only a few years ago Arthur Miller, an American writer much less critical of our society than Pasternak is of his, was summoned before the House Un-American Activities Committee, submitted to humiliating interrogation, and threatened covertly with perjury charges unless he recanted his past political views. Even today the one movie house in Washington which has revived the old Chaplin classics runs an apologetic note in its advertising.

It is easier for a critic of capitalism and the cold war to live in this country than for a critic of communism to live in Russia. But an unofficial blacklist still bars some of our best artists and actors and directors in Hollywood and from radio-TV work.

The closest analogue to Pasternak is Howard Fast, and until he broke with the Communists he was forced to publish his own books. All of us who are more or less heretical in our society are forced to live on its margin, grateful that we are able to speak (at the cost of abnormal exertions) to a small audience.

Pasternak has universal meaning, for he embodies the fight the artist and the seeker after truth must wage everywhere against official dogma and conformist pressures. Not a few of our intellectuals in Hollywood and elsewhere on their psychoanalysts' couches may say the very words Pasternak puts into the mouth of Dr. Zhivago.

"The great majority of us," he protests, "are required to live a life of constant, systematic duplicity. Your health is bound to be affected if, day after day, you say the opposite of what you feel, if you grovel before what you dislike and rejoice at what brings you nothing but misfortune. Our nervous system isn't just a fiction, it's a part of our physical body, and our soul exists in space and is inside us, like the teeth in our mouth. It can't be forever violated with impunity."

In another passage Dr. Zhivago tells his beloved, "The main misfortune, the root of all evil to come, was the loss of confidence in the value of one's own opinion. People imagined it was out of date to follow their own moral sense, that they must all sing in chorus, and live by other people's notions, notions that were being crammed down everybody's throat." This applies equally to present-day America.

Unlike Ehrenburg's pedestrian *The Thaw* and Dudinstev's wooden *Not by Bread Alone,* the other protest novels of the post-Stalin period, *Doctor Zhivago* is a work of art. Giving it the Nobel prize was a political act in the best sense of the word, for it put world pressure behind the struggle of Russia's writers for greater freedom. If the masters of the Kremlin were wise they would have let Pasternak go to Stockholm and they would publish his book in Russian; such magnanimity and the book's complete negativism about the Revolution would have been a telling answer to its thesis and their critics. Bigness, obviously, is beyond them.

Whatever their folly, let us examine the mote in our own eye and remember that an American Pasternak who accepted a Soviet prize would be hauled up before the Un-American Activities Committee and blacklisted in Hollywood and on Madison Avenue. And few, *very few,* of those who are now praising Pasternak would then say one word in defense of the right to a free conscience.

In Defense of the Campus Rebels

Here is a deeply *personal* essay. Its theme is the importance of dissent as a driving force for social and political improvement; the specific application, to the campus radicals of the Vietnam era; the point of view, that of "a premature New Leftist" who came of age in the 1930s and '40s and views the long-haired rebels of the '60s with a bemused mixture of admiration and alarm. In the end, Stone supports the radicals—not because he agrees with all of their positions or tactics, which he clearly does not, but because he recognizes the value of "a little *un*-reason" in forcing change on a hidebound establishment, and has enough faith in human nature to take a few chances on behalf of freedom.

. . .

May 19, 1969

I HATE TO WRITE ON SUBJECTS about which I know no more than the conventional wisdom of the moment. One of these subjects is the campus revolt. My credentials as an expert are slim. I always loved learning and hated school. I wanted to go to Harvard, but I couldn't get in because I had graduated forty-ninth in a class of fifty-two from a small-town high school. I went to college at the University of Pennsylvania, which was obligated—this sounds like an echo of a familiar black demand today—to take graduates of high schools in neighboring communities no matter how ill-fitted. My boyhood idol was the saintly Anarchist Kropotkin. I looked down on college degrees and felt that a man should do only what was sincere and true and without thought of mundane advancement. This provided lofty reasons for not doing homework. I majored in philosophy with the vague thought of teaching it but though I revered two of my professors I disliked the smell of a college faculty. I dropped out in my third year to go back to newspaper work. Those were the twenties and I was a pre-depression radical. So I

45

might be described I suppose as a premature New Leftist, though I never had the urge to burn anything down.

In microcosm, the *Weekly* and I have become typical of our society. The war and the military have taken up so much of our energies that we have neglected the blacks, the poor and students. Seen from afar, the turmoil and the deepening division appear to be a familiar tragedy, like watching a friend drink himself to death. Everybody knows what needs to be done, but the will is lacking. We have to break the habit. There is no excuse for poverty in a society which can spend $80 billion a year on its war machine. If national security comes first, as the spokesmen for the Pentagon tell us, then we can only reply that the clearest danger to the national security lies in the rising revolt of our black population. Our own country is becoming a Vietnam. As if in retribution for the suffering we have imposed, we are confronted by the same choices: either to satisfy the aspirations of the oppressed or to try and crush them by force. The former would be costly, but the latter will be disastrous.

This is what the campus rebels are trying to tell us, in the only way which seems to get attention. I do not like much of what they are saying and doing. I do not like to hear opponents shouted down, much less beaten up. I do not like to hear any one group or class, including policemen, called pigs. I do not think four-letter words are arguments. I hate *hate,* intolerance and violence. I see them as man's most ancient and enduring enemies and I hate to see them welling up on my side. But I feel about the rebels as Erasmus did about Luther. Erasmus helped inspire the Reformation but was repelled by the man who brought it to fruition. He saw that Luther was as intolerant and as dogmatic as the Church. "From argument," as Erasmus saw it, "there would be a quick resort to the sword, and the whole world would be full of fury and madness." Two centuries of religious wars without parallel for blood-lust were soon to prove how right were his misgivings. But while Erasmus "could not join Luther, he dared not oppose him, lest haply, as he confessed 'he might be fighting against the spirit of God.'"* I feel that the New Left and the black revolutionists, like Luther, are doing

*Froude's *Life and Letters of Erasmus.*

God's work, too, in refusing any longer to submit to evil, and challenging society to reform or crush them.

Lifelong dissent has more than acclimated me cheerfully to defeat. It has made me suspicious of victory. I feel uneasy at the very idea of a Movement. I see every insight degenerating into a dogma, and fresh thoughts freezing into lifeless party line. Those who set out nobly to be their brother's keeper sometimes end up by becoming his jailer. Every emancipation has in it the seeds of a new slavery, and every truth easily becomes a lie. But these perspectives, which seem so irrefutably clear from a pillar in the desert, are worthless to those enmeshed in the crowded struggle. They are no better than mystical nonsense to the humane student who has to face his draft board, the dissident soldier who is determined not to fight, the black who sees his people doomed by shackles stronger than slavery to racial humiliation and decay. The business of the moment is to end the war, to break the growing dominance of the military in our society, to liberate the blacks, the Mexican-American, the Puerto Rican and the Indian from injustice. This is the business of our best youth. However confused and chaotic, their unwillingness to submit any longer is our one hope.

There is a wonderful story of a delegation which came here to see Franklin D. Roosevelt on some reform or other. When they were finished the President said, "Okay, you've convinced me. Now go on out and bring pressure on me." Every thoughtful official knows how hard it is to get anything done if someone isn't making it uncomfortable *not to.* Just imagine how helpless the better people in government would be if the rebels, black and white, suddenly fell silent. The war might smolder on forever, the ghettoes attract as little attention as a refuse dump. It is a painful business extricating ourselves from the stupidity of the Vietnamese war; we will only do so if it becomes more painful *not to.* It will be costly rebuilding the ghettoes, but if the black revolt goes on, it will be costlier *not to.* In the workings of a free society, the revolutionist provides the moderate with the clinching argument. And a little *un*-reason does wonders, like a condiment, in reinvigorating a discussion which has grown pointless and flat.

We ought to welcome the revolt as the one way to prod us into a better America. To meet it with cries of "law and order" and "conspiracy" would be to relapse into the sterile monologue which precedes all revolutions.

Rather than change old habits, those in power always prefer to fall back on the theory that all would be well but for a few malevolent conspirators. It is painful to see academia disrupted, but under the surface were shams and horrors that needed cleansing. The disruption is worth the price of awakening us. The student rebels are proving right in the daring idea that they could revolutionize American society by attacking the universities as its soft underbelly. But I would also remind the students that the three evils they fight—war, racism and bureaucracy—are universal. The Marxism-Leninism some of the rebels cling to has brought into power a bureaucracy more suffocating than any under capitalism; the students demonstrate everywhere on our side but are stifled on the other. War and imperialism have not been eliminated in the relations between Communist states. Black Africa, at least half-freed from the white man, is hardly a model of fraternity or freedom. Man's one real enemy is within himself. Burning America down is no way to Utopia. If battle is joined and our country polarized, as both the revolutionists and the repressionists wish, it is the better and not the worse side of America which will be destroyed. Someone said a man's character was his fate, and tragedy may be implicit in the character of our society *and* of its rebels. How make a whisper for patience heard amid the rising fury?

The Crisis Coming for a Free Press

The Pentagon Papers were a 47-volume, 7,000-page history of the U.S. involvement in the Vietnam War, secretly compiled by the Defense Department and leaked to the press in early 1971. The papers revealed, among other things, that the government had deliberately expanded its role in the war by conducting air strikes over Laos and raids along the coast of North Vietnam even as President Lyndon Johnson was promising not to escalate the war. Stone's essay responds to a 6–3 decision by the Supreme Court (June 30, 1971) upholding the legality of the papers' publication. It was a victory for the free press. But in the larger historical arc that led to the Pentagon Papers case, Stone detected a troubling trend away from openness and accountability and toward secrecy and deceit—a trend subsequent years have done little to alter.

.   .   .

July 9, 1971

IN THE PENTAGON PAPERS, the government had a poor case on the facts. It had an even poorer case on the law. It is a pity that the upshot was not the kind of historic defence of a free press that the weak pleading and the grave circumstances called for. *The press did its duty but the Supreme Court did not.* Its splintered opinions left a bigger loophole than before for prior restraint—something English law abandoned in 1695 and the American press has never experienced. In addition five of the nine Justices encouraged the government to believe that they would give it wide latitude if it sought to punish editors for publishing official secrets *after* they did so instead of trying to enjoin them in advance. Two Justices indeed spent most of their opinions helpfully spelling out possibilities for successful criminal prosecution. It will be a miracle if this Administration, which is almost paranoid in its attitude towards the media, is not encouraged to include editors and reporters among the "all those who have violated Federal criminal laws" the Attorney General now says he will prosecute.

The coming attempt to prosecute for violation of the government's classification orders involves nothing less than the future of representative government. For if the government can continue to abuse its secrecy stamps to keep the press, the Congress and the people from knowing what it is really doing—then the basic decisions in our country are in the hands of a small army of faceless bureaucrats, mostly military. The struggle comes at a climactic moment when Hanoi's new peace offer and public weariness with the war make it all the more necessary for the bureaucratic machine to prevent new leaks by intimidating its own mavericks and the press. Duplicity is more requisite than ever when the other side makes it necessary plainly to choose between release of the prisoners or continued pursuit of a military-political victory in South Vietnam. From every indication, Nixon's answer, however veiled, will be to pursue the war. This will intensify his conflict with the media.

First, as to the facts: Trial of the government's action against the *New York Times* and the *Washington Post* proceeded on the assumption that two documents in their entirety were in the hands of these newspapers—a 47-volume Pentagon history of our involvement in Vietnam from 1945 to 1968, and a "Command and Control" report on the Tonkin Gulf incidents of 1964. The government was invited to "pinpoint" for the trial judges, the two Courts of Appeal and the Supreme Court precisely which portions of these documents were so sensitive that their publication warranted an order forbidding the papers to publish them. To give the government greater leeway, it was allowed to present much of its evidence in secret. This was the first secret proceeding of its kind ever held in the U.S. courts, itself a disturbing precedent for the future. Yet of the 27 Federal judges who passed on the government's pleadings not a single one thought the evidence impressive enough to warrant a preliminary injunction. The government was able to obtain nothing more than temporary restraining orders pending trial and appeal, and those who dissented on the appeals courts and the Supreme Court did no more than argue for a remand for further hearing. This is the best measure of just how dubious the government's system of classification looked even to sympathetic judges in secret hearings.

Some of the dissenting judges thought the case was disposed of too hastily, and that the government should have had more time. But the government had had ample time to review the two documents involved. The Senate Foreign Relations Committee has been negotiating with the Pentagon for the Command and Control document since early in 1968 and the so-called Pentagon Papers since November 1969. At least half a dozen letters have passed between Chairman Fulbright and Secretary Laird about these documents, and the Pentagon classification officer who was assigned to review them as a result of Fulbright's repeated requests testified during the trial. The government had plenty of time to decide what in the documents was really sensitive. Apparently the judges didn't think very much was. But only as this is written the Senate Foreign Relations Committee has finally received copies of both. It took a tidal wave of a leak to pry them loose but they arrived still stamped 'Top Secret'! The truth about the Tonkin Gulf incidents may be buried in the Command and Control report but the *New York Times* completed its series without disclosing what was in this document and the Senate Foreign Relations Committee is still forbidden by the 'Top Secret' stamp from discussing the contents publicly. It will be seven years next month since the Tonkin Gulf incidents occurred and we still don't know the full truth about them, though they were used to get a blank cheque for war from Congress.

The two dissenting judges who were most impressed with the government's case were Judge Wilkey on the Court of Appeals for the District of Columbia and Mr. Justice Blackmun on the Supreme Court. They felt that *if* the newspapers had, and *if* they published, certain documents dealing with diplomatic negotiations this would do great harm. But Dr. Ellsberg at his press conference in Cambridge 28 June said he withheld "several" of the 47-volume Pentagon Papers from the newspapers because they involved secret negotiations with Hanoi, Moscow and other foreign capitals. On N.B.C.'s *Today* show 2 July, he said he gave the full set to the Senate Foreign Relations Committee but did not retain any copy of these diplomatic volumes "since I had no intention of giving them to the newspapers at any time." In oral argument before the Supreme Court, the Solicitor General said he had "pinpointed" ten sensitive items in his secret brief and that one of them was made up of four volumes "all dealing with one specific subject." Are these the volumes Dr. Ellsberg withheld?

The newspapers provided the court with inventories of the documents in their possession. The Solicitor General told the Supreme Court that the government's experts had difficulty in matching this inventory against the 47-volume Pentagon Papers. There may have been difficulty in matching individual items but it is hard to understand why they could not match up an 'item' as large as four related volumes. A week before the oral argument, the *Christian Science Monitor* (19 June) carried a story from Washington saying that Pentagon experts, after they compared the published reports in the *Times* "with the still guarded and highly classified originals," decided that the disclosures were "something less than catastrophic." They informed higher officials "that some potentially damaging material, *particularly in terms of America's relations with other nations* (our italics) had been omitted." This sounds as if they spotted the material Ellsberg withheld. It is a pity the secret record cannot be opened up to resolve this mystery. The government's most impressive cause for alarm would have been eliminated by the admission that these volumes had never reached the newspapers at all.

All this may explain the curious vagueness and equanimity displayed by Deputy Under Secretary of State Macomber on the *Today* show 5 July, the day the *New York Times* series ended. He admitted that Dr. Ellsberg had withheld some sensitive documents and that the newspapers themselves had withheld others. When asked whether the *New York Times* or the *Washington Post* had published items "the government has pointed to as particularly sensitive," he replied, "I don't think the *Washington Post* has. I think the *New York Times* may have. I don't want to say it has. I'm not sure." So this is the molehill to which the government's mountainous original charges dwindled.

The government made an even poorer showing on the law. Solicitor General Griswold's argument was downright trivial and the few precedents he cited were irrelevant and quoted out of context. Unfortunately the newspaper lawyers were no better. Never was a great case argued so feebly. No one took the First Amendment as his client. The defence lawyers argued the case as narrowly as possible in order to get their newspaper clients off the hook. Professor Alexander Bickel whom the *New York Times* retained specially for the occasion, is no firm defender of the First Amendment; he holds the "balancing" view Frankfurter among others propounded. This holds, as Griswold flatly said during argument, that where the First Amendment says "Congress shall make no law . . . abridging freedom of the press," it does not mean what the plain words say but only that freedom of the press must be "balanced" against other public considerations. Bickel agrees with Griswold. This nullifies the intention of the Framers.

The crisis for which the bar and the press must mobilize lies in the fact that never before have the courts had to confront the freedom of the press issue in this form. The publication of secret government papers is hardly new. A patriot newspaper in Boston, thanks to a leak from Benjamin Franklin, published the Royal Governor's correspondence on the eve of the Revolution. The furore over the Sedition Act began in 1798 when John Franklin Bache (Benjamin's grandson) published secret diplomatic documents to attack the covert Federalist war against France. But this was before the days of "classification" and leaks of this kind were prosecuted as seditious libels intended to bring the government into disrepute. What we face now are the first prosecutions of the press for upsetting the government's system of classification. The freedom of the press issue is thereby entangled with the question of national security.

A government cannot be denied the right to some secrets, especially in wartime. But what makes this case so crucial is that Dr. Ellsberg's leak and its publication in the press represented the first open revolt against a system of secrecy which has reached cancerous proportions and threatens unless checked to destroy free government itself. The amount of information now stamped secret and withheld from the press and Congress is staggering. The *Washington Star* estimates (8 July) that Pentagon Xerox machines produce about 100 million documents a year. A recently retired Air Force security officer told a House Government Information subcommittee 24 June, "I would guess that there are at least 20 million classified documents, including reproduced copies, in existence" and added, "I sincerely believe that less than one-half of one percent of the different documents actually contain information qualifying even for the lowest defence classification."

The Pentagon Papers showed that the government has been carrying on secret warfare in Indo-China since 1954. They disclosed for the first time the full dimensions of the arrogance, duplicity and inhumanity with which successive Administrations got us into this horrible mess which is tearing the country apart and demoralizing the armed forces themselves. It was the height of Nixon-era banality for Chief Justice Burger to say that a newspaper editor, handed such documents, should, like a taxi driver who finds stolen goods in his cab, turn them over to the police! To reduce such historic revelations in the midst of an agonized public debate over the war to the dimensions of a simple case of larceny and receiving stolen goods is utterly to miss the function of a free press in a free society.

Representative government is menaced today by a cloud of secrecy. The Daniel Ellsbergs and Neil Sheehans are too few; a Senator like Gravel willing to challenge the classification system in which Congress has acquiesced for so many years, is unique. We need more such rebels, not fewer, if free government is to survive.

In the fight against government secrecy we need to apply in a fresh form the philosophy of risk which laid the foundations for real freedom of the press in the earlier struggle against the law of seditious libel. It is often forgotten that after prior restraint or censorship ended almost three centuries ago, the press was still shackled by the common law of seditious libel. Editors went to jail for bringing government into disrepute; the rule was that the greater the truth of their publications the greater the offence; royal governors decided the law and made conviction by the jury almost a foregone conclusion. The reformers sought to protect the press by making the jury the judge of the law as well as the facts, and to make truth a defence. The Sedition Act of 1798, so notorious in our history, actually embodied these reforms, though its purpose was repressive. Like Fox's historic Libel Act six years earlier in England, it made the jury the judge of the law as well as the facts; in addition the Sedition Act made truth a defence, something English law did not achieve until 1843.

But these long-sought reforms proved illusory. In the heat of partisan passion, only one jury failed to convict in a Sedition Act case and "truth" proved difficult to determine. It became clear that freedom of the press could only be secure if the press were allowed to propagate error. Otherwise censorship was only replaced by prosecution after publication. It was in the battle against the Sedition Act that the Jeffersonians for the first time* hammered out the libertarian doctrines which have made ours the freest press in the world. The philosophy to which we are indebted runs in a great line from Madison, the Father of the Constitution, to Brandeis, and from them to Black and Douglas. It says that freedom is impossible without risk of repression. This is what the best young people yearn for under Communist rule and this is what we are in danger of forgetting in the Nixon era.

We must apply the philosophy of risk to the new circumstances. Talk of reforming the classification system will soon evaporate. Successful prosecutions would only nail it down. The path of least resistance is that which Nixon has already charted: to cut down the number of persons with access to secret documents and to tighten up on security. It would in any case take a small army many years to review the classification of all our secret documents. The only hope lies in jury acquittals in the coming prosecutions, and in arguing that the only possible check on the abuses of overclassification and secrecy is to allow unpunished the leak and publication of documents like the Pentagon Papers. Congress by twice refusing to enact an Official Secrets Act in wartime has shown itself of a similar mind. Men of courage are all too rare; the circumstances which bring establishment papers to print such documents are even rarer. This is the only safety valve we have if the people's right to know is not entirely to disappear.

---

*One may find this ably developed in Leonard W. Levy's book, *Freedom of Speech and Press in Early American History.*

Part Two

A GOOD WAR—BUT FOR WHAT?

War Comes to Washington

It is always easy to project backward onto historical moments the conceptions and feelings of a later time. Decades after the entry of the United States into World War II, we think we recall an America instantly roused to righteous, united fury by the attack on Pearl Harbor. The snapshot offered in this article written at the time is subtly different. Stone writes of the impact of Pearl Harbor on the long-standing conflict between American isolationists and the "pro-war faction"; he notes "a sense of excitement, of adventure, and of relief" among the citizens of Washington, D.C., over the advent of war, and few signs of indignation directed toward the Japanese "treachery." Perhaps most surprising of all, he remarks, "We are going into this war lightly"—a startling comment from today's standpoint, knowing as we do the tragic sequels: Stalingrad, Dachau, Dresden, Auschwitz, Hiroshima.

.   .   .

December 13, 1941

I FIRST HEARD THE NEWS from the elevator man in the National Press Building. The ticker at the Press Club, normally shut off on Sunday, carried the first flash telling of the Japanese attack on Pearl Harbor. It was a beautiful late-autumn Sunday, the sky clear and the air crisp. At the entrance to the White House a small crowd had gathered to watch Cabinet members arrive. In the reporters' room inside a group was clustered around the radio. I talked to Ambassador Hu Shih by telephone, and he said he felt "really sad" and sounded as though he meant it. The Navy Department seemed busy but calm; the War Department less so. Soldiers in helmets, carrying guns with fixed bayonets, guarded the entrance to the War Department's half of the huge old Munitions Building. They looked awkward and uncomfortable.

The public-relations office of the War Department refused a request for background material on the comparative military strength of the United States and Japan on the ground that since four o'clock that afternoon all information on the composition and movement of troops abroad had been declared a secret. The Navy Department, less strict, was still giving out information already "on the record," thus saving reporters a trip to the Library of Congress. In the Navy Department reference room women employees, hastily summoned from their homes, sent out for sandwiches and coffee and joked about Japanese bombers. There as elsewhere one encountered a sense of excitement, of adventure, and of relief that a long-expected storm had finally broken. No one showed much indignation. As for the newspapermen, myself included, we all acted a little like firemen at a three-alarmer.

The first press release from the State Department spluttered. It said the Secretary of State had handed the Japanese representatives a document on November 26 stating American policy in the Far East and suggestions for a settlement. A reply had been handed the Secretary of State that afternoon. The release declared that Secretary Hull had read the reply and immediately turned to the Japanese Ambassador and with the greatest indignation said: ". . . I have never seen a document that was more crowded with infamous falsehoods and distortions—infamous falsehoods and distortions on a scale so huge that I never imagined until today that any government on this planet was capable of uttering them." I asked several other reporters at the State Department just what the Japanese had told Secretary Hull to make him so angry. Nobody seemed to know, and the release did not explain. Hull's language was later described by one reporter as being "as biting if not as deadly as his fellow-mountaineer Sergeant York's bullets." It is a long time since Secretary Hull was a mountaineer.

The Japanese memorandum, released later, made it easier to understand the Secretary's stilted indignation. One has to go back to Will Irwin's "Letters of a Japanese Schoolboy" to match this memorandum. "Ever since China Affair broke out owing to the failure on the part of China to comprehend Japan's true intentions," said one of the more humorous passages, "the Japanese government has striven for the restoration of peace, and it has consistently exerted its best efforts to prevent the extension of war-like dis-

turbances. It was also to that end that in September last year Japan concluded the Tripartite Pact with Germany and Italy." The memorandum indicates only the vaguest shadow of any American intention to appease
Japan. At one time the President seems to have offered to "introduce" peace
between Japan and China and then—I suspect after the visit to the White
House of Hu Shih and T. V. Soong—withdrawn it. But the kind of peace
the President might have "introduced" could hardly have been to Japan's
liking, though the idea may have made the Chinese uneasy. The Japanese
memorandum accuses our own government of "holding fast to theories in
disregard of realities," of trying to force "a utopian ideal" on the Japanese,
and of "refusing to yield an inch on its impractical principles." I hope these
compliments were fully deserved.

The proposals made by Secretary Hull in his letter of November 26 were
so obviously unacceptable to a government like Japan's that one wonders
why we negotiated at all. Japan was to withdraw all its troops from China
and not to support any other government there except "the National Government" . . . with capital temporarily at Chungking." Our War Department is said to have asked the White House for three more months in
which to prepare, and it may be that the Japanese were also anxious to delay
a crisis. It is suspected in some quarters here that the attack on Pearl Harbor
was the work of a minority in Japan fearful of further "stalling." The attack
came before the Emperor could reply to the President's personal appeal for
peace. If it forced the hand of the Japanese government, it also succeeded in
uniting our own country behind Mr. Roosevelt. The reactions of the isolationist press and of Senators like Wheeler are indicative. If Mr. Roosevelt
leaned too far in one direction to please the anti-appeasement and pro-war
faction, his tactics served to prove to the other side that he had done all in
his power to avoid war, that war was forced upon him. Lincoln in the same
way hesitated and compromised and sought to "appease" before war came.

We are going into this war lightly, but I have a feeling that it will weigh
heavily upon us all before we are through. The vast theater on which the
struggle between this country and Japan opens makes the last war seem a
parochial conflict confined to the Atlantic and the western cape of the
Eurasian continent. This is really world war, and in my humble opinion it
was unavoidable and is better fought now when we still have allies left. It is

hoped here that the actual coming of war may serve to speed up the pace of production and shake both capital and labor out of a business-as-usual mood far too prevalent. There has been a general feeling that the production problem could not be solved until war was declared. We shall see. It is possible that a whipped-up hysteria against labor and progressives will serve to stifle the very forces that could be used to bring about an "all-out" effort. It is also possible that the coming of war will open the way to greater cooperation in the defense program, to a broader role for labor in the mobilization of industry, to a lessening of attacks on labor in Congress, and to improved morale.

My own confidence springs from a deep confidence in the President. For all his mistakes—and perhaps some of them have only seemed mistakes—he can be counted on to turn up in the end on the democratic and progressive side. I hate to think of what we should do without him, and when I drive down to work early in the morning past the White House I cannot help thinking with sympathy of the burdens that weigh him down. On the threshold of war, and perhaps ultimately social earthquake, we may be grateful that our country has his leadership.

The Shake-up We Need

I. F. Stone was always immersed in the practical details of policy. In this column written within three weeks of Pearl Harbor, he discusses the kinds of personnel and administrative changes that he regards as essential to a effective war effort. Many of the specific details are now familiar only to historians of the period. (For example, in the second paragraph, "Knudsen" is William S. Knudsen, advisor for industrial production on the Advisory Commission of the Council for National Defense, which Roosevelt had established in 1940 to launch preparations for the inevitable war, while Jesse Jones was Roosevelt's Secretary of Commerce. Historians credit both men for their efforts at mobilizing American war production.) But Stone's larger theme—the need to remake domestic policies and reconsider long-standing assumptions about the sanctity of *laissez-faire* in support of the battle for national survival—remains relevant and fascinating today.

.   .   .

December 27, 1941

I AM RELIABLY INFORMED that recent events abroad have led our War College to the reluctant conclusion that the cavalry charge is no longer likely to be decisive. It is at least as important to overhaul our social as our military thinking. No official here will admit it in public, and few in private, but what this country needs is more interference with private enterprise. The military-naval revolution which has enabled a coalition of smaller, poorer, and hungrier powers to attack the British, French, Dutch, and American empires with such success is also the reflection of a social revolution, and requires the reexamination of the bromides which ordinarily pass among us for profound truths. When wars are fought with tanks and planes, defeat or victory is decided on the assembly line. We see the relationship between technology and military power, but we have only begun to recognize that technology is more than the fabrication of new weapons.

It also includes the way in which we organize our society to produce those weapons, for on that organization may depend the volume of our output, the speed of our production.

In all the talk here of impending shake-ups in defense, too little is heard of the need for a shake-up in fundamental ideas. Without it the effect of substituting Willkie for Knudsen or Wallace for Jesse Jones is likely to be less than miraculous. The war now unfolding marks the end of laissez faire, long honored more in the speech than in the observance, and the fate of free government depends on riding this tide, not bucking it. The root of our troubles, the basic defect of our war effort, the reason for our idle facilities lie in a system of ideas which leads us to regard the proposal to draft machines with horror while we look on the draft of men with equanimity. This is but the war-time reflection of the double standard which normally determines our attitude toward the rights of property on the one hand and the rights of human beings on the other. A society which regards it as proper in an economic crisis to throw men out of work at once but shameful to default on a bond until absolutely necessary is handicapped by its *mores* in mobilizing itself for war. The people who live in it are willing to order a man to risk his life for his country but reluctant to tell a factory owner that he must turn out parts for tanks—or else. Yet in a modern war we can no more depend on the profit motive to gear our economy for an all-out effort that we can depend on the profit motive to fill our army with enlistments at $21 a month and board. Until this is recognized, said publicly, and acted upon, we are headed for one unpleasant military surprise after another.

Just one year ago, in *The Nation* of December 21, 1940, I broke the story of the Reuther plan. Today's papers carry the news that 206,000 workers in Michigan will lose their jobs in the next seven days because no steps have yet been taken to convert automobile factories to defense production. This inability of a great and rich country to gather up sufficient will to mobilize its full energies for war is characteristic of empires in their senility. We are again the victim of want amid plenty, though this time it is a want of armament amid plenty of potential productive capacity. Solution of the problem has been hampered by a succession of complacencies in the capital. The first was the easy assumption that we were unbeatable because we had the greatest productive system in the world. When it began to be realized that this productive system was being largely devoted to a boom in consumer goods, it was assumed that it would transform itself automatically into a vast arsenal if we curtailed the output of automobiles, washing machines, refrigerators, and new houses.

A few months ago, however, officials and others began to see that curtailment alone was no guaranty that facilities made idle by scarcity of materials would be converted to defense production. Smaller industries found it hard to obtain orders from the big business men running the OPM [Office of Production Management] and hard to interest the conventionally thinking army-navy procurement officers in the possibility of turning out armament in factories normally used to produce washing machines. Now I find officials assuming that "December 7 changed all that." The attack on Pearl Harbor should have ended "business as usual," but it did not. To assume that it will without any action on our part is a curious, and comfortable, kind of fatalism. It is well to remember that bombs have been falling on the capital of the British Empire for two years without completely ending business as usual.

The truth is that while men like Stimson and Knox helped the President on the war issue by getting out in front, the top liberals and labor men in the defense setup have been more anxious to avoid fights than to exercise leadership. A fight is now brewing behind the scenes over the scuttling of the Victory Program by Knudsen and army-navy procurement, but at the SPAB [Supply Priorities Allocation Board] meeting at which the program was cut down by some 25 per cent neither Donald Nelson nor Leon Henderson nor Sidney Hillman put up an effective battle. All three have been good influences, but none of them is a fighter. Henderson is more smoke than fire. Nelson shines most by contrast with his fellow-business men. Hillman is able but not inspired or inspiring, and I was glad to see the Tolan committee take a rap at him in its excellent report on the measures needed to mobilize all our productive facilities for war. If Hillman had had the courage to go on the air last fall in support of the Reuther plan he would have looked a hero today. Unfortunately his is not the kind of leadership that will help us find our way to total effort for total war.

It is easy for a newspaperman writing for an independent weekly to talk of the need for interfering with private enterprise. It is hard for these men and other political leaders to do or say anything about it. Our government has political sovereignty under democratic processes, but in the sphere of our economy it is still in the position of a sovereign in feudal times and must deal with powerful economic overlords whose control over the means of public discussion make them formidable antagonists. Public officials who run afoul of these great interests take their careers in their hands, and few can be found to venture a head-on collision with them. Agencies like the Dies committee and the FBI play a valuable role here in keeping the progressives frightened and worried and thus in curbing the most useful forces in the war effort. In this connection I would like to point to Secretary Knox's statement that the most powerful fifth column since Norway operated in Hawaii and to ask why the FBI, with all the vast sums and great power at its disposal, seems to have been so ineffective in curbing it. Maybe if it spent less time tapping wires in an effort to get Harry Bridges* and scaring minor clerks in government offices by asking them what they think of communism and what their religious affiliations are, it would have more time left for the kind of detective operations we needed on Oahu.

---

*Militant labor organizer, head of the International Longshoremen's and Warehouse-men's Union, West Coast director of the C.I.O. From 1939 to 1955 the Justice Department tried unsuccessfully to deport him to his birthplace, Australia, as a Communist subversive.

Washington's Forbidden Topic

Here is I. F. Stone on the issue of the "second front," the assault on western Europe that would not begin until D-Day in June, 1944, more than a year and a half after this column. The technique here is classic Stone, from the opening sentence (which encapsulates the journalistic method for which he is most renowned, the discovery and analysis of a public but little-known document) to the typically open-minded, even contrarian viewpoint: Though a strong supporter of Roosevelt, Stone is happy to endorse a minority opinion from the pen of George H. Bender, an obscure Republican congressman who clearly represents the sort of "Main Street" conservatism Stone often held up to scorn. Note how Stone, as usual, places the urgent immediate issue in the broadest historical context: Will the Allies mount a truly united effort to defeat the Axis, and thereby lay a solid foundation for victory and a cooperative post-war world, or will they be defeated by their own mutual suspicions and antagonisms?

.   .   .

October 31, 1942

I WANT TO CALL ATTENTION TO an extraordinary document that seems to have been completely overlooked by the daily press. I refer to the "Additional Comments" of Representative Bender which are appended to the report on man-power issued by the Tolan committee last Tuesday. Bender is a Republican Congressman-at-large from Ohio. He was first elected to Congress in 1938 and only recently became a member of the Tolan committee. Little is known of him, and that little gives no indication that he differs much from the average Middle Western Republican. All "Who's Who" reveals is: "Pres. George H. Bender Ins. Co.; editor and publisher the *Ohio Republican* and the *National Republican* since 1934; mem. Ohio State Senate, 1920–30; pres. Ohio Fedn. of Rep. Clubs; chmn. Rep. Central Com. of Cuyahoga County." This certainly smacks of Main Street, and it is as a

Main Streeter that Bender chooses to speak in his "Additional Comments," which are really a separate and sharper minority report. "Since the winter of 1941," he declares, "it has been clear to every Main Street American that what is needed is a second front in Europe to split the Axis forces. Spring, summer, and fall have come and gone without a second front."

Representative Bender's advocacy of a second front is less important than his courage in being the first public figure here to speak out in plain language on the deeper issue behind the question of a second front. This is not whether we are to open an offensive in France next Tuesday or next month or next spring. The real question is whether we are to plan this as a war of the United Nations, with a Western offensive geared into the supply needs of the British, Russians, and Chinese, or whether we are to plan to fight the world alone. The truth is, as every important official here knows, that the President's dominant military-naval advisers are already operating on this latter assumption. The corollaries of this assumption are (1) the addition of several million men to our army, (2) the curtailment of lend-lease aid to our allies in order to outfit that army, and (3) postponement of the offensive until the enlarged army is ready. All three corollaries are already reflected in official action, and informed persons here say that the plan is to stage no real large-scale offensive in 1943.

The Bender report is a hard-hitting six-page summary of the basic manpower, military, and production problems facing us in this war. The full committee report is the ablest and most comprehensive analysis of war needs and war planning ever to appear here, and I hope to discuss it in some detail in my next article. The value of Mr. Bender's "Additional Comments" is that they bring some of the points in the full report into sharper focus. "Our military," Bender says, "have never decided when, where, and with what they are going to fight. For this reason they have not and cannot give to the War Production Board [WPB] and to the War Manpower Commission, respectively, schedules of their requirements for military products and man-power. Without these schedules it has been impossible to plan production, to allocate materials and man-power. And because we have not planned the elements of production, we cannot manage or control the flow of armament. Without such scheduled flow of weapons the military cannot undertake to plan its strategy." The result of this vicious circle is that "we are always on the defensive." And now we are really preparing to dig in on the defensive on a gigantic scale.

Will the reader bear with me while I quote more fully from that passage in which Representative Bender touches upon the capital's most important Forbidden Topic? "At the present time," Bender writes, "the army is demanding a huge increase in man-power." A fantastically high proportion of present production now goes to supply ordinary civilian items for our present army. "When the army is asked," Bender continues, "if it expects to obtain trucks and other equipment in the same proportion to this larger army as it now obtains, no answer is forthcoming." Why do we need an army and navy of about 10,000,000 men? "*The demand by the military for a huge army,*" Bender answers, "*is based in part on the assumption that one or more of our allies will collapse in the coming year.* Upon this assumption, it is then argued that we can rely only on ourselves." Since the Tolan report went to press, Secretary Stimson has cut his estimate to 7,500,000 men, but a continuation of the present defensive and defeatist strategic thinking will make necessary an army much larger than that, perhaps as large as 13,000,000.

"To equip such an army with training weapons alone," Bender goes on, "would require practically all of our present war production. Therefore, these advocates of a huge army move logically to the next point—the reduction or stoppage of lend-lease shipments to our allies." By assuming the defeat of our allies we are compelled vastly to enlarge the army. By mobilizing a vastly larger army we help to insure their defeat. "When it is pointed out to these advocates of a 13,000,000-man army," Bender says, "that our allies may collapse if we stop lend-lease shipments, they have no answer"—that is, no answer that could safely be made in public.

Behind these defeatist calculations are a complex of considerations and motives. Among them are not merely political dislike for the Soviet Union but considerable elements of anti-British feeling. As deep, if not deeper, than the more obvious anti-Soviet feeling, which wide sectors of our leadership and upper classes have overcome, is a kind of anti-British isolationist-imperialist attitude on the part of some of our foremost military men. An important man in this category is General Brehon B. Somervell, chief of the Services of Supply, the most powerful single figure in war production today and a man who has done his best to cut down lend-lease aid to Britain, the Soviet Union, and China. He feels that we have to "prepare to do this job ourselves."

This kind of thinking would make the Atlantic and Pacific seaboards our first lines of defense. It would cost many millions more in lives and many billions more in money. It means that we would have to defeat the Axis with our men and boys alone instead of with the aid of British, Russians, and Chinese. It would leave them to die in vain rather than as part of a world strategy for victory. "The international implications of army demands for man-power," Bender points out, "are seldom understood. But they are as important as the need to consider man-power requirements of industry and agriculture." It is these broader implications which the dominant military have failed to understand or chosen to ignore. Popular pressure is needed to support the efforts of powerful forces here, including I believe the President himself, to combat this dangerous trend. The moment is approaching when it will be decided whether these are indeed to be United Nations fighting a United Nations war, or each waging its own struggle in desperate and foolhardy isolation.

One Year After Pearl Harbor

In this overview of the international and domestic fronts one year into the American phase of the war, Stone attempts, as so often, to offer a sweeping historical perspective on the current political to-and-fro. The underlying question: What is America fighting for? Is our national objective simply to defeat the Axis and then return to business-as-usual, or is social reform part of our broader agenda?

. . .

December 12, 1942

LOOKING BACK ACROSS THE YEAR since Pearl Harbor, the President has much with which to be pleased. The task of mobilizing a fairly prosperous and contented capitalist democracy for war is like trying to drive a team of twenty mules, each stubbornly intent on having its own way. Only by continual compromise with the ornery critters is it possible to move forward at all. Examined closely, by the myopic eye of the perfectionist, Mr. Roosevelt's performance in every sphere has been faulty. Regarded in the perspective of his limited freedom of choice and the temper of the country, which has never really been warlike, the year's achievements have been extraordinary. The curtailment and conversion of civilian industry for war, the peaceful resolution of capital-labor difficulties, the preservation to a remarkable extent of both social gains and civil liberties, the great expansion of arms output, the successful launching of our first major offensive represent stupendous and back-breaking tasks. The President is only a man, with twenty-four hours a day at his disposal, and amid the clamor of criticism, much of it justified, it will not hurt to pause a moment in gratitude for his work in the service of our country.

Someone has said that politics is the art of the possible, and Mr. Roosevelt achieved what he did largely by taking the easiest route; the easiest was difficult enough. He let big business mobilize our economy for war pretty much on its own terms, and established what is in effect a government of coalition with the right. Just as King John had to sign on the dotted line for the barons before they would fight, so the President had to come to terms with the quasi-independent corporate sovereignties that control so much of our productive resources. In criticizing him for this, we must also in fairness criticize ourselves. Had labor and the middle-class progressives been better organized, politically more astute, less divided, more competently led, they would have exerted more pressure in the national tug-of-war. The last Congressional elections were an adequate if rough test of just how much influence the labor and liberal elements have in national and local politics. The things that count are not our speeches or our pieces in the paper but the votes we can muster in Congress in support of the measures we demand. It is easy to identify ourselves emotionally with "the people." At the moment the people are not identifying themselves with us.

The Attorney General is the first public official here to say this publicly, at least by implication. "Is the sentiment of the public," Mr. Biddle asked despondently at Charlottesville last Friday, "really moved by the vision of a better world or is it merely disturbed by anxiety about increased taxation and the threat of unemployment after the war? Do the people of our land fight only to win the war and have it over—or to use the war for great and democratic ends?" The answer of big business had been given at the convention of the National Association of Manufacturers two days before. "I am not making guns or tanks," the president of the N.A.M. said, "to win a 'people's revolution' . . . I am not fighting for a quart of milk for every Hottentot or for a TVA on the Danube." In this the N.A.M. spoke also for the War Production Board [WPB] and for most of our military-diplomatic bureaucracy. Is the answer of the people very different? The Attorney General made it clear that he is afraid that the dominant feeling toward fighting the war is to "get it over." Congress already reflects this desire for "normalcy."

The trend toward the right has gone to ugly extremes "on the hill." In executive committee sessions on the new War Powers bill, the principal objection to the measure was the fear that the President might use it to let in a lot of "non-Aryan" refugees after the war was over. The old slur about the Jew Deal has made a covert reappearance. Sumners of Texas on the floor of the

House Wednesday attacked New Deal administrators as "this bunch of people who . . . do not much more than get into this country before they are trying to tell us how to run this government." It would be a mistake to identify "Send 'Em to the Electric Chair" Sumners with the voice of the American people, but there are enough like him in the Democratic Party and in Congress to cheer the Axis and bedevil the Administration. The one part of the war machine generously left to New Dealers is that in which they are certain to become unpopular—the political-suicide assignment of price control and rationing. Sumners and his kind are making the most of it to set the farmer against the New Deal. Wait till they get started on how Lehman is taking food from Americans to feed foreigners!

Coffee of Nebraska thought the Sumners speech "wonderful." Cox of Georgia rose to suggest that perhaps the time had come to break away from party lines in order to get rid of these "carpetbaggers." Rankin of Mississippi and Hoffman of Michigan joined in, unrebuked, though next day Hook of Michigan gave Hoffman a drubbing in debate. Hoffman suggested that Congress set up a new committee to investigate the Marshall Field publications, the left and liberal weeklies, and the Washington *Post* for attacking Congressmen of this odorous variety in the last campaign. Hook threw Hoffman into confusion by asking whether this meant that the latter had lost faith in the Dies committee. Hoffman replied lamely that Hook and others had criticized the Dies committee so much that "they now have too big a job on their hands to handle all this."

As Congress moves right, the Administration may move with it, if only out of necessity. The precarious course of the Panama agreement through the Senate last week showed how dependent the President and his party leaders are on right-wing Democrats. The debate and the vote were a foretaste of what is coming when we begin to make the peace. The power of a Cordell Hull, who can swing Southern votes, is likely to increase, that of a Henry Wallace to wane, as the drift continues. In a sense we are already losing the peace more rapidly than we are winning the war, for the shape of our society is being determined by the undemocratic and monopolistic fashion in which it has been mobilized for war production. This trend will only be reversed if the Axis staying power proves much greater than, in the present optimistic mood, is now expected.

Is the outlook for the liberals hopeless? Not at all. The pendulum now swinging away from social reform will swing back. At present, in the full flush of boom employment, after twelve years of the New Deal, the country is ready for a change, and 1944 may see a right-wing Republican elected. The reaction is likely to go too far. Workers and farmers will not easily give up what they have won through Mr. Roosevelt since 1933. The idea of social security is too potent to be stifled. The Republicans must either submit to these currents or go under in trying to combat them. The immediate outlook for progressivism is dark, but it has been dark before, and it is some comfort to know that its future is nowhere near as bleak as Adolf Hitler's.

Relaxing Too Soon

For those not immersed in the history of World War II, it's startling to realize that in April 1943—two years away from ultimate victory and more than a year away from the belated opening of the second front in Normandy—many American voices were already calling for a relaxation of war production efforts. Savor the classic I. F. Stone "gotcha" in the last paragraph—the sentence quoted from a *Fortune* article by General Lucius D. Clay, in which the easy-to-overlook clause italicized by Stone unintentionally exposes the shakiness of the government's entire industrial strategy.

.　　.　　.

April 24, 1943

A CURIOUS ATMOSPHERE IS VISIBLE in the world of business. Though we are as yet only ankle-deep in the war, the impression is growing that the job of war production has passed its peak, and that we can now begin to think of a return to greater civilian production. The service-equipment division of the War Production Board [WPB] has prepared a plan for resuming the manufacture of office machinery. The WPB has issued an order easing its prohibition against the use of steel for non-essential purposes. Manufacturers may use stocks of partially or wholly fabricated steel parts in the production of a wide variety of gadgets ranging from electric hair-curlers to shoe buckles. Trade papers began to talk last fall of the possibility of obtaining materials for renewed civilian output, and the same sort of speculation has now reached the daily press. The financial section of today's New York *Times,* for example, carries no fewer than three articles on the prospect of greater civilian output.

William J. Enright, who covers business circles for the *Times,* says "war agencies intend to start the reconversion of industry to the production of essential civilian goods by the end of the summer." Kenneth L. Austin, who reports on finance and heavy industry, declares New York and Washington are hearing "forecasts that the supply of steel for military, naval, and ship-building needs soon will appear to have been more than amply covered, and . . . metal will be available for non-essential civilian needs within the next six months or less." C. F. Hughes, who writes the enlightened and well-informed Merchant's Point of View for the *Times,* reflects widespread opinion at the capital when he says, "In guns, bombs and shells, motor ve-hicles and tanks we have already produced more than enough for any rea-sonable requirements of [our] armed forces or those of our allies."

This feeling that the job of war production is in its declining phase has found expression in the ranks of both capital and labor. Walter D. Fuller, president of the Curtis Publishing Company and chairman of the executive committee of the National Association of Manufacturers, said here last week that the country was suffering from overproduction of certain types of war materials. Fuller declared that we had built up a sufficient backlog of weapons to justify more emphasis on civilian needs. Philip Murray, presi-dent of the C.I.O., told the Institute of Women's Professional Relations that the United States is confronted with mass unemployment because we have produced more war materials "than the United Nations can use or the United States can transport." He was unwise enough to speak of difficulties created by "a mad desire to expedite war materials."

There are many parts of the earth in which talk of this kind must make painful and puzzling reading. Our men in the Southwest Pacific are not suf-fering from an excess of supplies. Australia is worried about a possible Japan-ese offensive. Last year's widely ballyhooed offensive in Burma has subsided, for lack of material, into the faintest kind of nudge. The Chinese, who have done more with less than any of the United Nations, must think us mad. Our French allies in North Africa, from latest reports, are still using out-moded equipment. The Soviet Union, still the only nation fighting Hitler on a major scale, continues to look for a second front, a military enterprise that will require huge amounts of material if it is to be successful. Granted that we may be producing more than we need on the present scale of our op-erations, granted even that in some items we have produced enough for any scale of warfare, is it possible that in the over-all picture we have reached a stage where we can relax and turn back to more normal production?

There is evidence that even on the present scale we are still far from the point where we can begin again to make gadgets. Expansion of steel-making facilities is behind schedule and is being curtailed on the general view that we now have enough steel not only for war but for more civilian output. Yet WPB [War Production Board] Chairman Donald M. Nelson said last week that ordinary carbon steel had now become our most serious bottleneck. Production for the third quarter of this year, according to Nelson, will be only about 14,450,000 tons. The demands of our various military and lend-lease agencies and essential civilian supply for that quarter total 20,830,000 tons. There is a deficit of more than 5,000,000 tons, or 25 per cent.

The full significance of those figures becomes more apparent if we recognize that the President's Victory program of January, 1942, has been quietly revised downward not once but several times. "The earlier question of whether we would need eighty billions in war output this year," C. F. Hughes writes, "is on the way to being answered with a flat 'No.'" The phrase "on the way" is an understatement. Except in shipbuilding, even in aircraft, we not only are failing to meet those goals but have reduced them. In this connection I should like to call attention to an authoritative article on the Army Supply Program by Major General Lucius D. Clay in the February issue of *Fortune*. Major General Clay is assistant chief of staff for matériel in the General Staff Corps. His article is extraordinary reading. It shows how long the War Department waited before drawing up plans for an all-out effort and how soon it relinquished them.

"Immediately after Pearl Harbor," General Clay writes, "the Supply Division of the General Staff recognized the necessity for the revision of the Army Supply Program for all-out war. By early February it had completed the first Army Supply Program for this purpose." The Pearl Harbor mentality seems to have dominated the General Staff as well as the commanding officers in Hawaii. General Clay says this first program "was based on the mobilization rate and the composition of troops deemed desirable at that early stage of war, and it included large quantities of matériel that our allies had ordered or requested the year before." This first program called for $62 billion in supplies "through the calendar year 1943" or $31 billion a year in 1942 and 1943. This was reduced, according to General Clay, to $45 billion in April, 1942. Later it was reduced again, to $38 billion. In November, 1942, it was further reduced—to $31 billion. "For 1943," General Clay reports, "our problems in materials and facilities appear to be solved—*to the extent that objectives have finally been brought within the limit of available supplies and facilities*" (my italics). The production problem was solved by reducing the production program! It is measured by these reduced goals that we now have "overproduction of war material." It is on the basis of these reduced goals that plans for expanding production in steel and other basic materials are being curtailed and the resumption of non-essential production is planned. The monopolies which fought expansion have succeeded in cutting the war effort down to size, and "business as usual" is again raising its head. This is a dangerous tendency, which may yet prove costly in terms of lives.

How Washington Took the News

At last, the opening of the second front. Stone offers a marvelously atmospheric collage of scenes from Washington, D.C., on the day when news of the invasion broke, from "the couples making love . . . in Lafayette Park" to the shaking hand of Roosevelt, "happy and confident but tired," as he addressed a packed news conference.

.   .   .

June 17, 1944

MOST OF THE WASHINGTON PRESS CORPS, like most of official Washington, slept peacefully through the early hours of D-Day. The first announcement that the second front had been opened came at 12:37 A.M., long after the usual deadlines of the morning-paper bureaus and long before that of the evenings. The German source of the news and the absence of any confirmation here or in London made bureau chiefs skeptical, and decided them against staff mobilizations. The few who came down town after the German broadcast noted the usual sights—an occasional light in the darkened Navy Department, the lonely sentries before the White House, the couples making love across the way in Lafayette Park. The moon was full, the weather mild.

The Secretary of War and the Chief of Staff had left their offices at 5 P.M. the day before and were safe abed. The big military secret was that Elmer Davis, on leaving the National Press Club at 9:30 that night, had gone back to his office at the OWI [Office of War Information]. The one exciting place in town was the foreign news bureau of the OWI in the Social Security Building near the Capitol, but in the huge adjoining press room as late as 3 A.M. there were only two reporters waiting for the big news—Libby Donahue of *PM* and Joe Laitin of the United Press, neither certain that anything would turn up. There was a guard at the door to keep them away from Elmer Davis's office, and a terrific clatter and clang issued from the foreign news room, with its huge battery of tickers, each with a bell that rings when particularly hot news comes over the wires. The bells rang often and the place was a mad scramble of OWI foreign staff members, but as Libby says, "those boys are crazy even on a clear day," and one couldn't be sure. Five minutes before United Nations confirmation of the second front at 3:32 A.M. Miss Donahue was confidentially informed from an authoritative source that she might as well go home as there would be a long delay. She decided, however, to stay.

By the time news of the invasion was confirmed, a Philadelphia *Inquirer* reporter and an Acme photographer had also arrived, and all were ushered into Elmer Davis's office to hear General Eisenhower's broadcast over short wave. Davis looked tired and dazed but perked up over General Eisenhower's delivery, which was good. "That man could go places on radio when the war's over," Davis said admiringly.

The State Department moved its regular press conference from noon to II A.M. on D-Day, perhaps out of a sense of the urgency of the occasion. On the way there we saw a group of curious people, police, and photographers waiting to get a glimpse of the visiting Polish Premier. He had an appointment with Under Secretary Stettinius at 10:30, and the latter, in full protocol, walked across the street to escort Mikolajczyk over. What they said to each other, then or later, remains a secret, but the Soviet Ambassador arrived at the department an hour afterward. In between, the Under Secretary met the press. Hull was away resting at Hershey, Pennsylvania, and as always it was a pleasure to see Stettinius's youthful face and quick smile in his place. The Under Secretary read a prepared statement, "The liberation of Europe has begun . . . "—one of many like it on D-Day from departmental and embassy mimeographs. Then he went on to announce recognition of the new Ecuadorean government, the arrival of the Gripsholm at Jersey City, an agreement by the Japanese government to pick up supplies at Vladivostok for interned Allied nationals.

From embassies and department heads, press releases on the invasion began to appear, but aside from these synthetic reactions there was little excitement in the capital and—significant item—bond sales actually fell off. J. Edgar Hoover called for alertness on the home front, and the War Department asked Congress to establish sixty-nine new national cemeteries. All over town, in government offices as well as in churches, there were special prayer services, and many who do not ordinarily pray joined in them with a sober sense of the struggle on distant beachheads and its human cost. But on Capitol Hill, where some of us seemed to feel prayer was most needed, it had little effect. The galleries were well filled, mostly with visiting service men, but there were only eleven Senators and a scattering of Representatives present when the day's session opened. Minority Leader Martin told the house that "partisan politics . . . disappear as we think of the heroic deeds of our men and women" but this must be put down to poetic license. The Republican-Southern Democratic coalition soon got back to work in both houses with unabated enthusiasm. "I felt humble this morning when advised of the invasion," Majority Leader McCormack said. "A strange feeling came over me." The feeling was not widely shared.

Celler of New York tried to block a resolution to speed up the trial of Kimmel and Short* by pointing out that Pearl Harbor was in part due to an attitude of public "indifference and callousness . . . influenced by some of the isolationist remarks made in this very House . . . by the gentlemen who are the sponsors of this bill." Said Celler, "I have due respect for the gentlemen and I do not charge them with anything . . . they had a perfect right to their opinions." Retorted Dewey Short of Missouri boldly, "We still have them." The House passed his resolution for trial of Kimmel and Short within three months by a vote of 305 to 35, though trial may disrupt military-naval operations. The Senate went ahead on a bill which promises to hamstring the OPA [Office of Price Administration].

The big local event of the day was the President's regular press conference at 4 P.M., which drew a record crowd. Most of the President's official family, from Fala to Judge Rosenman, seemed to be with him in the executive offices, waiting in a kind of holiday mood to watch the old maestro handle the press. The President was happy and confident but tired, and he has aged. His hand shook a little when he lifted it to the same jaunty

---

*Rear Admiral Husband E. Kimmel and Major General Walter C. Short commanded, respectively, the U.S. naval and military forces at Pearl Harbor at the time of the Japanese attack.

cigarette holder. He answers questions slowly, looking up at the ceiling, occasionally wriggling his face and scratching his chest between phrases. Our faces must have shown what most of us felt as we came in. For he began, after an extraordinary pause of several minutes in which no questions were asked and we all stood silent, by saying that the correspondents had the same look on their faces that people all over the country must have and that he thought this a very happy conference. I asked him toward the close to tell us what hopes he felt on this great day, and he said to win the war—100 percent.

I thought the President's prayer that night a gauche affair, addressing God in familiar, conversational, and explanatory tone, as if it were a fireside chat beamed at heaven. But I am inclined to be charitable when I think of what D-Day means to Franklin D. Roosevelt, of the years since the "quarantine" speech in which he tried to awaken the American people to their danger and to gird them against enemies they so long refused to recognize. How different it would have been could we have gone into France before it fell; how much easier our task. And how different it would have been if the Germans had turned west and south toward Africa and South America instead of east. How poorly prepared we were in 1941 to resist, and how poorly prepared we are even today to understand. D-Day's events in Congress, the slash last Saturday in UNRRA [United Nations Relief and Rehabilitation Administration] funds, the unseemly and ungrateful uproar over the lend-leasing of a cruiser to the Soviet Union indicate how backward public opinion continues to be, and how formidable is the task the President will face in making the peace. D-Day served to remind us that we are heavily in debt to the man in the White House as well as to the boys on the beachheads.

The Same Old Codgers

A vivid snapshot of the opening of the United Nations conference in San Francisco. The war is all but won, Roosevelt is dead, and the new challenge is to forge a more durable peace than the one that followed the First World War. Stone's acerbic evaluation of Truman and the other leaders of the day—the "same old codgers to whose fumbling we owe World War II"—differs from today's consensus, which credits that generation for creating such lasting if imperfect institutions as NATO, the Bretton Woods system, and the UN itself, and for at least establishing a world order that helped prevent a third global conflagration. But for Stone, the magnitude of the opportunity demanded statesmen of true greatness, and he was disappointed to find statesmanship in short supply.

.   .   .

May 5, 1945

THIS IS A SPLENDIDLY VIGOROUS and beautiful city. Its lofty hills, great bay, clear skies, and fresh breezes make it an exhilarating place. The cable cars that crawl up and down its steep streets provide almost as exciting a ride as the chute-the-chutes of Coney Island, and the view from luxurious Nob Hill, where one feels closer to the stars at night, goes to one's head. For the press this has been a glamorous week spent scooting around between press conferences and plenary sessions. We saw and heard the bright, bird-like Dutch Foreign Minister, Van Kleffens; the school-masterish Deputy British Prime Minister, Clement Attlee; the monolithic but quick-witted Molotov; Nehru's fragile but intense sister, Mrs. Pandit; dapper Georges Bidault, the French Foreign Minister, who looks more like a care-free boulevardier than an underground leader; and, of course, Mr. Stettinius, our matinee-idol Secretary of State, whose press conferences are remarkable chiefly for his extraordinary facility in remembering the faces and names of reporters. It's the old apple sauce, but we lap it up just the same.

The press is housed in the huge Palace Hotel, on Market Street, down near the wharves, and the correspondents, for whom this is a kind of old-home week, obtain much of their mysteriously authoritative inside information by interviewing each other at the crowded bars and in the high glass-ceilinged dining-room. We are perpetually in transit, like skating bugs, from the Palace to Union Square, which is neat and fashionable and quite unlike its New York namesake; there, at the St. Francis, the Russians and the French are housed. Thence we go to Nob Hill, where the British and the Chinese are in the de luxe Mark Hopkins, with its famous rooftop bar, and the American delegation in the equally plush if less famous Fairmont. Down-hill again we speed to the domed Opera House, where the conference sessions are held, and the big Veterans' Administration Building next door, which is the "press room" of the conference; there are batteries of typewriters and telegraph machines and a most delightful clatter.

Hollywood, as though fearful of being outshone, is well represented here. Your correspondent, as goggle-eyed as any movie fan, was introduced to Charles Boyer by a member of the French delegation and later that night in the lobby of the Palace to Edward G. Robinson. "Well," Robinson asked with that overtone of quiet menace for which he is famous, "is our side going to win?" It was definitely an "or else" question, and I hastened to assure him that all would be well.

The main event, the opening of the conference Wednesday afternoon, might have been an M-G-M opening. Crowds strained against the ropes for blocks around the Opera House to watch the arriving notables; the press flashed its cards with pride; the foreign delegates poured out of their black limousines, trying hard to look dignified and unmoved. Within, in an interior that seemed to have been done by Maxfield Parrish, floodlights lit up the gilded gesso, red plush, and stainless steel; against the blue background of the huge stage stood four brown pillars, symbols of the four freedoms, connected at the top by what appeared to be large segments of a boa constrictor. The press was with difficulty confined to the triple-tiered galleries by the feminine elite of San Francisco, among whom many heart-rending battles were fought for the honor of ushering at the occasion. But down below camera men swarmed among the delegates of the forty-six nations, kneeling in the aisles and all but hanging from the boxes to get their shots.

Flashlight bulbs kept going off like summer lightning, and statesmen obediently composed their faces for the camera.

The affair itself was sobering. The speeches at the opening session were as banal as the juke-box music which was piped into the Opera House as the delegates arrived. The President's address was disappointing. The occasion called for either Lincolnian eloquence or plain, common-sense statement. Mr. Truman is fully capable in private of the latter, but he seems to have been prevailed upon to indulge instead in windy moralisms, turgid periods, and the kind of untruths which are regarded as inspirational. I pick one of the many examples from the speech. "None of us doubt," Mr. Truman said, "that with divine guidance, friendly cooperation, and hard work we shall find an adequate answer to the problem history has put before us." Mr. Truman would never talk that way in private to a visitor. Why does he in a speech? The statement is not true; some of the wisest of the delegates here certainly do doubt whether we shall find the "answer to the problem history has put before us." The rhetoric is false, the effect is hollow; it is hooey. In private Mr. Truman would say, "It's a tough job. I'm not sure we can do it. But we're going to try our best." Why not say that in public? That kind of plain talk inspires confidence. The tawdry and flatulent rhetoric which marked most of the speeches depressed me. The occasion was so momentous; the danger so grave; the need so great; the utterance so mediocre.

The San Francisco conference is as important as Versailles or the Congress of Vienna. But one's first impression of it is how mediocre is its leadership. The second is how little the cast of characters have changed since Geneva. To be quite frank about it, the conference, for all its glamour, is a meeting of pretty much those same old codgers to whose fumbling we owe World War II. They are still dishing out the same old platitudes and thinking in the same old terms. And so, I suspect, are many of the people they represent. The war, for all its terror and destruction, has not brought about that long-overdue revulsion against nationalism which can alone provide the basis for world order and security. The delegations assembled here indicate that the political parties and the dominant classes of the Western countries and of China are emerging from the conflict momentarily sobered, perhaps, but little changed. Except for the French and Yugoslav delegations, there is no sign here of the new men and forces which welled up from underground in continental Europe to fight fascism. The basic idea at San Francisco is that the big powers must stick together to maintain the peace; this was Metternich's idea in 1815; it is the kindergarten stage in education toward world security. The problem is how to keep the big powers together; it is the problem that these same men—the Halifaxes, the Edens, the Paul-Boncours, the Van Kleffenses—failed to solve at Geneva. Given the same men, the same parties, the same social systems, can one expect a different result?

These men lost the last peace, and unless they are replaced they will some day lose the next one. They can give us the first tentative framework of a world order; it is the job of progressive forces to take over from there as soon as possible. For whatever these men do on paper, they do not have the capacity to withstand and deal with real crises. The weak handling of the Polish issue, the clerical power politics focused upon it, the covert anti-Soviet urges associated with it, are indicative of the stresses and strains which peace will put on the relations of the big powers. It will take new leadership, deeper understanding, and firmer resolution if big-power unity is to be maintained when peace comes and trouble begins.

Brass Hats Undaunted

I. F. Stone applies his classic technique—close textual analysis informed by thorough knowledge of the historical facts and deep understanding of the ways of bureaucracy—to the army and navy reports on the disaster at Pearl Harbor, and issues a scathing attack on the "stupidity" they reveal. What would Stone say if he could evaluate our nation's preparation for a possible terrorist attack prior to the events of September 11, 2001?

.　　.　　.

September 8, 1945

THE REPORT OF THE NAVAL COURT OF INQUIRY on Pearl Harbor begins by explaining that the Pacific Fleet was organized in three main task forces. The operating schedule was so arranged that there was always one task force at sea, and usually two. "At no time during 1941," the Court of Inquiry assures us, "were all the vessels of the Fleet in Pearl Harbor." In accordance with this operating schedule, only Task Force One and part of Task Force Two were in Pearl Harbor at the time of the Japanese attack. Reading thus far, one feels that naval operations were wisely planned to avoid a situation in which the entire Pacific Fleet might have been destroyed in one enemy attack on the Hawaiian base. But then we read that "the preponderance of the battleship strength of the Fleet" was in Task Force One, and that all three of the battleships of Task Force Two were also in the harbor, and finally that "all battleships of the Pacific Fleet, except one undergoing overhaul at the Puget Sound Navy Yard, were in Pearl Harbor on 7 December." The Naval Court of Inquiry concludes, however, that this was "purely a coincidence." The disingenuous approach and the fatuous conclusion are alike characteristic of the report turned in by the three high admirals, Kalbfus, Murfin, and Andrews.

Despite this solemn rigmarole about the three task forces, the fact is that the Japanese attack had the effect, as the Army Board of Inquiry reports, "of immobilizing and substantially destroying the Pacific Fleet, which was a major threat to Japan's left flank in its southward move." To dismiss as "coincidence" the crucial blunder that concentrated all our battleships and most of the Pacific Fleet in Pearl Harbor that ghastly morning is to demonstrate the continued presence in the armed services of the brass-hat mentality responsible for that disaster. Admirals and generals are supposed to avoid "coincidences" of this kind when they know war is an imminent possibility, as they knew in the fall of 1941.

On a par with this Naval Court of Inquiry conclusion is its finding that "condition of readiness No. 3," in effect at the time of the attack, was "that best suited to the circumstances." This deserves to rank with the medical gag about the operation being highly successful though the patient died. It draws from Admiral King the tart comment that "condition of readiness No. 3" is that "normally maintained in port." In other words the high admirals of the Court of Inquiry still think the condition of readiness observed by a ship in Brooklyn in peacetime was "best suited" to the circumstances in Pearl Harbor on December 7, 1941. This finding will read better in Japanese.

As can be seen from these samples, the naval report on Pearl Harbor is hardly a masterpiece of forthright self-criticism. The report of the Army Board of Inquiry is by comparison a vigorous and outspoken document. The mealy-mouthed naval report is accompanied by separate statements from Admiral King, as commander-in-chief of the United States Fleet and Chief of Naval Operations, and from Secretary Forrestal. Both King and Forrestal indicate their displeasure with the Court of Inquiry and speak out with manly frankness on the navy's responsibility for Pearl Harbor. On the other hand, the army board's report is accompanied by a separate statement by Secretary Stimson which seeks to soften the criticism in that document and to rebut findings which place on the General Staff in Washington and on General Marshall, its chief, a substantial share of the blame for our unpreparedness at Pearl Harbor. The net effect of the reports and their accompanying statements is to leave the impression that the services as a whole are still far from prepared fully to admit the errors which made Pearl Harbor possible. That attitude does not promise well for the future.

Both the army and navy reports do a great deal of buck-passing. The prize specimen is the naval court's finding that "constitutional requirements that war be declared by Congress" made it difficult to prevent the attack on Pearl Harbor. This was neatly deflated in Secretary Forrestal's dour report, "The constitutional inhibition . . . did not preclude long-distance reconnaissance." The army board's report blames the state of public opinion and isolationism, but itself contains isolationist overtones; noteworthy is the statement, in discussing contradictory tendencies at home, "we were arming our forces for war and at the same time giving away much of such armament." Both reports have given fuel to the isolationist press by blaming Secretary of State Hull for not continuing to stall and appease the Japanese in the fall of 1941. That public opinion bears a heavy share in the responsibility for Pearl Harbor is indisputable, but irrelevant. For the question before the army and navy boards was whether the armed services did all they could to prevent the disaster *with the means at their disposal* and within the existing circumstances. The answer to that question is sharply negative. It is only the criticism of Hull, and by implication Roosevelt, which merits serious consideration.

Hull is blamed for presenting his ten-point proposal to the Japanese on November 26, 1941, over the objections of General Marshall as Chief of Staff and Admiral Stark as Chief of Naval Operations. Marshall and Stark, supported by Stimson and Knox, said we were unprepared for war and seemed to feel that Hull's proposals were so drastic as to make war unavoidable. It is implied that Roosevelt ignored or overruled this warning. But it is hard to see how Hull could have stalled the Japanese any longer without in large part accepting their proposals of November 20, and those proposals would have made us a partner in Japanese aggression. The Japs wanted us to supply them with all the oil they needed, to unfreeze Japanese accounts in this country, to end all aid to China, to "cooperate" with Japan in acquiring "these goods and commodities which the two countries need in the Netherlands East Indies." To accept such terms would have been to risk the complete collapse of China and the dominance of the Dutch East Indies by Japan. There was no assurance that paying this kind of blackmail would have prevented further Japanese advances and an eventual attack upon us anyway. It is to the credit of Hull and Roosevelt that they refused to participate in a

Far Eastern Munich and insisted, in the ten-point proposal, on the evacuation of China as a condition for resuming friendly relations with Japan.

The army and navy wanted more time, but we had already been stalling and appeasing the Japanese for ten years. The price asked for more time was so large that it would have benefited Japan more than the United States. The refusal to pay that price undoubtedly precipitated the long-prepared Japanese attack, and we were poorly prepared for war. But the real point involved in the Pearl Harbor inquiry was whether that disaster need necessarily have happened. And one test of the army-navy plea for more time is what use the armed services made of the time they did have. The services regarded the ten-point proposal as a virtual ultimatum to Japan, and since they so regarded the proposal they were under obligation to take steps immediately for war. But their record, as disclosed in the army and navy inquiries and in the earlier Roberts report, is one of unpardonable negligence and appalling stupidity. We would have had to fight a defensive war for months in any case, but we need not have lost our Pacific Fleet at Pearl Harbor and our air force at Manila in two quick, crushing surprise attacks. For the facts disclosed indicate that it was not a lack of knowledge but sheer stodgy unimaginative bureaucratic complacency at Washington, Pearl Harbor, and Manila which made the Japanese blitz possible.

In the first place, the joint army-navy defense plan for Hawaii signed on April 9, 1941, was, as the army board said, "prophetic in its accuracy." It was based on the assumption that the Japs would attack without warning, and the men who drew up that plan accurately forecast every basic detail of what happened at Pearl Harbor: the time of day, the type of task force used by the Japanese, the form the attack would take, even the fact that it might be preceded (as it actually was) by a single submarine foray in the harbor just before the big blow. The only trouble is that this army-navy defense agreement was neither implemented nor taken seriously by the military-naval command in Washington and in Hawaii. In the second place, President Roosevelt told the heads of the army and navy at a White House conference on November 25, the day before the ten-point proposal, to expect a surprise attack "perhaps as soon as next Monday," which was December 1. In the third place, from the time of that White House conference until December 7, "the record shows" (says the army report) "that from informers and other sources the War Department had complete and detailed information of Japanese intentions." Finally, at 9 o'clock on the morning of December 7, the War and Navy Departments were tipped off (four hours before the attack) that the Japanese would present an ultimatum or declaration of war at 1 P.M. Washington time. And a Commander Kramer in the navy was quick to point out that 1 P.M. Washington time would be dawn at Pearl Harbor, the very time at which our war plans predicted a surprise attack there.

General Marshall as Chief of Staff and Admiral Stark as Chief of Naval Operations failed to see to it that proper defense measures were taken at Pearl Harbor between November 25 and December 7. And they failed to react quickly enough to the advance knowledge that they had on the morning of Pearl Harbor. Stark didn't think the information was worth passing on and Marshall sent it to General Short by commercial cable when faster means of communication were available. The last warning left Washington 22 minutes before the attack and did not arrive until several hours after the attacking force had departed. Marshall could have telephoned Short, but his excuse was that he was expecting an attack on the Philippines rather than in Hawaii and telephoned MacArthur instead. This throws additional light on MacArthur's extraordinary incompetence as a commander at that juncture. For despite the pleas of subordinates to disperse his planes, MacArthur left them on the ground at Clark Field outside Manila, where almost his entire air force was destroyed by the Japanese ten hours after their attack on Pearl Harbor. MacArthur was more culpable than Kimmel and Short, and it is scandalous that there should never have been an investigation of his bungling in the Philippines.

Our military-naval command acted with indecent sedateness. Lacking daring itself, it did not expect daring from the Japanese. Even now, when we know how meticulously and minutely (and, let us confess, brilliantly) the Japanese planned their attacks, we still find the Army Board of Inquiry talking nonsense about "the Oriental mind" and attributing the Pearl Harbor blitz to "the violent and uncivilized reasoning of the Japanese." Our military-naval command did not keep abreast of new developments in warfare, notably the use of torpedoes from planes in shallow water. This was how the Japs did most of their damage at Pearl Harbor, and naval intelligence warned of this possibility months in advance. Our military-naval command under-estimated the intelligence of the Japanese and they made the equally crucial mistake of underestimating the loyalty of our Japanese-American popula-tion. For it was the latter error which led General Short to institute the alert against sabotage instead of the alert against attack from without. Under this type of alert planes were parked wing to wing and unable to get off the ground in less than four hours. The attack on Pearl Harbor took only three, and most of the planes were destroyed.

Perhaps the crowning example of military stupidity is in the revelation that while our army's mobile anti-aircraft artillery was in state of instant readiness, it had no ammunition. The ammunition was in a crater a mile away. General Short and Ordnance had rejected pleas for artillery shells sev-eral days earlier on the ground that "they didn't want to issue any of the clean ammunition, let it get out and get dirty, and have to take it back in later on and renovate it." The slogan of the Pearl Harbor high command seems to have been, "Praise the Lord, but don't muss the ammunition."

The End of the War

How eloquently and thoughtfully Stone takes the long view here, showing what
the end of the war *might* mean if only humanity chooses to absorb fully its terrible lessons.

. . .

August 12, 1945

MORE TERRIFYING THAN THE ATOMIC BOMB is the casual way we all
seem to be taking the end of the war. It has been clear since Friday morning
that there would be a Japanese surrender within a matter of a few days, if
not a few hours. But the news seemed to stir extraordinarily little excitement. The finish of a World Series evokes more talk at the lunch counters.

In part this is because, as before V-E Day, there was no clear-cut announcement. Victory, expected and discounted, is no longer news. In part,
this phlegmatic response may reflect the fact that people are punch-drunk
on horror and sensation. Imagination has been dulled by the demands
made upon it.

The cables indicate that this is not true in those countries where the war
has been experienced directly. In London, Paris, and Chungking, news of the
Japanese surrender offer sent rejoicing crowds pouring into the streets. There
the end of the war was the end of something people had themselves felt, seen,
heard, and suffered—not a distant drama played out in the headlines.

I do not feel like writing the standard editorial today in the face of all
the agony the last few years have seen. Terrible things have been done to
human bodies and to human minds. I think of the picture of the Chinese
baby crying alone in the ruins of Nanking. I think of the German woman
who said all this would not have happened if those damned British had
only surrendered in 1940. And I think of the American airman who came

back from dropping an atomic bomb over Nagasaki to report that the results were "good."

I am worried by the casualness with which we in America are greeting the peace, because this failure of the imagination does not bode well for the future. I wrote down "The most terrible war in human history is coming to an end," and scratched it out because I felt that to most people who read it the words would have but a pallid reality, and seem only another editorial cliché.

This is terrifying because the task of preventing another world war is a difficult one. If people do not achieve some vivid conception of what hell has reigned in parts of Europe and Asia during the past decade or so, how can one expect them to think hard enough and act firmly enough to prevent it from happening again?

Since 1931, when peace began to crumble in Manchuria, there has been war, civil war and world war, at an increasingly furious tempo: from those first shootings in Mukden and the first beatings in Dachau to the bombing of Shanghai and the civil war in Spain, from the first blitz on Poland to the use of the atomic bomb over Hiroshima and Nagasaki. What a vista of blood and cruelty!

But not blood and cruelty alone. As in some gigantic symphony played on human hearts for the delectation of a mightier race, agony has blended with a beaten-down but irrepressible, mounting, and finally victorious heroism and aspiration. These are only gaudy words to us. We and our orators have rung the changes on democracy and freedom until the words have grown shabby and nauseating. But to certain men the war's ending comes as the end of a struggle against fascism begun long before war was declared, fought in the underground hideaways of Japan, Italy, and Germany, in occupied China and in Spain, in the Vienna working-class suburbs and in the Warsaw ghetto, humbly and obscurely but as bitterly as on the broader battlefields.

Those who understand that this was in truth, for all its contradictions and compromises, a war against fascism, a successful war against fascism, a war that is slowly but surely letting loose the forces of freedom the world over, cannot take the end of the war casually. One of the reasons for the apathetic reaction to victory in our own country is that so few felt and understand this. To too many of us the war was a kind of horrible accident, disrupting families and lives for no good reason; a distant quarrel, into which we were somehow drawn.

One cannot understand what one has not suffered. How many of us are thankful that our own country was spared, that our children did not jump from their beds as the warning air-raid sirens screamed in the nights, that we did not huddle with our families in the subways, that our daughters were not shipped into slavery and our mothers sealed into death cars for the extermination camps, that our cities are not gutted by bombs, our children's faces pinched by hunger?

I know that if a Gallup poll taker came among us tomorrow 99 percent of us would vote for a permanent peace. And I know that this feeling is not to be lightly dismissed; it has already had its effect in concrete steps toward peace such as the ratification by the Senate of the United Nations Charter. But preventing war is not that easy.

Some of the causes of this war went deeper than any enemy men or movements. They were not removed by the death of Hitler and they will not be removed by the execution of Japanese generals. Some of these causes lie in our own minds and hearts as well as in those of our defeated enemies.

A small group of scientists can unlock the secrets of uranium and leap into the future. But it is harder to break a prejudice than an atom. Hundreds of millions of men the world over must take thought, must take time off from workday cares to perform a far more difficult task than that involved in the mastery of U 235 if peace is to be preserved, if the new horizons of science are not merely to provide a new and immense stage for destruction. They must shake loose from ancient nationalist egotisms; the world has grown too small for them. They must grope forward past cherished preconceptions to a better-organized society in which all men may be assured of their daily bread; the world cannot afford a renewal of the economic insecurity in which war and fascism grew, and can grow again.

I wish it were possible to throw on some gigantic screen for all to see some fraction of the suffering, the treachery, the sacrifice, and the courage of the past decade. For how are we in America to fulfill our responsibility to the dead and to the future, to our less fortunate allies and to our children's children, if we do not feel a little of this so deeply in our bones that we will be unswervingly determined that it shall never happen again?

Organization for Peace . . .
Or Against the Soviet Union?

Stone sees the seeds of the Cold War being sown even before the conclusion of the fight against the Axis.

·   ·   ·

May 4, 1945

IT IS VERY DIFFICULT at a conference of this kind to see the forest for the trees, to disentangle the realities from the rhetoric, but I think I am beginning to get my bearings.

I am inclined to believe that what is going on here becomes a good deal clearer if one keeps in mind that action is proceeding on two planes. On one, the formal and public plane, a final draft is being prepared for a world security organization. On the other, the informal and private plane, quite a different tendency is at work.

That tendency, which is very strong, if not dominant, in the American delegation, is to regard the United Nations Conference on International Organization as a conference for the organization of an anti-Soviet bloc.

This is not my own opinion alone. It is the opinion privately held by some of the most astute newspapermen here, irrespective of their own political orientation. In my own case, this opinion is the net product of my own estimate of the basic forces at work, of conference gossip, and of an attempt to find some pattern into which all the diverse pieces will fit.

But I did not set this down on paper until I found confirmation in trustworthy official American quarters I may not here identify. I can only say that among the younger and more progressive men attached to the American delegation there is increasing apprehension over the extent to which the conference begins to take on the aspects of an attempt by our delegation to build an anti-Soviet world coalition.

The maintenance of the unity of the powers as a first essential of world peace is a principle to which everyone agrees. But whenever one sets out to explore some specific problem, the future of Germany, the fate of the Rhineland and Ruhr, the course of the Far Eastern war and the settlement which will emerge from it, one finds this principle forgotten.

One finds, instead, that the main question in the minds of many State, War, and Navy Department officials, and too many members of the American delegation, is the balance of forces between the USA and the USSR, an implied assumption that war between them is inevitable and that it is our job to maneuver for as strong a position as possible in anticipation of that conflict.

This dangerous belief that war between the two remaining great powers of the earth, the USA and the USSR, is inevitable—a belief which can make it so—has diverse roots.

The defeat of Germany has upset the world balance of power. The strength of the Soviet Union has both surprised and frightened many leading figures in the War and Navy Departments; the bureaucracy of both tends to be either politically naive or socially reactionary.

The divergencies of outlook between a great Communist power, dominated by a one-party dictatorship and a still revolutionary mentality, and a capitalist democracy like our own are very great, and it will take much forbearance and good will to bridge them. There is less forbearance and good will visible since Roosevelt's death.

I think we must also recognize that there is no alternative between the achievement of full employment in America by peaceful means and new imperialist adventures and war. This is recognized by the progressives among the technical staffs and consultants of the American delegation, who fear a tendency—an almost unconscious and organic tendency—to find a way out of a new postwar unemployment crisis by armed conflict instead of the peaceful, but painful, process of adjusting our economy to full employment.

American progressives must keep in mind that however "correct" the attitude of the Soviets and however conservative the policies Moscow may impose on Communist parties abroad to conciliate capitalist opinion, the contrast between full employment in the USSR and a new unemployment crisis after the war in the USA would be explosive. Many people fear the impact of so socially dangerous a contrast, but, while some of us conclude from it the necessity of a full-employment program, others may think the contrast would best be avoided by an attempt to destroy the USSR. I do not believe that anyone would advocate this publicly, and very few would even admit it to themselves. Yet there is a natural drift in that direction in some circles.

I do not set this down to be alarmist; I do not think such a conflict is at all inevitable. But I think it time that people became aware of this danger- ous undertow and took steps to counteract it lest we wake up one day to find that we have permitted our representatives here to lay the foundations for a third world war—a war against the Soviet Union—while going through the motions of establishing a stable peace.

That is a rough way to put it. It by no means does justice either to the motives or the actions of many members of the American delegation, but I am convinced that it provides a true picture of what is developing here.

As early as April 26, Walter Lippmann noted a tendency to assume "that because Germany is prostrate, the German problem is no longer the para- mount problem of the world." He found this reflected in "the fact that the main preoccupation of so many here has been not Germany, but the Soviet Union." And he warned that our relations with the USSR would become hopeless "if we yield at all to those who, to say it flatly, are thinking of the international organization as a means of policing the Soviet Union."

I think it is no exaggeration to say that since last week, when Lippmann wrote what I have quoted, the anti-Soviet atmosphere has grown. It is no longer a question of not "yielding" to the men Lippmann has in mind. They are, if not running the show, at least playing the dominant part in the American delegation and in the conference.

Some of them have been very open and very indiscreet in voicing their anti-Soviet views at the social functions in which celebrity-dazed San Fran- cisco has been lionizing them. They have been equally open in spreading anti-Soviet propaganda "off the record" to correspondents who are their confidants or mouthpieces.

One correspondent, on a conservative paper with more access to these circles than I, says the only two members of the American delegation who have not been spreading an anti-Soviet line are Commander Stassen and Dean Gildersleeve. I cannot vouch for that information and it may be unfair to one or two others, but I do not think it is far wrong.

In an atmosphere of this kind one may be sure that the realistic Russians, who understand perfectly well what is going on, will make few concessions on Poland and other areas important to the security of the USSR. They are no more willing than are the French to rely for their security solely on a new world organization, especially one born in such circumstances.

If this seems wicked of them, it may well be kept in mind that the United States Navy, on the question of international trusteeship, is equally unwilling to accept the new organization as a substitute for effective American control of the Pacific islands and perhaps some of the African territories where it considers bases necessary to our own security.

Whether President Truman is aware of, and supports, the kind of maneuvering in which the American delegation is engaged I do not know. Since the death of Roosevelt, the leadership of the American delegation seems to have fallen to Senator Vandenberg.

Truman's own attitude is not clear. It is noted that the day after the Nazi attack on the Soviet Union he issued a particularly unfortunate statement that is now being recalled with perhaps unjustified apprehension.

The *New York Times* of June 24, 1941, carried a story by Turner Catledge in which he said Congressional reaction to "the newest turn of the European war was reserved except among isolationists. . . ." I do not think that term was fairly applied to Truman, but Catledge went on to quote Truman as one of those isolationists.

"If we see that Germany is winning," Catledge quoted then Senator Truman as saying, "we ought to help Russia and if Russia is winning we ought to help Germany and that way let them kill as many as possible, although I don't want to see Hitler victorious under any circumstances. Neither of them think anything of their pledged word."

What Truman said in 1941 may be no index of his ideas in 1945, but what he said in 1941 reflects the kind of thinking which has a strong hold on too many of the members of our delegation in San Francisco.

Part Three

TWILIGHT STRUGGLE

Unnoticed News Bulletin

The last sentence of this story says it all. In a seemingly innocuous report from a committee of the House of Representatives, Stone unearths telling signs that, driven by a resurgence of the anti-Communist fervor that produced the "Red scares" of the inter-war period, American political and business interests are moving to block Soviet development—and support rearmament of Germany—in preparation for an inevitable war with the U.S.S.R.

.   .   .

December 31, 1946

THE PRESS GENERALLY SEEMS to have overlooked two salient points in the so-called "progress report" on "economic reconstruction in Europe" made public here over the weekend by the influential House Special Committee on Postwar Economic Policy and Planning.

One is that the committee not only proposes to raise the level of industry allowed Germany under the Potsdam agreements but suggests the wisdom of permitting the Reich to retain its two key war industries, synthetic oil and synthetic rubber.

The other is that the committee at the same time not only proposes to restrict private American sales to the Soviet Union but to institute a world-wide trade war under American leadership against the USSR.

One extraordinary parenthetical reference in this report would seem to indicate that the committee would even allow the Germans to do research in atomic and bacteriological warfare, so long as they were subject to "inspection." Reports of the Allied Control Commission after the last war showed that inspection was circumvented and thwarted even under a Social Democratic regime in the Reich.

The report urges the State Department to initiate steps to prevent other nations, as well as ourselves, from supplying the Soviet Union with the materials needed for the reconstruction of its war-ravaged industries.

"Merely to refuse a loan to Russia," the report says, "is not enough."

The report proposes that all sales to Russia be subject to export license control by the Department of Commerce "under conditions set by the Department of State," with a special view to preventing the Russians from obtaining "American know-how and some of the most secret processes in fields of radar, electronics, communications, catalytic chemistry, etc., basic in the superiority of American defense."

That the influential House committee is thinking not merely of defense secrets but of blocking industrial development in the USSR is to be seen in its further recommendation:

The committee "urges upon the State Department the exercise of the maximum pressure upon other systems to follow this lead, and calls specific attention to the danger of having Britain, Sweden, Switzerland and France operate along these lines, to supply Russia with an industrial development that can only be deleterious to the interests of a secure and peaceful world under present Russian policies."

The committee objects in particular to the arrangement by which Sweden will supply a large part of its billion-kroner trade credit to the USSR in electrical equipment. It urges the Civilian Production Administration not to wait for Congressional authorization but to use its export licensing powers to shut off shipment of these and other "capital goods items" to Russia.

While objecting to industrialization of Russia, the committee throws doubt on the necessity of forbidding Germany in the future to operate two of the key synthetic war industries built up by I. G. Farben between the two first world wars. These are the synthetic petroleum and synthetic rubber industries. The Reich has been most susceptible to blockade in rubber and oil in the past and the Wehrmacht could not have fought as long as it did without synthetics at its disposal.

The report is critical not only of the Russians but of the British and the French as well for alleged unfair treatment of the Germans, and says: "Germany is the special responsibility of the Western powers, and on its fate mainly depends the future of Europe in relation to Communism."

Thus the old familiar Nazi line of the need to strengthen the Reich as a bulwark against Bolshevism reappears in a Congressional report, less than two years after the second World War ended, and it reappears in a context suggesting that America's principal postwar concern is preparation for a third world war, this time against the USSR.

Mr. Smith Pleads for Peace

Stone is generally thought of mainly as an investigative reporter and polemicist, but, as this piece illustrates, he also had a wicked gift for satire.

. . .

January 24, 1949

IN TAKING OVER THE HIGH OFFICE to which I have been elected as head of the Smith family, I want to pledge myself to peace.

We Smiths, unlike the Joneses, are peaceful people. A new war would ruin us. There are three mortgages on the old house already. We couldn't afford another scrap in this neighborhood. That's why I'm going to do all I can for peace.

So far as I can see, the prospects for peace would be excellent, were it not for the Joneses over in the next alley. They lie, cheat, steal, pick their noses in public, and forget to put the top on their garbage can.

As everybody knows, Smiths are righteous folk. We meet the interest on our mortgages, shovel the snow off our sidewalks, and we're in our pew at church every Sunday morning. We stand foursquare with God and we have reason to believe that God stands foursquare with us.

We're Presbyterians. The Joneses are different. They're Baptists. We have statistics to prove that 6,349,742 Baptists every year die from total immersion. That's the kind of people we Smiths are up against in trying to make this neighborhood a safe one.

We Smiths believe every man should be free to worship God as he pleases, so long as he doesn't turn Baptist, or spread total immersion. We're prepared to lend money to anyone on the verge of becoming a Baptist if only he'll desist from damnation.

One of the troubles with the Joneses is they're too darned suspicious. They keep insisting that we are getting ready to attack them. I have no hesitation in saying that this is a complete fabrication, highly exaggerated, only partly true, and something of a misconception.

It is true that in return for friendly loans to neighbors of the Joneses we have arranged to set up sandbag emplacements in all the backyards adjoining theirs, and are ready at a moment's notice to let loose with a new gadget of which we Smiths are right proud, the addled egg.

These eggs, as prepared by a secret process of our own, are so hard when thrown and so gaseous when broken that a fusillade of them is guaranteed within ten minutes to break every window in the Jones home, kill Mr. Jones, drive Mrs. Jones out of her head, and asphyxiate all the Jones children. But these preparations of ours are purely defensive. The refusal of the Joneses to believe this is another example of that stubborn wickedness to which Joneses are predestined.

Far from plotting war, we are anxious for peace. The front door of our home is always open to Old Man Jones. He's a crooked old scoundrel, with a nose like a tomato and a breath that would knock over a horse. Everybody knows he's an embezzler, chicken thief, bigamist, and prevaricator, but any time he wants to crawl over to my door on that dirty belly of his *I'll* talk peace with him.

We're going ahead on our own peace plans regardless. We're going to erect a ten-foot-high picket fence around the Jones house. We're building up the biggest stockpile of addled eggs in the history of our neighborhood. And we're negotiating with little Willie Jones, who's just crazy about lollipops, to supply him with all-day suckers for life, if he'll set fire to the Jones place next time his old man's sleeping off a bender.

We Smiths want peace so bad we're prepared to kill every one of the Joneses to get it.

Shall We Take the Gamble Hitler Lost?

This article was written in reaction to a special issue of *Collier's* weekly devoted to the fantastic supposition of a war in which the Soviet Union is quickly and easily overthrown by Western armies. (It's hard to ignore the similarity to the neo-con predictions of a "cakewalk" in Iraq, in which American soldiers would be greeted as liberators by the grateful Iraqi people after a quick and painless military triumph.) Thankfully, most American policy makers in the Cold War era retained enough of a grip on reality so that this hair-raising scheme was never actually tried.

·   ·   ·

October 25, 1951

IN THE FIRST DAYS OF THE NAZI ATTACK upon the Soviet Union, when General George C. Marshall himself thought the USSR might collapse within a few weeks, *Time* magazine spoke of the "pathetic fallacy" that Hitler could be stopped by the same defense-in-depth and scorched-earth tactics which defeated Napoleon.

Events proved this was no fallacy. The pathetic spectacle was the hitherto unbeatable Wehrmacht after two winters on the vast frozen Russian plain. The experts who drew up the blueprint for *Collier's* special issue on "Russia's Defeat and Occupation" did take note of Napoleon's defeat and Hitler's, but only to fall into as serious an error.

They realize that an invasion of Russia has proved fatal on three occasions. Napoleon, Wilhelm II, and Hitler alike were fatally enfeebled by their attempts to invade Russia. To meet this problem—quite a problem—*Collier's* assumes that Russia can be defeated without being invaded!

This needs to be read to be believed. Hanson W. Baldwin in his contribution, "How The War Was Fought," says, "No deep land penetration of Russia was ever attempted—or indeed ever seriously contemplated."

The main drive eastward halts at the Pripet marshes, i.e. on the ancient natural border dividing Russia from the Western lands. "Spearheads" move into Finland and the Baltic states and establish advanced air bases. A southern drive through Turkey ends "in a lodgment in the Crimea, where the last formal battles" are fought.

"In the meantime," Baldwin explains, "as the Red armies fell apart in the West, Siberia, and Red China, . . . limited amphibious operations, many of them made against little opposition, put United States and allied troops ashore in Korea, Manchuria and China."

As easy as that!

This picture of the Red armies falling apart and of the Moscow regime collapsing is based on the notion that the Russians are a kind of faceless enslaved mass of what Robert E. Sherwood calls "docile flesh and blood."

The impression *Collier's* creates is that Russia is one vast slave labor camp where we need only shoot the guards and wreck the gates to be hailed as liberators. The Communist regime, as Arthur Koestler explains in his contribution, "was simply a rule of terror."

Millions of lives have twice been staked—and lost—on Koestler's view that the Soviet dictatorship is "simply a rule of terror." The first time was in the years of armed intervention which followed the Revolution. The second time was when Hitler attacked the Soviet Union.

The same factors on which our anti-Soviet experts rely today—hatred of the secret police, the harshness of the Bolsheviks in dealing with dissident elements, dissatisfaction among the Ukrainians and other non-Russian peoples, "religious longings," etc.—also figured in the earlier calculations.

Twice the collapse failed to occur, though Russia was invaded and large portions occupied. *Collier's* would have us believe that this time a collapse would occur without an invasion. This is quite a gamble.

A great deal is being written in the American press about the danger of some "miscalculation" in a Kremlin blinded by its own propaganda. There is at least as great a danger of a miscalculation in a Washington blinded by *its* own propaganda.

Much that is being culled from Soviet newspapers and Soviet refugees is undoubtedly true, as much is true that can be culled about American weaknesses from the American press and American radicals who have gone abroad. But in neither case is this likely to be the whole truth.

A Russian whose head was full of stories about American lynchings and slums—both realities—might well imagine that at the approach of Soviet armies to our shores the Negroes would revolt and the American workers would hail their liberating brothers. An American whose head is full of stories about forced labor camps and secret police—both realities—can well imagine, as the contributors to *Collier's* imagine, a fervent welcome for the Western armies in the Soviet Union.

There is wishful thinking on both sides, and a fear on both sides of becoming politically suspect if one dwells on the sources of strength in the other country. Even amid the hostile propaganda here, there are glimpses which explain Soviet capacity to survive and which warn against reliance on theories of easy collapse.

Margaret Mead in her new book on *Soviet Attitudes Toward Authority,* a study financed by Cold War funds, speaks of "the reserves of zest and energy which the present population [of the Soviet Union] displays." A nation of cowed slave laborers does not show "zest and energy."

Ambassador Alan G. Kirk, just back from two years in Moscow, spoke here October 18 of a trip he made across the Soviet Union. He pictured "imagination and driving force at work" in Siberia. He spoke of the Soviet peoples as "a young race, virile and vigorous, with imagination and inspiration."

Regimentation is undeniable but "despite regimentation the individual is made to feel that he is a contributing member of society—a feeling that adds purpose and happiness to life." The quotation is not from the Dean of Canterbury. It is from the book written by the wartime director of American lend-lease in Moscow, General John R. Deane's *The Strange Alliance.*

Collier's blueprint calls for round-the-clock bombing but assumes we can fight Russia's masters without fighting her people. There is no way to bomb with such pinpoint accuracy as to hit only card-carrying Communists. There is no way to wage a war of liberation with atom bombs. History shows foreign attack tends to solidify Russians against the invader rather than against their rulers, whether czars or commissars.

Let us listen to a bitterly anti-Communist writer, who himself advocates American aid to counter-revolutionary movements within the Soviet

Union. "If," Boris Shub writes in his book *The Choice,* "through the continued absence of a positive American peace program toward Russia, the
Kremlin does convince the majority that we intend to wage genocidal war,
they will have to rally behind Stalin as the lesser evil."

"For no matter how much they hate the police state," Shub continues,
"they cannot welcome mass extermination by American hydrogen bombs."
War against the Soviet regime would inescapably be war against the Soviet
peoples and their allies in China and Eastern Europe. That is a lot of
people, about three quarters of a billion of them. It will take the lives of a
good many American boys to subdue them, if instead of collapsing (as in
the *Collier's* blueprint) they resist.

A Chill Falls on Washington

When Joseph Stalin died on March 5, 1953, after nearly thirty years as leader of
the Soviet Union, it created a power vacuum in the Kremlin and an atmosphere
of anxious uncertainty on the world diplomatic scene. I. F. Stone seized the opportunity to call on his own country to adopt a more realistic and accommodating
stance toward the other great power of the post-war era.

.   .   .

March 14, 1953

AMID THE BURST OF BAD MANNERS and foolish speculation, there was
remarkably little jubilation. A sudden chill descended on the capital. If
Stalin was the aggressive monster painted in official propaganda, his death
should have cheered Washington. Actually the unspoken premise of American policy has been that Stalin was so anxious for peace he would do nothing unless Soviet soil itself were violated. With his death, the baiting of the
Russian bear—the favorite sport of American politics—suddenly seemed
dangerous. Even Martin Dies rose in the House to say that while Stalin was
"utterly cruel and ruthless, he was more cautious and conservative than the
younger Bolsheviks." Few would have dared a week earlier to dwell on the
conservative and cautious temperament of the Soviet ruler, much less imply
that this was favorable to world stability and peace. Now this theme leaked
from every State Department briefing. There was apprehension that after
Stalin there might come someone worse and more difficult to deal with.

The cold war claque was critical of Nehru for calling Stalin a man of
peace, but Washington's own instinctive reactions said the same thing. The
stress put by the White House on the fact that its condolences were merely
"official" was small-minded and unworthy of a great power. After all, it is
fortunate for America that when Stalin's regime met the ultimate test of
war, it did not collapse like the Czar's. The war against the Axis would have

lasted a lot longer and cost a great many more American lives if there had been a second Tannenberg instead of a Stalingrad. Stalin was one of the giant figures of our time, and will rank with Ivan, Peter, Catherine and Lenin among the builders of that huge edifice which is Russia. Magnanimous salute was called for on such an occasion. Syngman Rhee, ruler of a satellite state precariously engaged in fighting for its life against forces supplied by Russia, demonstrated a sense of fitness in his own condolences which Washington seemed afraid to show.

It is difficult to pursue dignified and rational policy when official propaganda has built up so distorted a picture of Russia. Many Americans fed constantly on the notion that the Soviet Union is a vast slave labor camp must have wondered why the masses did not rise now that the oppressor had vanished. The Bolshevik Revolution is still regarded here as a kind of diabolic accident. The necessities imposed on rulers by the character of the countries they rule is ignored. To understand it would be to put the problem of peaceful relations with Russia in quite a different perspective and to dissipate febrile delusions about "liberation." The wisest of the anti-Communist Russian émigrés of our generation, Berdyaev, in his *The Origins of Russian Communism* has touched on the way bolshevism succeeded because it was so deeply rooted in Russia's character and past. Bolshevism "made use," Berdyaev wrote, "of the Russian traditions of government by imposition. . . . It made use of the characteristics of the Russian spirit . . . its search after social justice and the Kingdom of God upon earth . . . and also of its manifestations of coarseness and cruelty. It made use of Russian messianism. . . . It fitted in with the absence among the Russian people of the Roman view of property. . . . It fitted in with Russian collectivism which had its roots in religion."

Every great leader is the reflection of the people he leads and Stalin in this sense was Russia. He was also the leader of something new in world history, a party: a party in a new sense, like nothing the world has known since the Society of Jesus, a party ruling a one-party state. It is this difference which makes nonsense of prediction by analogy based on the principle of legitimacy in monarchy or the later history of the Roman empire. Struggle among the party leaders occurred after the death of Lenin and may occur after the death of Stalin, but the party itself provides a cement strong enough to hold the state together despite such struggles. To regard this as a group of conspirators may prove a fatal error. This is a movement, with a philosophy comparable to the great religions in its capacity to evoke devotion, and based on certain economic realities which give it a constructive function. It has proved itself capable of industrializing Russia and opening new vistas to its masses, and this is its appeal to similar areas in Asia. This is a challenge which can only be met by peaceful competition, for only in peace can the West preserve what it has to offer, and that is the tradition of individual liberty and free thought.

It is time in the wake of Stalin's death to recognize two basic facts about the world we live in. One fact is Russia. The other is the Communist movement. The surest way to wreck what remains of capitalism and intellectual freedom in the non-Communist world today is blindly to go on refusing to recognize these facts and refusing to adjust ourselves to coexistence on the same planet with them. Eisenhower in leaving the door discreetly ajar to possible negotiations with Stalin's successor was wise, and the lesser powers should seize on the sobering moment to urge Washington and Moscow to get together.

First Call for a Test Ban

In 1954, Indian Prime Minister Jawaharlal Nehru proposed a ban on the testing of nuclear weapons as a way of slowing the global arms race. The idea gained little traction in the atmosphere of suspicion and hostility then dominating the Cold War powers. Not until 1963, in the aftermath of the Cuban Missile Crisis, did the U.S. and U.S.S.R. agree to a limited test ban treaty, which prohibited nuclear weapon test explosions and any other nuclear explosions in the atmosphere, in outer space, or underwater (but did not prohibit underground nuclear explosions). Somewhat ironically, India is today one of a handful of nations actively resisting the ban's current form, the Comprehensive Nuclear Test Ban Treaty of 1999, and insisting on their own right to develop and test atomic weapons.

. . .

November 1, 1954

THE PICTURE IN OUR MINDS of the atom bomb is of something that we have stockpiled in a kind of dark closet, which can be taken out and used if we so choose. But enough is known to indicate that this is misleading, that the atom bomb is not just another new weapon which can be held in reserve like poison gas or germs; it is a revolution in warfare.

There is now a whole growing family of atomic and hydrogen weapons adapted for use in various situations by various branches of the armed services. And if atomic weapons are being adapted to the strategic and tactical needs of the various services, then these services in turn must be adapted to the use of atomic weapons.

If one prepares to wage atomic war, one must recast one's army, navy and air force radically. This means that we are confronted with a decision of policy quite different from taking a bomb out of a stock pile. Once the basic decision is taken to make the next war atomic, many other decisions follow

115

which make the first difficult, and perhaps in practice impossible, to reverse. For the war begins with armies, navies and air forces trained to attack with, and defend themselves against, fission and fusion weapons. The die that may mean the destruction of civilization is not only cast but loaded in advance.

It is against this background that attention should be called to a talk given in London a week ago by Field Marshal Lord Montgomery. With Generals Gruenther and Norstad, Montgomery is one of the triumvirate which commands the NATO forces. He spoke on "A Look Through a Window at World War III." And what he said, according to the London *Times,* was that "at Supreme Allied HQ they were basing all their operational planning on using atomic and thermonuclear weapons in their defense, and this called for a certain reorganization of their forces and in their strategy."

It is sometimes assumed that we will not use nuclear weapons unless the enemy does. But Montgomery made clear in London, as he did in a speech a few weeks earlier at Ankara, that we would use nuclear weapons for defense against attack, whether that attack was atomic or not. The decision has been made, the armed forces shaped, for atomic war.

In the light of these military realities, the renewed debate at the UN over atomic disarmament between the United States and the U.S.S.R. takes on a new significance. This debate is again plunged into another lengthy and arid veto-and-inspection controversy. This controversy—pitched in these terms—is insoluble. For there is no way to convince either side that any system of inspection and control may not be evaded or abused by the other.

The whole controversy in some ways is nonsense. Atomic weapons cannot be made in washtubs, nor launched without the most extensive measures of mobilization, dispersion, and defense in preparation for the retaliatory blow from the other side. As Montgomery said, the purpose of having active forces "in being" in peacetime "would make it impossible for the east to launch an attack successfully without a preparatory build-up of their forces, which we would know about." No iron curtain could hide the preparatory measures required to launch an atomic world war.

Nevertheless there is no way to convince the American public that the Russians might not make and catapult bombs in secret from some hideaway in Siberia, nor convince the Russians that the Americans might not utilize inspection to spy out the prime bombing targets of the U.S.S.R. In this atmosphere to debate veto-and-inspection, as Lodge and Vishinsky now are doing, is worse than hopeless. The world public is lulled into a false sense of complacency by the debate, while the real decisions have already been taken, the military vested interests on both sides built up, a juggernaut created which can move in one way only, the way of the A-, the H- and soon the C-bomb.

It is this which makes the Krishna Menon proposal of last week so crucial. There was a kind of cosmic comedy in the way the United States and the U.S.S.R. hastily joined hands in shelving and thus shutting off General Assembly debate on the Indian proposal for a "truce" in the testing of new atomic and hydrogen weapons. This proposal, which was first made by Nehru last April and endorsed by Indonesia and Burma, alone offers a simple and enforceable way to put a stop to the atomic arms race, to ease tension and thereby to create an atmosphere in which further agreement may become possible. A "truce on tests" is self-enforceable because the new weapons are so powerful that if exploded their radioactivity is detectible anywhere on earth.

India spoke for mankind when its representative challenged the criminal rubbish on our side about using the atomic bomb "only in defense against aggression." Both sides in every war always claim to be *aggressed*. Menon uttered what may prove to be the prophetic epitaph of our civilization when he said use of H-bombs would prove "suicide for the nations who used them, genocide for those against whom they were used, and infanticide for posterity." If there is still a peace movement left in America, this must be its platform. As a first step away from mutual destruction, no more tests.

National Suicide as a Form of Defense

A sharp protest against the "ultimate delusion of the atomic era"—the idea that the suicidal launching of a nuclear war could somehow serve the cause of national defense. Thomas E. Murray was a member of the Atomic Energy Commission who proposed, in a speech on November 17, 1955, that the U.S. detonate a hydrogen bomb as a staged demonstration before representatives of the nations of the world in order to underscore the dangers of nuclear weaponry. The proposal was quickly denounced by the other members of the commission and soon forgotten.

.   .   .

November 28, 1955

THE REAL REASON WASHINGTON rejects Atomic Energy Commissioner Thomas E. Murray's proposal for a world H-bomb demonstration is not for fear of what it might do to Them but for fear of what it might do to Us. The basic decisions of atomic warfare have been made from the beginning without consulting public opinion. At first from necessity and later from considerations of military security and finally from fear and habit, atomic decisions have been and are being made in secret, without popular consultation.

Democratic processes have been one of the first victims of nuclear fission. The decision to try and make the bomb and the decision to drop it on Japan were, of course, made privately. So was the decision to go ahead and make the H-bomb; had it not been for a slip by former Senator Ed Johnson of Colorado the public would never have known of it. Finally the decision to use "tactical" atomic weapons, and to refashion the armed services for atomic warfare, has also been made by the inner circles of the government without debate in Congress or elsewhere. The current Sagebrush military maneuvers in Louisiana show how far that transformation has gone.

The atomic thunderbolt is no longer a final weapon to be held in reserve for use only under the gravest circumstances on presidential decision, but *the* weapon around which all our military planning and training now revolve. Though atomic warfare means national suicide and humanity's final holocaust, the decision to engage in it has been made. We have been consulted as little about it as if we lived under a dictatorship.

Only once has there been a great national debate on atomic policy and that came when the aroused atomic scientists descended on Washington like a flock of Paul Reveres to raise the alarums against military control of atomic energy. That great debate, right after the war, was made possible because (1) Congress had to be consulted if an atomic energy act were to be passed, and (2) the atomic scientists had not yet been frightened away from political activity by the loyalty-security mania. In this case political activity meant an attempt to fulfill the highest moral responsibilities in the society to which they had made so fatal a gift. But that was before the onset of the cold war, and since that time the government has succeeded by one means or another in shutting off real debate.

Every attempt by the Russians from the Stockholm peace petition to the latest Molotov proposals for a world pledge against atomic warfare has been hooted down. Discussion of foreign policy has been made to seem somehow unpatriotic; talk of peace, suspect. Mr. Acheson's call for "total diplomacy" in January, 1950, merely put this into a vivid and sinister phrase; it sought at home the same kind of "disciplined" attitude toward foreign policy on which dictatorships pride themselves. Oppenheimer's ordeal, of which the atomic scientists knew long before the public, provided the scientific elite with a chilling object lesson. The decisions were to be made by our "betters"—though these self-appointed "betters" included some of those generals with prognathous jaws and Neanderthal minds who adorn the covers of our news weeklies and wield the power of world, life and death through our ever-ready Strategic Air Command. The reality has been the subordination of the best scientific minds to military control through the rich carrot of military research grants and the heavy stick of possible loyalty proceedings. In a period when no general ever makes a speech any more without giving God a plug, and self-righteous moralizings ooze from every political pore, real morality has been completely abandoned in our imbecile fascination with these new destructive toys. The atom is our totem; the bomb our Moloch; faith in overwhelming force is being made into our real national religion.

The Pentagon and State Department have feared public debate lest it interfere with the task of recasting our armed forces, our moral standards and our minds. There is evidence that this remolding process is far from complete and irreversible. The latest Gallup poll shows that peace far outranks every other problem in the public mind (42 percent answered peace—the farm problem, which was next, drew only 8 percent). To hold an H-bomb demonstration in the Pacific, as Mr. Murray proposes, with the world press and all other governments represented, would be not merely to frighten Them but to awaken Us out of our lethargy.

Thanks to Mr. Murray, we are now authoritatively warned that the atmospheric and soil contamination from large thermonuclear explosions is a far graver menace than had hitherto been supposed; apparently there is a limit to the safe amount of thermonuclear explosion even without war. A new substance, radioactive strontium, not hitherto present in the air or earth, has been created and released. Its contamination continues long after the blasts. As it passes from the soil into food and the human body, it can create bone tumors and fatal effects. Commissioner Murray says that estimates of how much radioactive strontium can safely be absorbed "have changed almost wildly" in the past year. A year ago it was said that we had little to fear because the amount would have to increase by one million times; now the estimate has been reduced to ten thousand times. Mr. Murray thinks this figure will be lowered. His four fellow commissioners, in rejecting his proposal for an H-bomb demonstration, significantly fail to deny these figures. Their official statement merely says that until further study has been made "it is impossible to be definite about the genetic effects." This is quite different from the statements of a year ago that fear of radioactive fall-out was exaggerated. Why should these matters be cloaked in secrecy, the decisions on them made without popular discussion?

The lack of real debate has allowed a thick deposit of dubious ideological fallout to contaminate the public mind. A whole series of doubtful propositions have been rubbed in by official statement and their echoes in a well-coordinated press. There is first of all the notion that but for the bomb the

Russians would have overrun Western Europe after the war. This is highly doubtful in view of the terrible wounds they still had to heal from the last war, the enormous headaches occupation of Western Europe would have added to their problems, the civil war it would have provoked and the world war it would have unleashed.

America has twice been plunged into world war unprepared, and twice won despite that initial handicap. The Russians are not fools; they do not underestimate the huge industrial capacity and human resources of the American people. It is, I believe, the most dreadful nonsense to say that they would have overrun Western Europe if we had not had the bomb. The same is true, in my opinion, of the equally prevalent notion that there would be world war today but for fear of our bombs. The Russians and the Chinese have enough to do at home; and even without the bomb, war with America would ruin them for a generation. Then there is the newer notion that we must not give up nuclear warfare because only the bomb counter-balances the "hordes" at the disposal of Russia and China. But this completely overlooks the fact that these "hordes" now have the A-bomb and the H-bomb, too. So we no longer have an advantage. Would it not be better for both sides to see if some means cannot be found to ban nuclear warfare for humanity's good?

In the past, certain terrible weapons have been held in reserve by both sides, and neither have used them; poison gas is an example. It is one thing to have the bomb in reserve. It is quite another to equip whole armies with atomic weapons so that they are no longer able to fight any other kind of war. That is what we are doing. We are thus deciding in advance that a new war shall be a war without mercy and limit. The notion that atomic war can be limited; that atomic weapons can be used, as Eisenhower once said, like "pistols," fosters the most dangerous misconceptions. Once such a war begins, neither side dares hold back its worst and biggest bombs, though this may mean total mutual destruction.

Atomic war means national suicide. The ultimate delusion of the atomic era is the notion that national suicide is a feasible means of defense; how apparently sensible and sane men could drift into such beliefs will astound future historians, if there are any. All this has been underscored by the Sage-brush maneuvers. They have shown how easily radar defenses can be jammed by an attacking air fleet; we can wreck Russia's cities but Russia can wreck ours. And the whole human race may be ruined by the aftereffects. Is it not irrational, then, to decide for atomic warfare when atomic warfare means mutual suicide? Should such a decision be made without the fullest national and world debate? How much security is there in plans for defense which could do no more than assure our dying people that the enemy was dying, too? The Strategic Air Command can destroy the enemy, but it cannot defend us.

To set off on the path of atomic warfare is to set off on a path from which there is no return, toward a goal where there can be no victory, into a hell where none could survive. Until now the worst wars have been, to some extent, limited—if not by human intention and hatred, then at least by human capacity to destroy. But this war, the war we have been trying out in Operation Sagebrush, the atomic war must become unlimited war, against Us as well as Them. On those whom the bombs spare the radioactive dusts will fall, gently and impartially as the rain.

Natasha's Ready Answers

In May 1956, I. F. Stone traveled behind the Iron Curtain for six days in Moscow and three in Warsaw. During this brief trip, he visited a collective farm, took in the usual tourist spots such as St. Basil's Cathedral and the tombs of Lenin and Stalin, interviewed Soviet journalists, and spoke with as many ordinary Russian citizens as possible. This article is the second of four dispatches Stone sent back from the visit in which he tried to offer an objective picture of America's great Cold War rival and the subject of so many demonizing fantasies in the American press.

.   .   .

May 14, 1956

ON OUR WAY BACK FROM our visit to the Kremlin, I asked Natasha, my tourist guide, whether she had any questions to ask about America. She wanted first to know why Paul Robeson could not get a passport. I said I had criticized the government's action in refusing him a passport. She then wanted to know what I thought of the condemnation of the Communists in the United States. I said I had criticized that in public speeches and in my paper. She asked whether many people agreed with me and I said unfortunately not many did. When she looked triumphant, I asked her a question. "How many people in this country," I asked, "would be willing to defend the right of oppositionists to speak against the government?" To this she had a ready answer.

"We have no oppositionists," replied Natasha.

"But suppose you did?" I insisted.

"How could we have oppositionists?" she said. "A man cannot be an oppositionist for himself alone."

"Tolstoy was an oppositionist on his own," I countered.

"No," Natasha replied, "he spoke for the people."

"But the people were voiceless," I replied, "until a few such men had the courage to speak for them."

"Well," Natasha said, "if we had oppositionists, someone would defend their rights."

To illustrate she began to tell me about her trade union.

"In our union," she said, "some people are timid but most of us speak up. Why the other day we even got the reinstatement of a fellow worker who had been fired."

"We have unions in America, too," I said, "and they often get workers reinstated."

"Yes," she said, "but in America unions cannot strike."

"That's not true," I said, "there are lots of strikes in America."

"No," she said, "under the Taft law, workers cannot strike."

"That's not true," I argued. "The effect of the Taft-Hartley Act has been very much exaggerated. We have strikes all the time."

"But union leaders are afraid to call strikes," Natasha insisted, "because they may be heavily fined."

"There have been fines," I said. "But that has not stopped strikes."

By this time we were back to the Metropol and the conversation was over. Natasha looked at me with condescension as a benighted heathen. The idea that something she had read in her party press might possibly be wrong obviously never occurred to her.

I got a different sort of question about America and a different reaction from a Red Army officer. I saw him sitting by himself in a café. I walked over and asked, "*Sprechen sie Deutsch?*" He answered in German, "A little." He spoke no English or French and communication was difficult. He was a friendly man, with clear intelligent eyes, and the face of a kindly person. He wanted to know—after I told him I was an American journalist on my first visit to Moscow—how many rooms the ordinary worker has in the United States. This was his first question. I said in a city like New York even well-to-do people might have small apartments but that in many cities like Philadelphia workers owned their own homes, and that these were five- or six-room homes. He did not look at me with pity as a victim of capitalist propaganda. He looked pleased, as if I had told him something which buttressed his own convictions. I asked him why there were still so many pictures of Stalin around and he said this would soon pass away. He said Russia was "going back to Lenin," and that many bad things had happened under Stalin. He looked incredulous when I said I liked Moscow. Trying hard to express his feelings in his inadequate German, he said—as if in a few words he was distilling the product of long thought—"*the peasant here has a hard life.*" He said, "I am a soldier but I believe in peace." Then he pointed to his uniform and said, "I cannot speak freely." He paid for his drink and left.

I visited two government buildings, the offices of Tass, for copies of speeches made at the Twentieth Congress, and a Ministry of Culture office on Zhdanova Street where the Soviet Information Bureau publishes its Daily Review of the Soviet Press. In both there were uniformed police guards inside the door and no one could get by the guards without showing a pass with a photograph on it. Workers coming down the elevator on errands in the lobby showed their passes each time they passed the policeman. It reminded one of the Pentagon in wartime Washington.

I went to the Ministry of Culture because I wanted a translation of the full text of a long editorial which *Pravda* published on April 5. The fragmentary reports I had seen of it in the foreign press on my way to Russia were disturbing. What was most disturbing was the vagueness of the editorial. I talked to the official in charge of translations at the Ministry of Culture. I told him after reading the text that I could not make head or tail of it. "Suppose," I said, "I were a Soviet citizen, honestly trying to understand what was permissible free speech and what was slanderous and antiparty and therefore impermissible, how could I find out from this editorial? It would only leave me confused and afraid." His answer was that all these matters referred to in the editorial had already been explained at party meetings. "Anyone who attended these meetings will know what the article means," he said. "But," I insisted, "what is the use of a newspaper article which can only be understood if the reader attends a private meeting to hear the explanation?" His reply was that this was an internal party matter. "In your country," he said, "there is free discussion—no," he interrupted himself, "that is not a good word—in your country problems are first discussed in the press but in our country they are first discussed in party meetings and in factory meetings and then we decide how much should go into the press." The talk was held in the English translation bureau, and some of his fellow workers had a hard time trying to keep a straight face during this conversation.

The Russians like their contacts to be organizational. They like visits by delegations rather than individuals. Organization contacts relieve the individual of responsibility. If a visit turns out badly, the fault lies with the organization. In addition, contacts between delegations facilitate that exchange of slogans, safe generalities and non-political pleasantries which the Russians prefer to real talk, which may become dangerous. If you reach a man directly in his office, he will call in a colleague to take part in the conversation, and provide a witness to the talk.

I succeeded in starting impromptu discussions with Russians everywhere. I was not rebuffed once, and this—other foreigners told me—was a complete change from a few years ago when it was simply impossible to talk with Russians at all except on strictly official business. But I never succeeded in making a date with a Russian for a further talk alone. One man I met through an official organization for a group talk seemed most intelligent and most eager for real discussion. I asked him if he would come to my hotel for tea next day and continue our talk. He said he would like to and that he would call me up and let me know. A half-hour before the appointed time he telephoned to say he couldn't come because his wife had a bad cold but he would call me within the next day or so and make another date. I never heard from him again.

I had a talk with two journalists on a well-known Soviet publication which circulates widely abroad. One man, a top editor, was well-tailored, slick, and intelligent but not an attractive type; he seemed very much like the Hollywood intellectuals in the film industry, a born yes-man, with a sharp nose for any change in the wind. One felt that he would never stick his neck out for any man or any principle. He was well-stocked with glib answers for the freedom of the press questions he expected from foreign journalists; what these glib answers boiled down to was that the "capitalist" press faithfully echoed the line of its government, too. The existence of some independent voices and of some independence even in the conservative and conventional press was conveniently passed over. The other man, a subordinate, was more independent-minded. I asked whether Soviet writers and journalists in the future would have more freedom but I never did get a clear answer.

"It would be wrong," said the first journalist, "to say that writers felt restricted. The young people were a new Soviet generation which expressed what it sincerely had been feeling. Now that the party thinks it necessary for writers to be more independent and to write more naturally and from within, they will do so. But it would be wrong to say they were restricted."

"So," I suggested, "it is a question of changing the habits of writers?"

"Yes," was the answer, "and of revising some conceptions."

Then he added what I thought was a most appalling commentary. "Our writers," he said, "thought that to criticize our life was not their affair. They thought only to be happy and not to criticize."

When I asked whether there would be more freedom of speech, the first man said there had always been free speech in Russia. But when I asked whether any Soviet journalist had criticized the earlier attitude toward Tito or the "doctors' plot" he shifted his ground and said that the press in America or England on a subject like the German problem all followed the same line, too. "Our newspapers," he said, "defend our line, too."

I said this was not entirely true in the West. I said the *New York Times* had criticized the padlocking of the *Daily Worker* just before I left. I said I had criticized the "doctors' plot" in my own paper because I felt there was something fishy about it. I asked whether in the future, if there were a similar frame-up, some Soviet journalist would criticize it, too.

"If you ask us about the 'doctors' plot,'" the journalist explained, "now we know. The facts were distorted and invented by the Beria gang. Now that the facts have been made known, we have attacked the 'doctors' plot.' But you have to know the facts."

He never did answer my question about the future. When I cited the fact that one man, like Zola, could force open the Dreyfus case in France, I struck no response. The idea of getting the facts on one's own and of opposing the government in a political or criminal prosecution was completely foreign to his mentality. I felt not merely opportunism but genuine submissiveness in his attitude.

The other journalist seemed to feel that something more was needed to satisfy my questions. "We lived in a besieged fortress," he said. "I am now forty-two. All of my generation were accustomed to believe in the security agencies because these were our shield against real enemies. When we heard of measures taken by these agencies, we were sure they must be true. No revolution ever had so many enemies as ours.

"Now," he continued, "we know that these revolutionary bodies like the security police can also make mistakes. The result is a new atmosphere. Our party and the government have hardened their control over these agencies and put new and good people into them to improve them."

I suggested that one way to "improve" the secret police was to give the individual citizen more rights against them, to establish safeguards like our habeas corpus against the police.

"In the West," the second journalist explained, "it was different. You had a very long experience and got used to defending yourselves against the bourgeois state. But here from the beginning it was a people's state and there was no practical need for such protective procedures. The last few years, however," he conceded, "have showed the need for some such safeguards."

On the question of Tito, the second journalist also had something interesting to add. He said, "Only a small number of our people ever went abroad. We had no way to judge for ourselves. Now that thousands are beginning to go abroad and see for themselves, it will help to prevent such mistakes in the future."

Everywhere I found Russians went out of their way to be helpful as soon as they learned I was a foreigner, and there seemed to be no prejudice against me when I said I was an American. I got to the Bolshoi Theatre just as the performance was starting and the ushers were closing the doors. I didn't know where to go or what to do and was on the verge of being shut out when I told an usher, "*Ne panamayou parusski*" (Don't understand Russian). He at once caught on that I was a foreigner, found me a vacant seat in the darkness and then after the first scene came back and took me to my proper place.

I went to two performances in Moscow. The first was at the huge Bolshoi Theatre where a ballet named *Laurenciana* was being played that night. I liked the enormous, brightly-colored theatre, the gay sets, the music and the audience, which was enjoying itself. But I found the ballet itself conventional, and the story corny; peasant boy saves peasant girl from advances of arrogant knight in medieval village. I was so bored I left after the first act. I didn't think it half as much fun as just walking the streets and looking at the people.

The other performance was a sheer joy. I saw *The Girl with the Fluttering Eyelids,* a satire on Hollywood, done at the puppet theatre of Abrasov. It had been on a triumphant tour in England, and someone should bring it to America. I had never seen anything like it before—a full-length play written for puppets, and the puppets specially designed for the play. The satire was terribly clever—I heard later that our Ambassador Bohlen had enjoyed it immensely. In one scene there are three puppet stenographers taking dictation at once from three collaborating writers in the best frenetic Hollywood manner. An elderly usher who spoke English kindly explained the plot to me before the play began; it was a take-off on *Carmen.* But after the second act, when I saw the smugglers being executed with a flame gun and I asked her to explain, she suddenly went dead on me. She hadn't seen that act, she didn't know what had happened, she practically couldn't speak English any more. I gathered later that Abrasov was satirizing the Marshall Plan and American military policy in that scene. The usher was afraid of offending me if she explained.

I BELIEVE THAT subconsciously or unconsciously every American in Moscow must feel a slight uneasiness, even a little anxiety. These are our rivals and imitators; the subway and the skyscrapers and even more so the booster spirit reflect their desire to imitate, to overtake and to surpass our own country. It is easy to see on the surface how far they yet have to go, and to sneer at their *nouveau riche* vulgarity as the nineteenth-century English visitor sneered (in much the same worried spirit) at the new brash giant growing up in America. But to see the building going on and the beautiful new department stores, to read the speeches of the Twentieth Congress and the stupendous figures of the new Five Year Plan, is to feel that this new rival is a giant, a gauche and slovenly giant whose manners it is easy to ridicule, but whose capacity for huge strides is not to be discounted.

The Legacy of Stalin

In this, the fourth dispatch from Stone's trip to Eastern Europe, he offers his summation of what he sees as the essentially repressive and dishonest nature of the Soviet system. Feeling personally sympathetic with the goals of socialism and strongly averse to giving support to the jingoist anti-Soviet element in American society, Stone found it painful to have to offer such a diagnosis, but his commitment to journalistic honesty—as well as his love of freedom as the single deepest human value—left him no alternative. Angry reactions by "fellow traveling" sympathizers with the Soviet regime are said to have cost Stone 400 subscriptions to the *Weekly*.

.   .   .

May 28, 1956

The way home from Moscow has been agony for me. I have been reading furiously in Russian history and a little in Russian law and in past Communist controversy in an effort to evaluate what I have seen. The deepest questions of history and morality are raised by Russia, the terrible intermingling of good and evil in the evolution of society, history's endless riddle of whether-it-might-have-been-otherwise. My knowledge is inadequate, my ignorance is vast, my only credentials are that these conclusions represent what one man has seen and felt.

All sorts of advice has poured in on me from my friends, and from what I know my friends would say. All the inhibitions of expediency have been urged upon me, the inhibitions of the most worthy expediency—the fight for world peace. But I hate the morass into which one wanders when one begins to withhold the truth because the consequences might be bad—this is, indeed, the morass on which the Russian Communist State is built. I am not wise enough, and perhaps no one else is either, to know how much truth may wisely be given the public with our eye-droppers. I am only a reporter and one does not go to Moscow every day. This is what I think, not what I believe may wisely be told the reader. It may be wrong but it is not synthetic.

I feel like a swimmer under water who must rise to the surface or his lungs will burst. Whatever the consequences, I have to say what I really feel after seeing the Soviet Union and carefully studying the statements of its leading officials. *This is not a good society and it is not led by honest men.*

No society is good in which men fear to think—much less speak—freely. I don't care how many tons of steel the Russians produce. It is not by the volume of its steel but by the character of the men it produces that a society must be judged. The kind of men Russia has produced is the kind which must always be wary, quick to sense any change in the wind and adjust to it, careful never to give way to the anguish of seeing injustice, always guarding one's tongue, alert to survive at whatever cost to one's neighbor.

This society is a paradise only for a rather stupid type of Communist party member, good but sharply limited. If you believe everything you read in the papers, lack imagination, and feel no need to think for yourself, you can be very happy in the Soviet Union and engage in useful devoted work. Or you can shut yourself up in a scientific laboratory and work on your own scientific problems and close your eyes and ears to what is going on outside or maybe even to your unlucky colleague next door. But for the journalist, the writer, the artist, the thinker, the man who cares deeply about the basic questions of humanity and history, the U.S.S.R. has been a hermetically sealed prison, stifling in its atmosphere of complete, rigid and low-level thought control. In this atmosphere has been bred a whole generation of sycophants, and yes-men, and writer-politicians.

It is impossible to imagine unless you have been there what it means to live in a country in which you do not know what is going on outside. The Soviet press is matchless for turgidity and obscurity; it prints only what the men at the top think people ought to know and it is written by uninspired hacks scared to add a thought of their own lest they get into trouble. I invite readers to check this for themselves by reading three authoritative expositions of the new line—*Pravda's* article of March 28, "Why Is the Cult of the Individual Alien to the Spirit of Marxism-Leninism?" (It can be found in full English translation in the March 30 issue of the now defunct Cominform weekly, *For a Lasting Peace, for a People's*

Democracy); *Partiinaya Zhizn's* article of March, 1956, "Wherein Is the Harm of the Cult of the Individual?" (English text in the April 12 issue of the Soviet Information Bureau's *Daily Review of Soviet Press*); and *Kommunist's* article of March, 1956, "Fully Re-establish and Develop Leninist Standards of Party Life" (English text in the April 4 issue of the *Daily Review of Soviet Press*). They are as alike as if all three were the results of a party briefing at which the writers took down the words from on high in as verbatim a manner as possible. The same thoughts, the very same phrases, reappear in the same kind of repellent gibberish.

When you ask in Moscow where foreign papers can be purchased, the answer is that your bookstall in the hotel carries all kinds of foreign papers. But when you watch the stall in the Metropol or the National or the Savoy (the three Intourist hotels) all you see are the East European and Chinese Communist party publications and that completely empty waste of paper, the *Moscow News*. I don't know what it was like when Anna Louise Strong edited it, but there is certainly no news in it today. I could not even buy Western Communist papers like *L'Humanité*. When I picked up a copy of the London *Daily Worker* in the Prague airport on the way back, I got the full flavor of what I had experienced in journalism. The London *Daily Worker* seemed like a bright, newsy, *real* newspaper after the Soviet press. In Warsaw, they have begun to sell Western "capitalist" papers. It will be a sign of real change when this happens in Moscow. It is indicative that a Communist intellectual with whom I discussed this problem in Eastern Europe admitted to me that he "couldn't live" without the *New York Times*. It was a confession and a tribute. Whatever the shortcomings of the Western press, there is no comparison between it and the Soviet press. Out of the variety of news and opinion in the Western press one can sift even the most unpopular truths. To read the Soviet press one has to become expert in decoding a peculiar kind of party language, developed to hide the facts rather than to make them public.

Again I invite readers to check this for themselves. I cite as an example the dissolution of the Cominform, a major news and political event of the Soviet world. The full text of the joint statement by the Bulgarian, Hungarian, Italian, Polish, Rumanian, Soviet, Czech and French parties explaining the dissolution may be found in the final, April 17, issue of the Cominform bulletin, which is on sale in New York. The front page also carries an article on the dissolution snappily entitled "For the Further Development and Strengthening of the International Communist Movement." I challenge anyone to read these two pieces of drivel and find in them any real explanation of why the Cominform was dissolved.

This is why I am compelled to conclude that the present leaders of the Soviet Union are dishonest. I mean dishonest with their own people, not only with the non-party masses but with their own Communist party members. If they want to make a clean break with the Stalinist past, they can best demonstrate it by telling their people what they are doing and why. How can you have "democratic centralism" in the Communist party, i.e., free discussion within the limits of party discipline (what Lenin meant by the phrase), when the party members themselves aren't told what is going on?

I cite as a major example the Beria business. No one outside a very small circle at the top really knows why Beria was executed. Those who study the tortuous, veiled and contradictory language of the various statements published in the Soviet press will find themselves completely confused. Only persons rendered permanently idiotic by complete submergence in party-line literature will take at face value the charge that he was a British or imperialist agent. This is how Stalin operated; he never met an opponent on the ground of honest discussion; first slander and then the firing squad were his answers. And *everybody* turned out to be a foreign agent!

Now, if the charge was meant seriously, why didn't the new rulers demonstrate their intention to operate differently by presenting their evidence against Beria in open court? Why was he tried secretly and so swiftly executed? Was not the treatment of Beria in the true Stalinist tradition? And nothing was more truly Stalinist than the obscure and slanderous verbiage of the various statements on Beria.

I cite as another major example the attack on Stalin himself. Nobody yet knows just why and how it was decided to go so far in the denigration of Stalin. After his death, the press began to play him down. But in 1954 and again in 1955 his picture appeared with Lenin's on the front page of the November 7 issue of *Pravda,* celebrating the anniversary of the Revolution. Zhukov in Red Square paid tribute just last year to the party of

"Marx-Engels-Lenin-*Stalin.*" As recently as last December 21, *Pravda* published a 2,000-word article on the 76th anniversary of Stalin's birth, an article full of the most lavish praise of the dead dictator in Marxist theory and in practice, in industry and in agriculture. The language was that of the Stalin cult.

What happened between the end of December and the Twentieth Party Congress in February? Indeed why did Khrushchev confine himself to generalities about the "cult of leadership" in his report to the Congress on behalf of the Central Committee February 14—only to make a savage attack on Stalin at a secret session eleven days later, on February 25? Why was it secret? Why did Communist newspapermen leak the gist of this secret session deliberately to other newspapermen in Moscow? Why was the Soviet censor so "sticky" about passing these reports until after they had leaked from abroad? No one knows. Indeed it is amazing how little anyone knows of what really goes on in Moscow.

What one does see is that somehow the attack on Stalin has the same crass, crude air as Stalin's own attacks on his own victims. Stalin had a series of scapegoats on whom he blamed the abuses of his regime in his periodic relaxations. His successors act the same way. Their scapegoat was Beria and then Stalin himself. By blaming all the evils of the regime on the dead dictator, they may hope to increase their own popularity. But to blame the evils of Stalinism on Stalin is obviously inadequate. It is not merely that they were his accomplices; their cowardice is understandable. It is that Stalinism was the natural fruit of the whole spirit of the Communist movement. The wanton executions, the frame-ups, the unjust convictions and exiles—these would not have been possible except in a movement whose members had been taught not only to obey unquestioningly but to *hate*. The average Communist was prepared to believe anything about anyone who differed with him in the slightest; the liquidation of the opposition was not just a duty but a savage pleasure. And if "errors" were occasionally made, these were the unavoidable sacrifices of the revolution. This was the spirit the Communist movement bred. Stalin embodied that spirit. To change it one must do more than hang Stalin in effigy, or defame him in self-serving panic as Khrushchev is doing.

The more one studies Russian history the more one sees how deep were the roots of Leninism in Russian radical thinking of the nineteenth century as well as in Czarist habits. Lenin was fashioned by the weight of many generations. But whether Lenin was right or wrong and whether so complete a dictatorship was really necessary is beside the point. The point is that the Revolution has succeeded; socialism in Russia is there to stay; capitalism will never be restored; even among the escapees the only major criticism is of collectivization. Russian industrialism, despite Russian slovenliness and that callous waste of men and manpower one feels in Russia, has advanced on giant boots, thanks to economic planning. Now Khrushchev, in revealing the extent to which the abuses had grown under Stalin, shows that these are not figments of hostile propaganda. ("Multiply all you have read abroad by ten," a Communist said to me, "and you will get the dimensions of Khrushchev's revelations about Stalin.") The problem has been posed by the new regime itself. How is a repetition of these terrible evils to be avoided? How indeed are they to be wholly eliminated?

It is in seeking the answer to these questions that I found Russia and its leaders most disappointing. These are the very competent managers of a great industrial empire; their speeches at the Twentieth Congress show their grasp of concrete industrial problems. They get down to brass tacks in studying steel output or railroad management. But they do not show the same spirit at all in grappling with the evils they have themselves exposed. These Socialist industrialists, these lifelong Marxists, drift off into vague mysticism and into worship of personality. When a system breeds monsters, as they say their secret police system has bred monsters for twenty years, then something must be wrong with the system. If Yagoda, Yehzov and Beria were all monsters, should not the ordinary citizen be given greater protection against the police in the future, greater rights of his own? Should not the public be educated to understand the reason for these rights and their existence? Should not the press be encouraged to criticize when it suspects frame-ups? The questions which confront Russia today under communism are like those which confronted the framers of our own Constitution. Individual rights are no less, perhaps more, necessary under communism than under capitalism; the coercive power of the new State is greater. These questions are not yet even being discussed in Russia.

Instead we come across a lot of vague talk about "collective leadership." But Stalin as well as Lenin talked of collective leadership and its virtues.

And what does collective leadership mean? Again I urge the reader to examine the basic documents for himself. An eleven-man Presidium may be just as wrong as a one-man dictator. *Pravda* said April 5, "Throughout its history the Party's policy was and remained a Leninist policy." *Pravda* says the Party's policy has always been "correct." (A revealing Bolshevik word; it implies an absolute standard of measurement, like a yardstick; how can this wooden mentality be reconciled with the rich, complex and dynamic views of a man like Marx?) But what sense does it make to say that the Party has always been correct when you admit that for the last twenty years of Stalin's life he used the Party as his vehicle for all kinds of injustices and abuses? Obviously the Party was incorrect when it allowed itself to be frightened into silence, acquiescence, collaboration and submission by Stalin. The Party and the Central Committee for these people are mystical concepts; the whole is different from its parts; the leaders may be rotten and the members cowardly but put them together and they are miraculously the bearers of the future! Instead of rights, guarantees, free discussion, Russia is told to repose faith in the Central Committee, that is in the eleven-man Presidium, in "collective leadership."

The speeches of the new leaders are wholly inadequate to the correction of the evils they have exposed. So long as there is only one party, and it has a monopoly of government and controls all expression, there cannot be freedom. Russia is strong enough, secure enough, to move away from the one-party system. We have two parties which do not differ in essentials; they could have two parties, too. Their society is stable enough for stable politics. The kind of one-party rule which may have been necessary to achieve the Revolution has become a positive hindrance; this is the real lesson of the revelations about Stalin.

I came away from Russia with the strong conviction that Khrushchev is more crude and vulgar than Stalin, and will if given the chance take over completely. I believe his colleagues have forced him into the attack on Stalin and talk of "collective leadership" to prevent a return to one-man rule. In the process they have intensified the ferment which began with Stalin's death and set in motion events whose momentum they may not be able to control. The new policies have opened Russia's windows on the West and given us a chance to resume contact with this huge and wonderful segment of humanity. In the interests of peace, and of peaceful change in Russia, we ought to strive to keep the windows open, and to help along the process which may some day carry Russia forward from the current relaxation to freer institutions. I believe not only her people but her rulers want peace; and I believe that given peace they will slowly liquidate Russia's terrible backwardness and unholy past.

But this process will not be helped by indulging in delusions, or by quickly forgiving and forgetting Stalinism in the belief that Russia has now fundamentally changed. Changes there are, and given the natural extremism of the Russian temperament, no one knows how much further they may go tomorrow. But we will not help the Russian people by letting this crowd of leaders soft-soap us; in any free country, after similar revelations, a whole new set of men would have been swept into power as earnest of real change. Nor will we help ourselves, and our power to fight for a better world and a better society, by joining hands with the poor deluded housebroken Communist parties of the West. They remain Russian puppets; they will jump back through the hoops as soon as they get new orders. Their members cannot be freed from intellectual bondage until the parties themselves have disintegrated. Nothing has yet happened in Russia to justify cooperation abroad between the independent left and the Communists.

Almost as Safe as Ivory Soap Is Pure?

For film-maker Stanley Kubrick, the only possible response to the insanity of the nuclear arms race was the mordant satire of *Dr. Strangelove*. In this essay, I. F. Stone responds with a dose of realism and moral common sense, exploding the ghastly "optimism" of war-minimizing propaganda in *Life* and the *Saturday Evening Post* with sober facts about the real levels of casualties to be expected from a nuclear war.

.   .   .

September 25, 1961

CRISIS IS PILING ON CRISIS, instabilities mount in an unstable world, frustration is added to frustration. At such a time it is dangerous to spread the illusion that thermonuclear war may be a way out, a cleansing thunderstorm in the planet's humid summer, or a cathartic that would magically purge our ills, if only we are ready to spend a cramped week or two in underground shelters, emerging on a world from which communism had happily disappeared but where free enterprise was all set to go again. As if orchestrated out of Washington, mass circulation media are beginning to condition the public mind for nuclear war. The *Saturday Evening Post* inaugurates a new department, "The Voice of Dissent," with a piece by that favorite iconoclast of the Air Force, Herman Kahn. The Associated Press sends out a series of interviews with Dr. Edward Teller on how exaggerated are fears of thermonuclear war. *U.S. News & World Report* runs a cheerful cover piece, "If Bombs Do Fall,"* with a side story from Japan on how well

---

*"What about money?" asks *U.S. News & World Report.* "Instead of destroying all old bills that are taken out of circulation, the Government is storing money away in strongboxes around the country. Enough $1 bills have been saved to last 8 months. . . . Bank accounts safe? Plans are being worked out to enable you to write checks on your bank account—even if the bank itself were destroyed."

the survivors of Hiroshima and Nagasaki are doing. *Life* magazine puts a civilian in a reddish fallout suit looking like a partially boiled lobster on its cover, with the glad tidings, "How You Can Survive Fallout. 97 Out of 100 People Can Be Saved. . . ."

No doubt the purpose is to make our threat of going to war over Berlin credible to Khrushchev, as indeed it should. Our ultimate weapon, Madison Avenue, may be able to sell anything to the American people, even the notion—why fool around with aspirin?—that one little bullet through the head and that headache will disappear. Some years back, the Pentagon and popular magazines were advertising how many Russian cities we could "take out" if necessary. Now the same moral imbecility is being applied to our own cities. "About five million people," *Life* says lightly, "less than 3% of the population, would die." It adds hastily, to anticipate any vestigial humane twinges, "This in itself is a ghastly number. But you have to look at it coldly. . . ." *Life* has been telling us righteously that the godless Chinese Reds put little value on human life. Mao is willing to see millions die to wipe out capitalism but Henry Luce is willing to see millions die to wipe out communism. Kennedy, like Khrushchev, prepares the public mind to gamble all, if necessary, on Berlin. This is the real mobilization. Our moral scruples and our good sense must first be conscripted.

Worse than the horror is the levity, the transparent mendacity and the eager commercialism. A happy family with three children is shown by *Life* in their well-stocked, assemble-it-yourself, prefabricated steel shelter, only seven hundred dollars from the Kelsey-Hayes Company (and soon to be marketed by Sears, Roebuck). A picture shows a girl laughingly talking on the phone from an underground shelter, as if to her beau, who is presumably in his own shelter and ready to take her to the latest movie as soon as the all clear sounds. Grandmother's old-fashioned remedies turn out to be best after all even in thermonuclear war. "The best first aid for radiation sickness," *Life* advises, "is to take hot tea or a solution of baking soda." Suddenly thermonuclear war is made to seem familiar, almost cozy. All you need is a shelter, a well-stocked pantry, some new gadgets like Geiger counters. The budding boom in these products promises to stimulate badly lagging magazine linage. *Life's* editorial hopes Khrushchev notices "our spontaneous boom in shelter-building" and concludes euphorically, "He cannot doubt our ability to wage nuclear war, or to erase his cities." Aren't we getting our people ready to accept the erasure of ours? We used to think thermonuclear war likely only if lunatics came to power. Well, here they are.

I am not arguing for surrender, a runout on Berlin, dishonor, national cowardice, appeasement or better-red-than-dead. I am trying to say that when a nation faces problems as complex as those which now face ours in Germany, the United Nations, the Congo, Laos and the resumption of nuclear testing, there is a duty on every publisher and every writer to help inculcate sobriety and the need for reflection. The President's power to maneuver and negotiate is not helped by piling delusion upon hysteria, by making people feel not only that we face a simple choice of death-or-surrender but that most of us won't die anyway—so why bother to negotiate?

Why should President Kennedy lend his name to *Life's* wicked stunt? Nowhere does *Life* tell us what level and kind of attack it assumes which need kill only 3 percent of our people. The latest Rand study in the new Holifield committee hearings shows 3 percent dead as the result of "a very small attack delivering 300 megatons" on military targets exclusively. Even this small attack, if aimed at our cities, would put inescapable death (with everyone in some shelter) up to 35 percent. The same study (p. 216, House Government Operations, Civil Defense, August, 1961) shows a 3,000-megaton attack on cities would put inescapable deaths up to 80 percent. The new Holifield report on these hearings says than an attack half this size, as assumed by Secretary McNamara, would kill fifty million Americans and seriously injury twenty million more. The report warns that the existing basement space on which the Secretary relies to save ten to fifteen million lives won't do. "All deaths from fallout can be prevented," the report says, "but not in existing buildings, even when improved. Nationwide, the largest number of structures do not afford even the bare minimum factor considered necessary to bring the radiation hazard down to tolerable levels."

Stewart Alsop's "Report Card" on Kennedy in the *Saturday Evening Post* September 16 disclosed that the President told congressional leaders a new war would cost 70,000,000 dead Americans. Even Dr. Teller did not go beyond saying that 90 percent of our population could be saved. Where did *Life* get that 97 percent? Was it a copywriter's bright flash? Just as Ivory Soap is sold as 99 percent pure, is thermonuclear war to be sold as 97 percent safe?

The Mythology of the
Anti-Missile Missile

This article exemplifies the remarkable quality of *déjà vu* that the contemporary reader repeatedly experiences when revisiting Stone's writings from the 1950s, '60s, and '70s. It wouldn't take much rewriting for this column to apply to the recent controversies over the Strategic Defense Initiative (often dubbed "Star Wars") initially launched by the Reagan administration and still being kept on life support by the second Bush administration two decades later. Stone would not have been surprised; as he notes, the logic behind such imagined techno-logical cure-alls is not novel but is simply "the mutually disastrous logic of any arms race."

.   .   .

February 19, 1962

THE ANTI-MISSILE MISSILE, which has become the excuse for resumption of nuclear testing, may usefully be examined from the standpoint of mythology, as a relic of belief in the supernatural. The anti-missile missile is only the latest of those ultimate weapons on which our hopes have rested for a military miracle, in this case for something like the invisible and impenetrable cloak which enables the hero in the fairy tale to emerge victoriously unscathed from amid enemy swords and lances. This belief in an ultimate magical weapon, like other superstitions, survives all demonstration to the contrary. We had the atom bomb years before the Russians and they had both the H-bomb and the ICBM before we did, but none of these earlier ultimate weapons enabled one side to force the surrender of the other. To the delusions of the irresistible offensive is now added the delusion of the insuperable defense. We think of the anti-mis-sile missile in terms of Buck Rogers. We see the tense comic strip panel in which our side (or theirs) says, "Their (or our) missiles are landing but our (or their) missiles have been halted in mid-flight by some mysterious new anti-missile device. There is nothing left to do but phone Khrushchev (or Kennedy) to surrender. Capitalism (or communism) has conquered the world."

This delusion reflects a faith in science which has nothing to do with a faith in the methods of experiment and reason. It is a faith in the magical potency of science, and thus little different from any primitive tribesman's belief in his witch doctor. We believe our wonder workers, if only given ample funds, will come up with some new weapon that will once and for all smash our enemies. From a sober military point of view, this faith in any one weapon is ludicrous. As General Bradley said in that speech at St. Alban's here in Washington November 5, 1957, which was so hastily buried by our opinion makers, "Missiles will bring anti-missiles, and anti-missiles will bring anti-anti-missiles. But inevitably this whole electronic house of cards will reach a point where it can be constructed no higher." The hope of an anti-missile rests on the fact that the ballistic missile follows a fixed trajectory. The hope of an anti-anti-missile rests on the possibility of changing that trajectory in mid-flight. The hope of both rests on the experience that for any weapon of war there is always a counter weapon to be found, and so on ad infinitum, that is, if the human race lasts.

All this is worth a closer explanation because the business of arranging a meeting in mid-air between a missile and an anti-missile is more complex even than arranging a meeting of minds between the White House and the Kremlin. This is how you start to construct an anti-missile. You know the missile follows a fixed curve. Therefore once it rises far enough above the radar horizon to enable you to map the beginning of the curve, you can determine the rest of the curve. The problem is to build an electronic device capable of computing this in the few minutes available, and automatically aiming your anti-missile to some intermediate point on that curve where it can hit the oncoming enemy missile before it reaches your territory. It is, as has been said crudely, like hitting a bullet with a bullet. This problem is hard enough. The real problem of the anti-missile however is much harder. It is the problem of designing an electronic network of anti-missile batteries which can cope not with one missile but with a flood of missiles accompanied by several times as many decoys, distinguishing the real from the false, and determining in split seconds which of your anti-missiles is going to be aimed at which missile.

Nobody knows whether this belongs in the realm of electronics or in Grimm's Fairy Tales as revised by General Dynamics. Dr. Hans Bethe, in that speech at Cornell on January 5 which set the arms race crowd gunning for him, said he did not think "any really effective" anti-missile was possible. "It is not very difficult," he said, "to design a defensive missile which will come close enough to an ICBM to destroy it by means of an atomic explosion. There is also no problem about providing atomic warheads for anti-missiles. But the offense can send decoys along with their missiles which are almost impossible to distinguish from the missiles, and they can send many missiles simultaneously which saturate the radars of the defense. Thus I think the AICBM [anti intercontinental ballistic missile] virtually hopeless." It is for this heresy, which threatens the biggest military boondoggle ever dangled before the electronic industry, that Dr. Bethe is under attack. The development of the Nike-Zeus anti-missile system would provide from fifteen to twenty billion dollars' worth of business. Who cares that it might be rendered obsolete before its completion by the next development, a means to change the trajectory of the missile in mid-flight, which would frustrate all the intricate computing and targeting mechanisms of Nike-Zeus?

It is in the perfection of these targeting and computing mechanisms, not in the warhead, that the secret of an anti-missile system lies. The warhead is essentially no different from the warhead of the missile. This is what makes doubly nonsensical the reports being leaked out of evidence that the Russians were testing an anti-missile. First, there is no way to determine from the debris or waves set off by a bomb whether it was being tested for missile or anti-missile purposes. Secondly, the testing of a warhead does not mean that either we or the Russians have solved the enormously intricate problem of targeting and computing for an anti-missile system. The explanations leaked out to the United States and British press are so varied as to create doubt. As in a criminal trial, too many alibis are worse than none. An accused who claims to have been (1) home in bed, (2) at a night club, and (3) only accidentally passing the scene of the crime when it happened is obviously a liar. One paper (the London *Sunday Times,* February 11) says "suspicions [i.e., of an anti-missile] have increased since the discovery that two of the Russian tests on Novaya Zemlya appear to have involved relatively small nuclear weapons above the atmosphere" while another paper (the London Sunday *Observer,* February 11) says the evidence of a Soviet anti-missile is "circumstantial." Since the United States last December successfully got a Nike-Zeus anti-missile to hit a Nike-Hercules missile "high above the White Sands proving ground in New Mexico" it is assumed (the *Observer* reports) that the Russians can do likewise!

The truth is that this anti-missile excuse for resuming testing is, as one scientist phrased it privately to us, "a publicity gimmick." The real rationale for test resumption was expressed by Assistant Secretary of State Harlan Cleveland on February 10 at Rollins College, Florida. "Given the technology of nuclear weapons," Mr. Cleveland said, "the first requisite of orderly change is to prevent our Soviet rivals from getting ahead, or thinking they can get ahead, in the hidden and costly game of nuclear deterrence." The logic is the mutually disastrous logic of any arms race. If each side aims to show the other it can never get ahead, this must push both into ever bigger arms expenditure and further along the way to garrison states; Russia, back toward Stalinism; we toward a parallel revival of paranoid suspicion and repression. But this Administration, like the Democratic party as a whole, remains committed to the arms race as the line of least resistance, as a grandiose WPA for perpetual prosperity until the bombs go off. This is what lies behind the President's impossible new condition that we will enter no new moratorium without a means to detect Russian *preparations* for new tests. (Would we be prepared to open *our* laboratories for surveillance?) We fear any proposal which might interfere with another round of testing now that the Russians have had theirs. This has to stop somewhere but we don't really want the arms race to stop. This explains the press briefings immediately held here to make sure that the release of Powers was not interpreted as an improvement in Soviet relations, and the near panic visible in the wake of Khrushchev's suggestion that the top leaders meet on disarmament. All that talk about our waging a peace race is blarney, a gift with which Mr. Kennedy is richly endowed. It is not a Russian anti-missile that the dominant alliance of the military and arms industry fears. It is their old enemy, relaxation of tension.

Fresh Light on the
Mystery of the Missiles

Written after a visit to Cuba just three months after the near-disaster of the missile crisis, this essay offers an unusual perspective on the U.S.-Cuban standoff,
analyzing it in the light of the growing rifts within the Communist bloc—an alliance that many hard-line Western observers still regarded as monolithically unified. Pointing out the strategic, ideological, and personal differences among
Russia, China, Cuba, and the Eastern European nations, Stone calls for a "flexible and pragmatic" American policy as the best long-term hope for peace.

.   .   .

January 21, 1963

THE ONLY TOP LEADER I SAW in my ten days in Havana was Armando
Hart, the Minister of Education. But this energetic and devoted young man
spoke only of the successful campaign against illiteracy and his mounting
problems as more and more Cubans began to go to school, and to stay there
for a higher education, all safely nonpolitical topics. I did not succeed in
talking with Prime Minister Castro or any other top leader capable of discussing foreign policy questions. Knowledgeable persons told me Fidel was
going through an agonizing reappraisal in the wake of the missiles affair,
that until he spoke on January 2 no one knew what the new line would be,
and that lesser men would hesitate to discuss such delicate matters. I found
my old friends in Havana asking the same question about the missiles affair
that I heard in Washington: Why did Khrushchev put them into Cuba in
the first place if he was so ready to take them out again? The consensus
among reporters with whom I spoke—and these included men from Soviet
bloc, uncommitted and Latin American countries—was that Khrushchev
had made a mistake. Nobody spelled this out but obviously the mistake was
to believe that he could get away with placing nuclear missiles in Cuba.

The removal of the missiles stirred anger among the Fidelistas, and I was told that Fidel had gone several times to the University to appeal to the students to be quiet. Cubans made up a little poem which went like this:

Nikita, Nikita,
Lo que se da,
No se quita

i.e., Nikita, Nikita, what you gave, you can't take back. In the eyes of the Fidelistas, the purpose of the missiles was simply to deter an American attack; they turned against us our own favorite theory of deterrence. But if I had had a chance to talk with top leaders I could have raised the questions which did not occur to the ordinary Fidelista: Did the Cubans realize that these missiles could be quickly observed, that theirs would be soft bases which could fairly easily be put out of commission by conventional attack, that their presence in Cuba would make Cuba a first target in the event of war between the United States and the U.S.S.R., that the missiles would raise tension and increase risk? The political questions were as delicate as the military. The Russians had agreed to remove the missiles without consulting Castro. For a man—and a people—as sensitive about their national dignity, this was an affront. An island besieged by the United States, and so dependent on the U.S.S.R., could hardly afford open discussion of such questions.

Now that Castro has made his long-awaited speech of January 2 and discussed the missiles affair, some illumination can be found by comparing the three versions now available, the Russian, the Chinese and the Cuban. Khrushchev's version, as set forth in his foreign policy address to the Supreme Soviet December 12, was that the missiles were placed there at Cuba's request, for "exclusively humanitarian motives." Khrushchev said, "Our aim was only to defend Cuba." The United States, he said, was trying "to export counterrevolution" and threatening Cuba with invasion. "We were confident," he said, "that this step," i.e., placing the missiles, "would bring the aggressors to their senses." Realizing "that Cuba was not defenseless," they would be "compelled to change their plans" and "then the need for retaining rockets in Cuba would naturally disappear."

This was the kindergarten version. What if the United States, once the missiles were removed, changed its plans again and invaded? If the Cubans were satisfied with this version, they would hardly have published the full text of Khrushchev in their press only to follow it up a few days later by printing first a partial and then the full text of the reply made by the Chinese in the Peking *People's Daily,* December 15.

The Chinese were anxious to answer Khrushchev's charge that theirs was a policy of adventurism which might well plunge the whole world into thermonuclear war. The Chinese replied that while they were opposed to "the imperialist policy of nuclear blackmail," they also saw no need whatsoever for Socialist countries to use "nuclear weapons as chips in gambling or as a means of intimidation." This implied that the missiles were emplaced by the Russians as "chips" in a strategic game. "To do this," the Chinese said, "would really be committing the error of adventurism." They went on to say that "if one has blind faith in nuclear weapons" and "becomes scared out of one's wits by imperialist nuclear blackmail, one may possibly jump from one extreme to the other and commit the error of capitulationism." The Chinese said the Cubans had committed neither but implied the Russians were guilty of both. They quoted with approval Castro's statement that the way to peace "is not the way of sacrificing or infringing upon people's rights," a sideswipe at Khrushchev, and praised the Cubans because "far from being frightened by United States nuclear blackmail, they insisted on their five just demands."

This must have been music to Fidelista ears. The Chinese went on to make a puzzling remark. "The whole world knows," the Chinese said, "that we neither requested the introduction of nuclear weapons into Cuba nor obstructed the withdrawal of 'offensive' weapons from the country."

The Chinese have an influential Embassy in Havana. To say that they did not obstruct the removal of the missiles is to say that they did not advise the Cubans to resist the removal. That much seems clear. But why should they feel it necessary to say that they had never "requested" the placing of nuclear missiles in Cuba? No one assumed that they did. Castro's speech of January 2 throws some light on this. He suggested that the emplacing of the missiles in Cuba had been requested by the Russians. "We agreed with the Soviet Union on the weapons which were set up here," Fidel said, "because we understood that we were fulfilling two obligations: one toward the country, fortifying its defenses in view of imperialist threats, and one obligation toward the peoples of the Socialist camp." This contradicted Khrushchev's account. It implied that Castro allowed the missiles to be set up in Cuba not only to deter United States attack but also because he was persuaded that in doing so he would be fulfilling an obligation to the Soviet bloc. Was it to help right the Soviet missile gap by placing IRBM's in Cuba? Castro did not say. But this reference in his speech would help to explain what the Chinese meant when they said *they* had not requested the placing of missiles in Cuba, and then went on to call the emplacement "adventurism" and the swift removal "capitulationism."

Castro in his speech of January 2 had no word of praise for Khrushchev. Castro did not say, as Khrushchev did, that with the United States no-invasion pledge, there was no further need of missiles to deter a United States attack. On the contrary Castro said that while "the Soviet government, in search of peace, arrived at certain agreements with the North American government" this did not mean that Cuba had renounced "the right to possess the weapons we deem proper and to take the international steps we deem pertinent as a sovereign country." He said over and over again that he did not believe United States pledges and he would not allow inspection. The Kremlin is not accustomed to such coolly independent language.

As for the Sino-Soviet struggle, Castro alone of all the Soviet leaders declared his neutrality between Moscow and Peking. This, too, is unheard of in the bloc. There personal rivalries have always taken on doctrinal forms, and questions of doctrine in turn have been debated in the intransigent tones of medieval theological dispute, in which the loser was doomed to be outcast as a heretic. Castro stood aside from this *furor theologicus*. In his January 2 speech the Cuban spoke of the split with sorrow. He said Cuba was forced to carry on its struggle for economic development in "a bitter situation" amid "discrepancies in the bosom of the Socialist family." The very word chosen must raise eyebrows in Moscow *and* Peking. Castro could hardly have picked a weaker word than "discrepancies" for what they regard as a mortal quarrel. He said, "We see with clarity here, from this trench ninety miles from the Yankee empire, how much cause for concern these discrepancies can be, how much unity is needed, how much all the strength of the entire Socialist camp is needed to face up to these enemies." He announced that "the line of our people" was to be "to struggle for unity" in the Socialist camp so that it could present "a united front to the imperialists." Unity "inside and outside" was his watchword. This neutralism in the Soviet cold war will be as unpalatable to Moscow and Peking as India's neutralism in our cold war has been to us.

There is no better place than Havana to listen in on the controversies shaking the bloc. I did not speak with Chinese but I did speak with Russians, Poles and Yugoslavs. They cannot dismiss the Sino-Soviet struggle as easily as Castro. For Castro the problem is to save unity so he can get help from both sides in his struggle against American strangulation. For these others the problem is more complex. "The Cubans wanted to join the bloc," one Yugoslav said bitterly, "to have its advantages but then did not wish to accept its obligations." He thought it sheer madness for the Cubans to expect the Russians to risk a thermonuclear conflict on their behalf. From the Yugoslav and Polish points of view, Castro fails to see that a Chinese victory would be the end of "different roads to socialism," and that Castro would be the first to find this unbearable. For Poles and Russians, the Cubans seem not to understand that while Khrushchev may be too cautious for their taste, his downfall would threaten the greater freedom within the Soviet bloc which followed the death of Stalin and the defeat of the Old Guard. In their opinion the very same Fidelistas who cheer China's "paper tiger" line would be the first to rebel if Chinese-style thought control were to be imposed on Cuba. As for the Russians, their friendliness for Cuba in no way interferes with their obvious desire for friendlier relations with the United States.

These talks in Havana showed me that wherever American policy was to some degree flexible and pragmatic, rather than rigidly ideological, this paid off. The Yugoslavs, the Poles, the Russians—none took as dark a view of the possibilities of peaceful coexistence as the Cubans or the Chinese. This difference does not have its origin in theory but in experience. We treat communism as negotiable—everywhere but in Cuba and China. We have diplomatic relations with most of the bloc. We do some business with them. We have cultural exchanges. We even extend aid to two Communist countries, Yugoslavia and Poland. But China and Cuba are outside the pale.

Is it any wonder that they, knowing only our rigid hostility, are rigidly hostile in return?

One way to look at the recent crisis is that we were brought to the brink of thermonuclear war because we had driven an island neighbor so far into fear and enmity that it was willing to emplace nuclear missiles against us. We can be back on the brink again very easily by misjudging our relations with Cuba. From all I could learn, the events of that awful weekend when the world came so close to destruction brought Castro new support from among his own people, as the Russian threat once evoked support for Tito. People who had never volunteered before came out for militia service. Those foreign observers who were in the front-line trenches when a United States attack was expected at any moment said they had never seen anything like it in their experience of war. "The sense of the people's courage," said one East European observer, "was a physical, tangible thing. You felt it in your skin and in your spine." Of course, he added, the Cubans have no conception of what a modern war, even a "conventional" one, would be like. "Everybody was running around with pistols, as in the Wild West," he said. "They did not realize that in a real war they might never see the enemy at all, much less engage in hand-to-hand combat with him." The Cubans are a brave people with a great tradition, fighting after a half century to complete a revolution we twice thwarted before, once after they defeated the Spaniards at the beginning of the century and again in 1933 after they overthrew Machado.

A visit to Havana for any foreigner today is both frustrating and inspiring. Red tape and inefficiency are suffocating, and in the middle echelons of the bureaucracy—the worst echelons everywhere—one meets officials who seem to arrive late and leave early and devote themselves in between to keeping up the morale of the cigar industry by smoking their way gloriously through the Revolution. Appointments are made and broken in the most maddening fashion. Petty officials drag out the simplest tasks to magnify their own sense of importance. One finds in oneself a sudden sympathy with the "imperialists" who have to do business in these Latin lands of a *mañana* that rarely comes. But then one encounters a very different type of official, some young guerrilla soldier turned administrator, whose sobriety and devotion are at once apparent. I was often reminded at such moments of the best *chaverim* (comrades) whom I had known in Israel in the greatest days of its struggle. Indeed Castro's Cuba often recalled Israel, in the courage of its people in the face of such great odds, and in the spirit of the Fidelistas. There is no way of knowing what portion of the Cuban people are with Fidel but everyone with whom I spoke felt that his support was substantial. The spirit of the Fidelistas is difficult to explain to persons like ourselves who live in a stable society, indeed a society which often seems stalemated at dead center. For the Fidelistas—and they are particularly strong among the youth and the Negroes—the Revolution is still in its first uncorrupted phase. For them the experience is like love. They live in a springtime of mankind when words which have grown overblown and empty elsewhere become meaningful—love of country, devotion, selfless-ness, readiness to sacrifice one's life for others, the joy of struggling to end misery and to build a better society. How speak of these things to the jaded intellectuals of Washington?

Elsewhere youth has turned beatnik in the shadow of the mushroom cloud. In Cuba the same youth still *believes*. A whole new generation of technicians, scientists, doctors and engineers are being developed from them to replace those who have fled. The best and most promising youth are being brought in as *becados*—50,000 of them—given scholarships (*becas*) and stipends to make it possible for them to study. It was the holiday season and I was unable to talk with them. But a girl who is teaching some of the premedical students English spoke glowingly of their enthusiasm and devotion.

Without hope, faith and charity, Castro's Cuba cannot be understood. We underestimate its grass roots strength and we overestimate its difficul-ties. A Britisher who had gone through the London blitz, a Pole who had seen his country forced to make a revolution in a land leveled by war and depopulated by Nazism, a Yugoslav who knew at first hand what the Parti-sans went through, a Russian who had seen war in all its appalling fury—such observers told me they regarded the Cuban Revolution as a de luxe affair, the standard of living as extraordinarily high, the food supply as phe-nomenal for a country undergoing so fundamental a revolution against the will of so powerful a neighbor. It is, thanks to the kind of buildings we Yan-kee imperialists left behind, the world's first air-conditioned revolution.

They keep the air conditioning on even in December when it is hardly needed. It is also, thanks to the existence of a huge Soviet bloc, getting a level of aid from abroad such as no other revolution has ever enjoyed. An American engineer who spent a lifetime in the automotive industry in Detroit and is now running a Cuban government laboratory for products research and automation told me the machine tools being supplied by the bloc are of very good quality. He said even a country like North Korea, so recently leveled by war, is sending Cuba first-class milling machinery. "They may be short of consumer goods," he told me, "but the task of supplying capital equipment and technicians for a country as small as this one is 'chicken feed' for the Soviet bloc." He is very optimistic about the future. He thinks Cuba will be growing its own food needs in three or four years and he says a geological survey has found not only many valuable metals like cobalt but petroleum. If Cuba can supply its own oil and food, it will really be independent.

The true Fidelistas are a pleasure to talk with. One of them was the young soldier in charge of the new fishing port. When I told him the United States fears this will be a Soviet naval base, he said, "We are building this port in Havana. We are building a refrigerating plant, a canning plant, a fileting plant. You will be able to see for yourself that our purpose is fishing." Traditionally Cubans have paid little attention to the food potential of the seas around them. In other quarters I was told that Cuba hopes also to fish the little-touched South Atlantic, that the Russians can fish the North Atlantic from their own bases but that for South Atlantic fisheries it will be advantageous to them to have fish-processing and ship-repair facilities in Cuba. Others spoke of the plans going forward for automation in the sugar fields. Part of the Revolution's problems arises from its success rather than its failure. Labor is growing short. The hard work of cane cutting is not popular and peasants are no longer forced by hunger and misery to take on such backbreaking tasks. They are also eating more, and supplying the cities with less. My own impression in the shops was that price control and rationing were working fairly well, and there was more available than I had been led to believe. In everything the children come first. Milk was impossible to get in Havana's best hotels but a Mexican reporter told me of visiting a fishing village in Oriente where every morning a truck came over bad roads to deliver twenty-eight liters of milk for the twenty-eight babies. Those people in Havana with babies all told me they got their milk ration regularly. If Havana is poorer, the countryside is richer. And in the hotels at night one sees a whole new class of Negroes and mulattoes, the men in dinner jackets, the girls in new-style half-bustle dresses, enjoying themselves where hitherto only the rich and the foreigner played. The sense of full racial equality and ease is one of the most pleasant experiences for the guilt-burdened white American in Castro's Cuba.

It was my sixth visit to Cuba—three times before and three times since the Revolution. I did not encounter enemies of the regime. I did not visit the prisons, or study the workings of the bloc system which is supposed to give the Castroites eyes and ears everywhere against the threat of sabotage and our CIA, but must work some injustice too. The Cuba I picture is a Cuba as it appears through friendly eyes. This, of course, is not the whole truth. A revolution is a complex phenomena, a tragic struggle to be fully grasped only when seen from many points of view with compassion for the exiles as well as the victors. But I believe it is dangerously misleading to make policy and form opinion, as we do back home, almost exclusively on the basis of hostile views. To look at Castro's Cuba only through the eyes of those who have fled, to concentrate on the negative aspects as our press does, to exaggerate these and even to falsify, is to make it almost impossible to fashion flexible and wise policy. For years we read in our press that the Russian Revolution and then the Chinese was on the verge of collapse. Every time we are confronted with a new revolution we take to the opium pipes of our own propaganda. Those who try to be objective or friendly are dismissed as dupes, and sometimes—as the Stalin years demonstrate—they were. But events have also shown that in the long run the dupes prove less misleading than the doped.

The Rapid Deterioration in
Our National Leadership

In this remarkable essay, Stone warns his readers about the apparent failure of
the still-young Kennedy administration to take seriously the lesson of the Bay of
Pigs invasion fiasco—namely, the danger when nations "take the law into their
own hands." And to illustrate the seriousness of the danger this failure poses,
Stone points to the administration's threat to embroil the United States in another anti-Communist crusade in a distant nation few Americans had then heard
of—Vietnam.

. . .

April 26, 1961

NEITHER MEN NOR NATIONS can take the law into their own hands
without paying a price. The price we are paying for our undercover war
against Cuba is a rapid deterioration in our leadership, and in our moral
standards. According to Chalmers Roberts in the *Washington Post* of April
23 the President made a significant remark at the National Security Council
meeting called the day before to discuss the Cuban debacle and the world
situation. He said of South Vietnam that the Vietminh does not have a
New York Times reporting how many people it is sending south to assassi-
nate officials of South Vietnam. "He had in mind," Mr. Roberts wrote, "the
pre-invasion stories in the American press about the Cuban fiasco," and
"what has come out of the Cuban affair has been a determination to meet
the Communist para-military tactics of guerrilla warfare, infiltration, sabotage and so on." General Maxwell Taylor's assignment "now is going to try
to figure out how to do it."

These remarks of the President, more cryptically reported in the *New
York Times* of April 24, are alarming in their implications. In the first place
they misconceive the situation in South Vietnam as seriously as our govern-

ment does that in Cuba. The real causes of the disintegration in South Vietnam lie in the failure of the Diem regime to build a viable government in the seven years since the Geneva settlement; its corruption, its false elections, its concentration camps, its suppression of democratic liberties, its mistreatment of minorities, are the causes of the growing rebellion. In the second place, the President's animus seems to be directed not at the follies exposed in the Cuban fiasco but at the free press for exposing them. The *New York Times,* and particularly staff members Tad Szulc and James Reston, has acquitted itself in recent weeks in the best traditions of a free press. It has brought to light conditions of which the President himself seems to have been but dimly aware. In the third place, the President's remarks are disturbing because they indicate he is out, not to rid our foreign policy of the CIA's incubus, but merely to improve our cloak-and-dagger methods, and to go further along the path of adopting the worst practices attributed to the Soviet bloc, even to the point of wistfully eyeing the advantages he thinks it derives from the absence of a free press.

The failure of the attempted invasion of Cuba, like so many of our failures in the postwar period, had its roots in an inability to understand popular feeling. But in the briefings held at the State Department during the first two days of this week for visiting editors—a kind of mass brainwashing operation in which no time was allowed for any but the official point of view and little time for questions or discussion—there was no evidence of a willingness to face up to this fact. From the conceited Berle through the discombobulated Stevenson to the smug Allen Dulles not a single official was willing to admit that our intelligence was wrong in assessing the mood of the Cuban people. Official Washington has learned nothing, on the contrary it has drawn all the wrong conclusions, from the failure in Cuba. The Kennedy Administration's swift slide back to the conventional viewpoint of the stuffed shirts who direct our intelligence, military and diplomatic bureaucracies is evident from the men chosen by Kennedy to investigate the failure. Only a few weeks ago, the President was enforcing a blue pencil on the inflammatory remarks of Admiral Arleigh Burke, one of the biggest windbags in the military establishment; now the Admiral is to assist General Maxwell Taylor in the investigation. Admiral Burke is a member of the Joint Chiefs of Staff; one of the points which ought to be investigated is the

poor advice given the President by them; how to get a real investigation
with the Admiral at General Taylor's elbow? Just to make sure that the inquiry will be equally impartial in assessing the role of the CIA, Allen Dulles
will also serve on this panel; he too will be in the happy position of investigating himself. In addition, Attorney General Robert Kennedy has been
added to the panel. Like his brother, he had been acting admirably until the
Cuban crisis came along. Now, in advance of the investigation, he has issued a disingenuous opinion which would so reduce the ambit of the Neutrality Act as to absolve the CIA and big business paymasters of the Cuban
counter revolution from complicity. General Taylor himself is superior in
intellectual capacity to most of the Pentagon crowd, but as a professional
soldier he is concerned with military means for dealing with social change;
events have over and over again demonstrated their futility. There is not a
single man on this panel capable of approaching the Cuban question and
the broader problems it illustrates with the independent mind and perceptive spirit they require.

The clearest sign of deterioration in national leadership lay in the tone,
the implications and the deceptions of Mr. Kennedy's speech to the American Society of Newspaper Editors. The tone in its arrogant and willful self-
righteousness sounded like an echo of Bismarck and Teddy Roosevelt; this
was the Monroe Doctrine nakedly restated as American domination of the
hemisphere; here was exactly that doctrine of unilateral intervention Latin
America so hates and fears. The implications were of a return to the worst
days of the cold war, with a readiness to extend the use of cloak-and-dagger
methods on a wider scale than ever before. The worst deception did not
come out until several days later. Mr. Kennedy spoke that Thursday, April
20, of the Cuban affair as "a struggle of Cuban patriots against a Cuban dictator." But on Sunday, April 23, in both Washington and Miami many
newspapermen heard but few dared to print the story of how the Cuban
Revolutionary Council was taken into custody in New York on the eve of
the Cuban invasion, kept in ignorance of it, shut off from all contact with
their own forces, and held incommunicado at a supposedly abandoned air
base in Florida while statements were drafted in its name by the CIA and issued through the Lem Jones advertising agency in New York. Despite
White House orders to the contrary, Batista men were not weeded out of

the invasion forces and the CIA's notorious Mr. Bender who is cordially hated by all but the extreme right-wingers still ran the show. Yet Mr. Dulles at the big private press briefing Tuesday (not having been invited we are not bound by secrecy) was brazen enough to claim that his intelligence estimates were correct and that failure was due solely to the poor Cuban exiles themselves!

Fidel Castro won in Cuba by provoking Batista into destroying himself; the dictator in his fear and frenzy set out on so brutal a course as to undermine all support for himself except among his partners in plunder. I have all along feared that if we allowed ourselves to be drawn into war with Castro, he would provoke us similarly to self-destruction. The chain reaction is already in motion, and all Americans of sense and devotion must speak up quickly while it can still be stopped. The bright promise of the new Administration is being quenched by its own panicky folly; the military and the right wingers have been strengthened within our own government. A moral obduracy like that of South Africa's is apparent in the unthinking clamor for get-tough policies. The danger of direct invasion seems to have passed for the moment, but the new emphasis on "para-military" methods has an ominous ring; para-military formations poisoned the life of the German Republic under Weimar, assassinated some of its best leaders, and paved the way for Nazism. We cannot set up government agencies empowered to act lawlessly without infecting the life of our own Republic. To fall back on the conspiracy theory of history is to assume that human convulsion and aspiration are but puppet movements on string from Moscow, to place our hopes in counter-conspiracy, is to misread man and history to our own ultimate undoing.

Part Four

THE WALL BETWEEN
BLACK AND WHITE

The Voice of America Falters

I. F. Stone began writing about America's failure to respect the rights of the "Negro" (then the accepted term) long before the advent of the modern civil rights movement. Here, he puts our failure to honor the constitutional protections of due process and color-blind justice in the context of our global rivalry with the Soviet Union.

. . .

February 8, 1951

PARIS—*Scene: the office of Voice of America; an imaginary interview.*

Q. Are you in charge of European broadcasts?

A. I am.

Q. I was wondering how you were going to handle two criminal cases involving American policy which attracted a great deal of attention in Europe during the past few days.

A. What cases do you mean?

Q. One was the reprieve of twenty-one Nazis sentenced to death for war crimes, and the release of Krupp and other prisoners condemned to long terms in jail. The other was the execution of seven Martinsville, Virginia, Negroes.

A. I don't see any connection between them.

Q. Clemency was granted in one case and not the other.

A. Yes, but what's the execution of some Negroes for rape in Virginia got to do with the reprieve of some Nazis at Landsberg?

Q. It will be said that American policy is more tender with Nazi war criminals than with American Negroes.

A. That's just Communist propaganda.

Q. But I thought it was the job of the Voice of America to counter Communist propaganda? How are you going to do it in this instance?

A. We're going to let people know the truth. Those boys in Martinsville had their day in court. They were found guilty. They had their full right of appeal. The case showed that today even in the South and even for the crime of rape Negroes can get a fair trial. We'll present the facts as they are—a triumph of American justice.

Q. The Nuremberg trials were also a triumph of American justice. The Nazis also had their day in court. They were found guilty, and the review board in recommending the reprieves reasserted the justice of the convictions but advised clemency.

A. I still don't get what you're driving at.

Q. Well, how are you going to answer when people ask why Nazis guilty of heinous crimes against humanity were considered worthy of clemency while Negroes found guilty of rape are considered unworthy, although no white man has ever been given the death penalty for rape in Virginia, and there are doubts both about the fairness of the trial and the actual role of the poor half-witted woman in the case.

A. Look, I'm on to newspapermen like you. We're engaged in the opening maneuvers of a vast war against the totalitarian evil you pinks help to cover up. I don't like those Nazis any more than you do and I wish to God they had freed those Negro boys. It makes my job a lot harder. But we've got to have the Germans on our side in the scrap that's coming, and we can't infuriate the South by reprieving some Negro boys who have had a fair trial instead of just being strung up as they might so easily have been. We can't change the South overnight and we need national unity more than ever.

Q. Then you think war against Communism so necessary and inevitable as to excuse clemency for Nazis and denial of clemency for American Negroes?

A. I certainly do.

Q. Why?

A. Because we're up against an immoral force which believes the end justifies the means, and will distort and pervert any and every human ideal to get its way.

Q. But didn't you just finish telling me that you were ready to excuse the Nazi pardons and the Negro executions, much as you regretted both, because you felt the end—war against Communism—justified the means? Aren't you condoning mass extermination of peoples and the ugliest side of "white supremacy" in the South because you think these immoral means justify the end—war against Communism? Where, then, does your kind of thinking differ from that you impute to the Communists? Where does it differ from those who supported Hitlerism on the same grounds, that objectionable as its methods might be, they were necessary for war against Communism?

A. Get the hell out of my office, you dirty R – d.

May 17, 1954

Here is Stone's on-the-spot reaction to one of the epochal events of twentieth-century history—the Supreme Court's unanimous decision in the case commonly known as *Brown v. Board of Education*, which struck down school segregation. As Stone immediately recognized, "The ultimate impact [of this decision] must revolutionize race relations."

.   .   .

May 24, 1954

FOR WEEKS ON MONDAYS, when opinions are handed down, the Supreme Court press room had drawn a full house, including an unusually large number of Negro reporters. Last Monday, after we had all begun to give up hope of a school segregation decision that day, an unusual event occurred. Ordinarily opinions are given out in the press room after word comes down the pneumatic chute that they have been read in the courtroom above. This time the light flashed and there was a different kind of message. The press aide put on his coat and we were all shepherded into the court chamber to hear the opinion read and receive our copies there.

In that tense and crowded marble hall, the Chief Justice was already reading the opinion in *Brown et al. v. United States.* He read in a firm, clear voice and with expression. As the Chief Justice launched into the opinion's lengthy discussion of the Fourteenth Amendment, the reporters, white and Negro, edged forward in the press boxes, alert for indications of which way the decision was going. "We come then," the Chief Justice read, "to the question presented: Does segregation of children in public schools solely on the basis of race, even though the physical facilities and other 'tangible' factors may be equal, deprive the children of the minority group of equal educational opportunities?" In the moment of suspense which followed we could hear the Chief Justice replying firmly, "We believe that it does." It was all one could do to keep from cheering, and a few of us were moved to tears.

There was one quite simple but terribly evocative sentence in the opinion. For Negroes and other sympathetic persons this packed the quintessence of the quieter misery imposed on members of a submerged race. "To separate them," the Chief Justice said of Negro children, "from others of a similar age and qualifications solely because of their race generates a feeling of inferiority as to their status in the community that may affect their hearts and minds in a way unlikely ever to be undone." So the fifty-eight-year-old ruling of *Plessy v. Ferguson* was reversed and the court ruled "Separate educational facilities are inherently unequal . . . segregation is a denial of the equal protection of the laws."

The unanimous ruling seemed too explicit to be whittled away in the enforcing decree. The rehearing next fall on the form of that decree, the invitation to the Southern states to be heard, offer a period in which tempers may cool and bigots be allowed second thoughts. At the best, Jim Crow will not be ended overnight. The clue to what is likely to happen in most cities, North and South, may be found in a clause of the questions on which the Court will hear argument in the fall.

The Court is to consider whether "within the limits set by normal geographic school districting" Negro children shall "forthwith be admitted to schools of their choice" or a gradual changeover be arranged. Since most Negroes in most cities already lived in more or less segregated Negro sections, these will still have largely Negro schools. It is on the borderlines that mixing will begin; ultimately the pattern of segregated schools will break down with the pattern of segregated Negro housing areas. The ultimate impact must revolutionize race relations and end the system of inferior status and inferior education which has kept the ex-slave a menial.

Among the audience streaming out of the chamber when the Chief Justice had ended, the lawyers for the NAACP suddenly began to embrace each other outside the doors. They had achieved a giant stride toward the full emancipation of their people. The growing political power of the Negro had prevailed over the growing wealth of the Republican party's newest recruits, the Texas oil millionaires. In a showdown, American democracy had proven itself real.

The Murder of Emmett Till

Stone reports on the stunning acquittal of J. W. Milam and Roy Bryant in the murder of Emmitt Till, a young black Mississippian accused of whistling at a white woman. Milam and Bryant were widely known to have committed the crime, and they admitted as much a year later in a *Look* magazine article. As usual, Stone puts the story and its revelation of American racism in the broadest possible context: "Basically all of us whites, North and South, acquiesce in white supremacy, and benefit from the pool of cheap labor created by it." And he closes with a prescient call for a black Gandhi to lead the nation out of its racial madness—two months before the start of the Montgomery bus boycott would bring the name of Martin Luther King, Jr., to national prominence.

.   .   .

October 3, 1955

NEXT TO THE PRESIDENT'S COLLAPSE, the worst news of the week was from Mississippi. The jury at Sumner brought in two verdicts, not one. The immediate and visible decision was that J. W. Milam and Roy Bryant were not guilty of killing a fourteen-year-old colored boy. The other, unspoken, unintended, unconscious but indelible was a verdict of guilty against all the rest of us and our country.

There are scenes at the murder trial which imprint themselves unforgettably: the Negro reporters, as they walked into court one day after lunch, being hailed by the Sheriff with "Hello, niggers." Mrs. Bradley, the mother of the victim, testifying that she told her son before he left for the South "to be very careful how he spoke and to say 'yes, sir' and 'no, ma'am' and not to hesitate to humble yourself if you had to get down on your knees." Moses Wright—we salute his courage—testifying that when J. W. Milam came to get his fourteen-year-old nephew Emmett Till, he asked, "You from Chicago?" and when the boy answered "yes" Milam said, "Don't you say yes to me or I'll knock hell out of you." Mrs. Bryant's sexy whopper (which Judge Swango to his credit kept from the jury) that this fourteen-year-old boy with a speech defect had grabbed her round the waist, solicited her with an unprintable expression and boasted, "I've been with white women before." J. A. Shaw, Jr., the foreman of the jury, asked by the press what the jury thought of Mrs. Bradley's testimony, replying, "if she tried a little harder, she might have got out a tear."

Emmett Till's broken body, with the bullet hole in the right temple and the gaping hole in the back of the head, as if broken in by a rock, testified to a maniacal murder. Those who killed him were sick men, sick with race hatred. The murder and the trial could only have happened in a sick countryside. Where else would a mother be treated with such elementary lack of respect or compassion? Where else would the defense dare put forward the idea that the murder was somehow "framed" by the NAACP? Where else would newspapers somehow make it appear that those at fault were not the men who killed the boy but those who tried to bring the killers to justice? There is a sickness in the South. Unless cured, there may some day spring from it crimes as evil and immense as the crematoria of Hitlerism.

If Milam and Bryant did not kill Till, then who did? Nobody in the South asks the question, at least publicly. Who was the third man with them? Where are the two missing witnesses? Nobody cares. Mississippi went through the motions, and the motions were enough to muffle the weak conscience of the northern white press. The judge was honorable; the special prosecutor tried hard; who can quarrel with a jury verdict? But the jury was all white, in an area two-thirds Negro. And of what use was an upright judge and a special prosecutor when the case was rushed to trial without adequate preparation or investigation? This was only the final scene of a lynching, hastily covered with a thin veil of respectability by a shrewd governor. The same governor, Hugh White, as chairman of the Legal Education Advisory Committee, has just put forward a six-point program to fight desegregation which calls for abolition of compulsory public schooling and legislation to "prohibit interference with state law under cover of federal authority." Hugh White is himself the leader of Mississippi's racists and nullificationists.

Before the war and the witch hunt, when there were still organizations like the Southern Conference for Human Welfare, there would have been public meetings of protest under mixed auspices. It shames our country and it shames white Americans that the only meetings, in Harlem, Baltimore, Chicago and Detroit, have been Negro meetings. Those whites in the South and in the North who would normally have been moved to act have been hounded out of public life and into inactivity. To the outside world it must look as if the conscience of white America has been silenced, and the appearance is not too deceiving. Basically all of us whites, North and South, acquiesce in white supremacy, and benefit from the pool of cheap labor created by it.

Will the Negro take this latest outrage? Unless Negroes rouse themselves to make their indignation felt in some dramatic way, nothing will be done in Mississippi or in Congress. A. Philip Randolph last Sunday suggested a march on Washington like that which dramatized the FEPC fight before Pearl Harbor. Were thousands of Negroes to converge on the Department of Justice and demand action against the murders of Till, and of the other Negroes whose recent murders have gone unpunished in the South, such a demonstration would have an impact. The American Negro needs a Gandhi to lead him, and we need the American Negro to lead us. If he does not provide leadership against the sickness in the South, the time will come when we will all pay a terrible price for allowing a psychopathic racist brutality to flourish unchecked.

Eisenhower Goes Neutralist—
On Civil Rights

The "neutralism" Stone refers to is that of the so-called nonaligned movement of nations that refused to choose sides in the Cold War struggle between East and West. Here he castigates the cowardice of mainstream American politicians like Eisenhower, eager to avoid alienating either northern liberals or southern racists, who refused to choose sides in the clear-cut moral struggle between Jim Crow and racial equality.

. . .

September 17, 1956

NEUTRALISM HAS BEEN MADE a dirty word in American politics. Both parties are against it. We are constantly being treated to homilies from the White House and the State Department on the wickedness of being morally neutralist. But apparently these high principles only apply to disputes between the United States (right) and the U.S.S.R. (wrong), in which Pandit Nehru (by refusing to take our side) demonstrates incorrigibility.

The President at press conference the other day delivered himself of an impromptu message on integration which was afterward filmed and is being shown in the movie houses. Mr. Eisenhower deplored the extremists "on both sides." We weren't hearing the people of good will in the South. "We hear the people who are adamant . . . they even resort to violence," he said, "and the same way on the other side of the thing, the people who want to have the whole matter settled today."

If we stop and translate this into realities, we will see that the President is adopting at home the moral neutralism he deplores abroad. Let us turn to Clay, Kentucky. There last week a mob of white miners and farmers massed near the Clay elementary school to prevent any Negroes from entering. These were the "adamant people" to whom the President referred. Several

171

school days in a row they turned back a lone Negro woman who tried to enter her son of ten and her daughter of eight. Mrs. Louis Gordon finally gave up, and sent her children to an all-Negro school six miles away. "I just couldn't continue to take them out there every day," she told reporters. "They were in too much danger." Mrs. Gordon is one of those people whom Mr. Eisenhower described as "on the other side of the thing, the people who want to have the whole matter settled today."

We would like someone to ask the President how he can take that mob and that one brave Negro mother, and lump them together as "extremists." The mob opposes enforcement of the law; the woman asks for her children the benefit of the Supreme Court's decree. By any standard, isn't the mob wrong and the woman right? Isn't Mr. Eisenhower's attitude "moral neutralism" of a real and obnoxious variety?

Is it fair to speak of Mrs. Gordon as wanting "the whole matter settled today"? Isn't this an invidious way to describe what is happening? The Supreme Court decision is three years old. Unless her children are admitted "today," i.e., at the beginning of this year's school term, they must wait another year. And another year means, for them, as for many colored children in the South, another year of traveling a long extra way from home to school. "Six miles away" is twelve extra miles of travel daily, no small matter for children of eight and ten. Do they walk or ride? And if they ride, who pays their fare? These are bread and butter questions in most Negro homes.

Mr. Eisenhower says we aren't hearing the people of good will in the South. Their voice is not heard because the same mob spirit which overwhelms the Negro also cows them into silence. If the President is afraid to speak clearly, what can they (themselves a minority) say with the mob outside? This is what Adlai Stevenson meant when he told the Liberal party in New York last week that it was the President's duty to create "a climate of compliance." This was what Adlai courageously was trying to create when he told a hostile, often booing, American Legion in Los Angeles the week before that we could not convince other nations that we believe in justice "when mobs prevent Negro children from lawfully attending school."

We were sorry Adlai had to spoil his Liberal party speech by invoking that double talk from the Democratic platform about rejecting "all proposals for the use of force to interfere with the orderly determination of these matters by the courts." There will be no orderly determination without some show of force. A false dichotomy has been set up about force and persuasion. Both are needed. Neither can succeed without the other. But mobs can never be merely persuaded. They will overwhelm the good people of the community unless dealt with firmly. What progress has been made in Kentucky and Tennessee was made because Governors Chandler and Clement to their credit called out the militia to show that they meant business. And both Governors were able to act because of the political realities in these border states, which differ sharply from the Deep South in two ways. The Negro votes in Kentucky and Tennessee. Both have a two-party system.

In the one-party Deep South, where the Negro if he votes at all has no real choice, integration has not made a dent. All those fancy compilations only hide the fact that outside of the western fringe of Texas, which is more western than southern, the only progress is in the border states. Everywhere from Virginia on, the South is preparing to nullify the law, to resist it, and there are too few places where Negroes have been able even to file suit. Unless some firm moves toward enforcing compliance are soon made from Washington, the lines may harden for a long, long fight in which the South, its destiny and its good people, will more and more come under the control of the worst elements and poison the political life of the whole country. Behind the school struggle is the shadow of a conflict as grave as slavery created. The South must become either truly democratic or the base of a new racist and Fascist movement which could threaten the whole country and its institutions. On this, more than any other issue, fresh leadership in the White House is urgent.

The Beginnings of a Revolution

In the fall of 1957, the focus of the nascent civil rights movement was on Little Rock, Arkansas, where the integration of all-white Central High School by nine black students was blocked on September 4 by National Guard forces called out by Governor Orval Faubus, ostensibly to avert violence provoked by "outside extremists." In fact, the only violence was threatened by local white mobs determined to prevent blacks from attending their schools. By the end of the month, President Eisenhower was forced to send in 1,000 soldiers from the 101st Airborne Division and to federalize the Arkansas National Guard. Under military guard, the nine black students successfully enrolled in Central High, although the battle for integration wasn't over: In 1958, the public high schools in Little Rock were actually shut for a year in a last-ditch attempt to prevent whites and blacks from studying together. Not until 1972 were all grades in Little Rock public schools finally integrated.

·   ·   ·

September 16, 1957

WHAT WE ARE SEEING IN THE SOUTH is something which resembles a revolution. The government is trying to bring about a deeply unpopular change. The moderates have been counseling peaceful resistance, and undermining respect for the agencies of government. The moment has now come when leadership passes to the extremists, who advocate force and violence. The street mobs have begun to take control.

The mobs are only a handful, and those who would resort to violence are still a minority. But that minority has so much power because its aims are the wishes of the majority—to block integration. The power of the mob may be measured by the silence of the South's normal leadership. Except for the Mayor of Little Rock, no public figure has spoken up for obedience to law. No senator from the South, no governor, no member of Congress, no leader of the bar, has dared publicly utter a restraining word. This dead silence may prove to be the inner "eye" of a hurricane.

It is whispered in Washington that unless something is done soon by the federal government the moderates will be destroyed politically. The southern senators only a few weeks ago looked like shrewd and skillful statesmen. Now they appear to be appeasers and quislings. How can they compete with a Governor who calls out the National Guard to prevent integration? The niceties of senatorial footwork would look ludicrous if explained to a southern audience which has just seen *action.*

The best the moderates offered was a long, slow, delaying action. To the extremists this was only a gradual form of surrender. They have taken the offensive in the border states of Arkansas and Tennessee where integration had already begun. They can claim to be pushing integration back, instead of retreating slowly before it. The extremists have outbid the moderates.

The moderates prepared their own downfall. In the state legislatures, the moderates enacted nullification. In Congress all last spring during the civil rights debate, the moderates helped to intensify in the South a pathological state of mind: suspicion of the Supreme Court, distrust of all federal judges, a feeling that alien and esoteric forces were plotting against the South and its "way of life." The moderates, when a little integrity and courage might still have counted, pandered to the view that resistance to law was an almost sacred duty for white southerners, a pious obligation they owed their past. Faubus, the mobs and the dynamiters are only acting out what the moderates taught them.

The mob itself is what mobs usually are, unstable fringe elements, eager for any occasion to vent long pent-up hatreds, hatred of their own ugly selves they spew outward on whatever their social conditioning makes the target. The South has more than the normal quota of such sick souls, as it has more than the normal quota of poverty, ignorance and shiftlessness plus a frontier habit of violence. The average southern white is probably more afraid of the mob than the average southern Negro, since the former fears his own good instincts, which might betray him into "nigger loving" opposition. The latter may regard the mob as an almost normal recurrence of white bestiality which one may avoid without loss of self-respect.

These human scarecrows and juvenile delinquents in the news photos and on the television screens might become a majority overnight. If they can provoke a race riot, if they can make the issue seem starkly North versus South, the United States could find itself in the gravest crisis since Fort Sumter. Every day's delay by the President, whose enormous personal prestige might be put to good use at this juncture, risks irreversible events.

Unfortunately we have a President who is nine-tenths figurehead. A figurehead must be manipulated. There seems to be no one around to tell him what to do, and so he turns up in the same picture pages, happily relaxing on the eighteenth green. "Mr. Brownell also informed the President," the *New York Times* reported almost tongue in cheek, "that a Nashville school had been bombed. Mr. Hagerty said the President's reaction to this had been 'the same as anyone else's would be—he thought it was a terrible thing.'" The gaping walls of the Hattie Cotton School are not as terrible as this gaping vacuum in the presidency.

If the situation were not so deadly serious, one would be tempted to satirize the contrast between the airlift swiftly unloading arms six thousand miles away in Jordan to meet an exaggerated crisis in Syria with the irresolution the government shows at home. The dangers of communism seem to arouse Washington much more quickly than those of racism, though the latter comes up in a form which is a fundamental challenge to law itself.

This is a time to see ourselves as others see us. The ugly hate-filled faces of the whites in Little Rock and Nashville, the bravery of the Negro children and their parents, the minister knocked down and beaten in Birmingham, the poor feeble-minded Negro emasculated by Klansmen just to prove their mettle, are giving the colored majority on this planet a picture of us it will be hard to eradicate. Whether here or in Algiers, the white race just doesn't seem as civilized as it claims to be.

The Wall Between

Here is Stone's review of *The Wall Between,* a memoir by Kentucky reporter and social activist Anne Braden, which focuses on the attacks she suffered after selling a house in an all-white Louisville neighborhood to a black family as a protest against segregation. In the decades that followed, Braden continued to work for racial peace and justice, founding Progress in Education and the Kentucky branch of the Alliance Against Racist and Political Repression to ease the stress of school desegregation in the 1970s. She died on March 6, 2006.

.　　.　　.

September 15, 1958

ANNE BRADEN GREW UP IN THE SOUTH on the right side of the tracks. She came, as they say in the South, of a good family. Very early she began to feel there was something wrong in the relations between the races. Her family was always kind to the Negro family who worked for them. "But something happened to me," Mrs. Braden writes in her book, *The Wall Between* (Monthly Review Press), "each time I looked at the Negro girl who always inherited my clothes. . . . She would sit in a straight chair in our kitchen waiting for her mother. . . . She would sit there looking un- comfortable, my old faded dress binding her at the waist and throat. And some way I knew that this was not what Jesus meant when he said to clothe the naked."

Anne became a newspaperwoman and married a fellow reporter, Carl, who came most decidedly from the *other* side of the tracks. His family was Catholic, the father an agnostic and Socialist who lost his job in the 1922 railway shopmen's strike. The family had known poverty ever since. Carl, at the age of thirteen, went into a pro-seminary to prepare for the priest- hood but at sixteen decided it was not for him. He became a newspaper- man in Louisville, Kentucky. "A police reporter," he once told his wife, "has to become one of three things—a drunk, a cynic, or a reformer." Carl chose the third course, and it led him in 1954 to agree when a Negro veteran, Andrew Wade, asked the Bradens to buy a house for him in a new white neighborhood in Louisville. The house was dynamited, and the state authorities, instead of prosecuting the dynamiters, indicted the Bradens and five other residents of Louisville for sedition. Braden, first to be tried, was sent to jail for fifteen years, and saved only by the miracle of the Supreme Court's Steve Nelson decision.

Anne Braden has told the whole story in her book, *The Wall Between*, and told it with the depth and objectivity of a first-rate novel. All that is happening elsewhere in the integration crisis is lit up for us by this story of what that attack on housing segregation did in and to liberal Louisville. Mrs. Braden writes with compassion for the prisons in which men seal themselves up. She sees the "paralyzed liberals" of Louisville, like its cross burners, as "trapped men." She even tried, in one of the most memorable episodes of the book, to understand her fellow southerner, the prosecutor, Scott Hamilton, who was trying his best to send her and her husband to prison on trumped-up charges he himself had come to believe. "If circumstances," she asked herself, "somewhere in the past of both our lives had been different, would I perhaps have been on his side of this battle or he on mine?" This was the same young woman who could firmly refuse to answer questions about the books she read and the organizations to which she belonged. "I think we have enough McCarthys in this country," she said defiantly when taken before a judge, "without the grand jury turning into one."

The Bradens walked through the valley of the shadow of the witch hunt. An FBI informer perjured herself to call Braden a Communist; he denied it under oath. The House Un-American Committee sent down agents to frighten Andrew Wade, the Negro they had risked so much to help, and got him to say things one only says about a man and a woman one does not trust. The transcript of what Wade said in a moment of weakness gave Anne Braden the most terrible moment of the whole experience, one in which she felt "that the things we had been working for—a world without segregation, a world of understanding and brotherhood—had turned to dust in my hand." But the moment passed. Both Wade and the Bradens recovered from it. Her book is a worthy record of a great experience, the warming story of a heroic couple's abiding faith.

When the Bourbon Flowed

As the Little Rock school integration crisis continues, Stone visits Arkansas and sketches a vivid portrait of two worlds, black and white—deeply intertwined yet mutually uncomprehending.

. . .

September 22, 1958

WE TOOK THE FIRST PLANE out of Washington for Little Rock after hearing Chief Justice Warren read a tense and crowded courtroom the order that integration proceed. The plane's first stop was at Nashville, and passengers came aboard carrying its evening newspaper, the *Banner.* A black headline across page one indicated that we had reached the South. It said, with White Citizens Council objectivity, "Mix Now, Little Rock Told." On the editorial page, under the caption "Education Be Hanged!" there was a cartoon which pictured the Chief Justice as a burly man leaning arrogantly on a huge gavel. Behind him was a blackboard on which he had triumphantly crossed out the word "deliberate" in the phrase, "all deliberate speed," and written in the word "breakneck." A page one Associated Press bulletin claimed that a "jubilant" Mrs. Daisy Bates, local leader of the NAACP, had "hinted" that she expected "more mixing" soon, though I was later to learn that Mrs. Bates in Little Rock was harder to reach than the Secretary of State on Duck Island and twice as cautious and that any such "hint" must have been deduced by the AP man from the way she said "no comment." A staff correspondent in Little Rock quoted the Reverend Wesley Pruden, the segregationist leader, as saying, "The South will not accept this outrage, which a Communist-dominated government is trying to lay on us." This was my introduction to a regional journalism which prints such statements matter-of-factly.

We sat forward on one of four seats. Two of them, facing each other, were occupied by a gray-haired elderly white woman and a middle-aged colored woman who seemed to be traveling together. Though the former, from her accent, did not appear to be southern, she turned out to be a gentlewoman returning from a summer in Massachusetts to her plantation home below Memphis with her Negro maid. When the maid, a sturdy woman, went to the rest room, the white lady told us her maid had been with her for twenty-five years and that she had given the maid a $2500 gift on the twenty-fifth anniversary of her coming to work for her. This was to illustrate her point that there were good relations in the South between the races. "There is real love between us," the white woman said of the Negroes who grew up on her plantation. She blamed the trouble in the South on "white riffraff." She said her great-grandfather had tried to free his slaves before "the war" but they pleaded with him that they would not know how to make their way in the world. (Later that evening in Little Rock I was to meet another woman who told me that her great-grandfather had tried to free his slaves but that they begged him not to. I began almost to believe that in the slaveholding South no one was a slaveholder by choice but only out of devotion to the welfare of their black wards.) Our gentlewoman friend told us how the "cream of the crop" on her plantation in her father's time and her husband's had been sent to college, and of the eminent positions they later reached in the Negro community. Though a Democrat, she had never once voted for Roosevelt, of whom she obviously disapproved. She voted for Eisenhower twice, but no longer felt the same way about him. She spoke with gentle cynicism of the machine politicians and senators she had known in Tennessee, as a well-bred lady discussing rather vulgar retainers. She and the maid got off the plane in Memphis, leaving behind an authentic whiff of the old regime.

Below us, in the deepening dusk on leaving Memphis, was the dirty, gray, serpentine Mississippi. At Little Rock, in its modern new airport, flash bulbs popped as Virgil Blossom, the school superintendent, got off the plane ahead of us looking heavy and tired, and said a few noncommittal words for the TV reporters. Little Rock, its main street lit up with green and red neon lights, its J. C. Penney Store and its big 5-and-10, seemed like any small Midwestern city, except for the "colored" sign in the rear as one passed the bus station. The one pleasantly different touch were the old-fashioned gas lamps on the streets, like those in Philadelphia a generation ago. On the way to the Sam Peck Hotel, we caught a glimpse of the haberdashery run by the Syrian, Karam, so prominent behind the mob scenes last year. The bellboy had that look of simulated imbecility Negroes often wear like a protective cloak in the South. The elevator was run by a pretty Negro girl.

A British newspaperman and myself were invited out that night to a party in a country home cluttered with heirlooms and good modern prints. Courtesy and political discretion forbid too close a description but after a night with a group of tortured southern liberals one acquired a new view of Tennessee Williams; he began to seem a camera-like realist. As with Negro intellectuals, all their talk came back obsessively and painfully to the race problem. These off-beat members of old families know their own political impotence and feel like aliens despite their family trees. Their self-deprecatory jokes are bitter; their talk often builds up to a kind of anguish. At moments they make one think of the nineteenth-century Russian intelligentsia distressed by the abyss between them and the people. Many of the women at least take their Christianity with deep seriousness and are torn by guilt. They are appalled by the race hatred which spills over from apparently civilized people they have known all their lives. They are despairing over those who know better but say, "Let it take its course," the "it" being the mob. They feel themselves a natural elite gone to seed, caught between the rabble (that's how most upper-class southerners think of common white people) and the rabble-rousers like Faubus, whom they despise. Yet as the bourbon flows more freely their whole environment draws them into compulsive imitation; they begin to say "niggers" and "coons" with the obscene pleasure of an adolescent using dirty words. One feels that the Negro doesn't just live in the South, he haunts it.

A liberal Little Rock newspaperman came to breakfast at the hotel next morning to give us a fill-in on the local situation. His most revealing remark, it seemed to me, came when I asked him what Negroes were thinking. "I just don't know," he said. The Little Rock story is covered almost entirely from the white side. In an effort to get the Negro side, I went to a white lawyer, Edward Dunaway, a Columbia graduate, who is head of the

Urban League, which may seem stuffily respectable in the North but is regarded as downright radical in the South. "People ask me if I am a Yankee,"
Dunaway said with some bitterness. "One side of my family came here
from Virginia in 1820 and the other from Kentucky in 1830." One of his
grandfathers was governor of Arkansas and Senator Joe Robinson was a
cousin. Dunaway's father, also a lawyer, ran unsuccessfully for Congress on
an anti-Ku Klux Klan platform in the twenties and defended Negroes condemned to death after the Elaine, Arkansas, race riots of 1919. These began
when a deputy sheriff put in an appearance at the meeting of a union being
formed by Negro sharecroppers. Several white men and more than one
hundred Negroes were killed; eighty-seven Negroes were sentenced to jail
and twelve to the electric chair. The latter were saved by a Supreme Court
decision reversing their convictions. "I remember as a boy visiting the condemned with my father in the penitentiary," Dunaway related. "They had
been put to work building and painting their own coffins. They showed us
the black boxes and then sang hymns." It left a deep impression.

Dunaway made a date for us to talk later in the afternoon with a Negro
doctor, and took us off for lunch to the Little Rock Club, a mausoleum-like
building which might have been taken for a large undertaking establishment. We sat around with a group having drinks, in a kind of neutral zone,
the talk coming around only slowly to The Question. A visiting Texas reporter said Dallas, when ordered to integrate, would make Little Rock
"look like a picnic." Another man said, "Well our whole problem might be
summed up by saying that Orval Faubus just didn't want to go back to
Huntsville, and if you've ever seen Huntsville it is hard to blame him." It
was interesting to see the different ways in which members spoke to the Negro waiters. Some addressed the waiters with unostentatious politeness.
There were others who ordered drinks with the cold look and lordly manner that seemed to reflect an idealized image of themselves as members of a
superior race, disposing of vast acres and accustomed to handling *nigra*
servitors. As one watched these men, one thought, "So this is the wine that
goes to the white man's head in the South."

We took a cab after lunch to Little Rock's Harlem along Ninth Street, a
district of dingy bars, dilapidated stores and hand-me-down houses. My
companion was a British reporter and we hoped the combination of his ac-

cent and mine would make it easier to get people to talk with us. But we drew a complete blank. A blind woman beggar said in a cultivated voice that she did not know what she could say that might not hurt her hereafter since she was on public assistance. "I will say this," she said, picking her words slowly, "everyone likes a good thing," meaning presumably better schools. Her son, also blind, also in a cultivated voice, said he was studying music. Farther down the street we got a less friendly reception: "White man takes what you say and uses it against you." On a side street, alongside a long unpainted barnlike building which turned out to be the upper class dorm of Philander Smith College, a Negro Methodist school, there were a number of Negro boys playing ball. They wouldn't talk either. We went inside the college, which seemed more like a run-down old high school, and were told politely but firmly by the young woman who handles publicity that the college was keeping strictly "out of it" and that nobody would comment. "No, the students even among themselves do not discuss the question." One got the feeling of extraordinary restraint and discipline, as of a community which felt itself besieged. No one even used the word "school" or "segregation" or "integration." We also had the feeling of a new educated generation, not at all the "darkies" of white stereotypes. The silence as it piled up seemed more eloquent than anything which might have been said.

We did a little better with a white pawnbroker who said he had been there twenty years. He understood the silence which had greeted us. "People don't say anything," he told us. "They're polite and friendly but never discuss it." But Negroes had been buying guns and knives and laying them away. "You get arrested if you carry them on the street," he explained, "but if you wrap them up in paper and carry them home for self-protection it's legal." The only other white man we had seen in our walk around the neighborhood came in and turned out to be the manager of the local Negro movie. "Business usually falls off just before school opens," he told us. "But I've never seen anything as bad as this year. Ever since the court in St. Louis overruled Judge Lemley people have stopped coming out on the streets at night. They keep their children home." The pawnbroker said his business was bad, too. There was a lot of unemployment in the Negro section. "People don't have anything left to pawn." But the Negroes weren't the only ones not talking. He owned six duplexes inhabited by whites and when he went around to collect the rent he found the same unwillingness to discuss schools or integration. "People on both sides just ain't talkin'." The pawn-broker summed up his own philosophy: "You gotta keep the nigger in his place or he'll run all over you." He had a permit and carried a gun. Even the Negro cops, as we had noticed, went on their patrols in pairs.

We went into a white bar near the Negro section for a beer on our way back downtown. The place was crowded and we sat down at a table with two ducktail haircut characters, one handsome and friendly, the other with flattish face and slow of speech but anxious to talk. He asked my British friend whether rock-and-roll had reached England and when assured that it had, confessed to us one of the painful experiences of his life. Elvis Presley had once been in Little Rock before he became famous and our new friend had never gone to hear him! He told us this was the worst skid row bar in town and recommended a better place uptown. He said he used to be a Methodist but was now a member of the Christian Church. He told us that about twenty years ago a Negro had assaulted a white girl and "they" had set him afire and dragged his burning body down Ninth Street and "they haven't forgotten." When we asked who he meant by "they," he said "the white folks" and repeated the story again, in the same melancholy tone. Then he told it a third time, as if it were a portent of things to come. What did he think of school integration, we ventured to ask. "It's coming," he said, shaking his head. "It'll be here in about ten years, and then as the Bible says, 'there will be wars, and rumors of wars' and war between the na-tions and the races." He did not speak with hatred but with a kind of dis-passionate fatalism. He shook hands as we left, but his friend looked on coldly, as if he weren't going to be taken in by any furriners.

The Negro neighborhood to which we went for our appointment with the doctor was quite different from Little Rock's Harlem. He lived in a modest but well-painted frame house, set on a wide lawn. The homes and yards all looked well cared for. A Negro neighbor was cutting his grass nearby, and there was a scamper of feet and a burst of giggles within when we rang the bell. Two sets of pigtails with hair ribbons ran into the rear of the house when the doctor's wife, a tall, handsome dark woman, opened the door. She asked us to sit down in the parlor and said her husband would be home in a few minutes. There was a piano and a hi-fi set in the living room. She said her oldest boy who had just graduated from junior high was one of the new applicants for Central High. "My husband and I tried to dissuade him. We told him it would mean giving up his saxophone." Apparently the school band at Central High is not integrated. "But he insisted." The boy himself came in before going out to serve his paper route. He was a slim, shy, gangling youth. Why did he want to go to Central High? "The science facilities there are better and I want to be a doctor. I'd get a better education and I'd be paving the way for others." (It is a strange world and time in which the future of a race depends on the pioneering courage and steadiness of its children.)

The doctor, when he arrived, turned out to be a pleasant young man, conforming to neither Negro nor southern stereotypes. We asked what was the feeling in the Negro community. "I can only speak for myself," he replied. "We feel apprehensive but hopeful. We hope everybody will come to their senses." He smiled when we told him of the silence which had greeted us in Little Rock's Harlem. "That's not exactly new," he said. "Even at the best there was never much communication between us." We asked whether any of his patients were white. He said about twenty percent. He said there were Negro dentists in the plantation country whose practice was eighty-five percent white. Were any of his white patients segregationists? He supposed most of them were, but that didn't make any difference when it came to choosing a doctor. There were six Negro doctors and about one hundred white in Little Rock and both sides had a racially mixed practice. The Medical Society had been integrated for five or six years and there had been Negro students in the Little Rock medical school since 1948. "The doctors meet together but not the wives," his wife interjected. Both said it was impossible to find any consistency in racial patterns. "In a store downtown," the wife said, "I will be standing near a white woman and she will talk to me pleasantly and long. But a few minutes later when I see her again outside at the bus stop where she is with white friends, she will look straight through me." She said there were no facilities in the stores for Negro shoppers, no rest rooms, no place to get a bite to eat.

Were there interracial groups in Little Rock? There was the Arkansas Council on Human Relations, a Thursday-morning mixed prayer group, a

Fellowship of Reconciliation chapter, a Bahai group, all small. All met at a Negro community center or in a Negro church. The previous Thursday, the day the Supreme Court heard final argument on the school case, there was an eighteen-hour mixed prayer vigil in a Negro Methodist Church, beginning at 6 A.M. and ending at midnight. (Later another reporter told me that a cameraman outside the prayer meeting asked a white minister going in, "Are you a nigger lover?" The minister replied, "I love God. God loves niggers. I guess that makes me a nigger lover, too." "Will you repeat that for the camera?" said the cameraman.) "Why do white people here come to interracial groups?" I asked the doctor. "Some have a guilt complex, I suppose," he answered. "They feel they and their forebears haven't treated Negroes right. Others just have deeply Christian feelings and want some way to express them."

On Sunday, with two British correspondents, I drove down to the delta country. Arkansas is half southern, half western. The mountainous country north and west of Little Rock has few Negroes; the people and the mentality of the area is more like Oklahoma and mountain Missouri. South and east of Little Rock is black country, "delta" in the sense that it gets an overflow from the Mississippi and from its tributary White and Arkansas Rivers. The land and the mentality here is southern. We decided to visit Helena, the state's only "seaport," a river town of which Mark Twain wrote in his *Life on the Mississippi*. The Negro boy who brought the rented car to the hotel for the trip and drove me back to the car rental office was friendly and said he came from that area. He followed us into the office to show us the best way to get there and the manager found him there marking the map with me. "Mandy Lee," he said, "you're getting out of your place when you come into this office." I explained it was all my fault and Mandy Lee stood aside, with a properly contrite expression. "Now, my friend," said the manager. "You're going down to nigger country. This is where they raise rice and cotton and niggers." He showed me the points of interest I would pass. "Right here," he said, "a Yankee gunboat came up the river and shelled a Confederate hospital." I thanked him and left thinking of the wondrous way in which all enemies in all wars always manage with unerring aim to hit hospitals.

The country is flat and not too interesting. We passed two Negro baptismals on the way; the women in bright Sunday clothes; many cars parked nearby, and some brother in a white gown being dipped in the water. We thought it would be rude to stop and watch, that a white man's presence would be disturbing and resented. But we did after several attempts and suspicious greetings manage to talk with one old Negro farm couple on their ramshackle porch with chickens running about in the yard. The old man said he had farmed there for sixty-eight years and the white folks thereabouts had always treated him right "and with respect." He had no complaint, the price of cotton was good but the price of victuals went up with it. "We work like oxes," said the fierce-looking old lady, his wife. Shrewd eyes looked out of her worn black African face. Their children were gone to St. Louis and Chicago, all except one daughter who sat there shyly reading in a hymn book. Good manners and journalism struggled but the latter won when we asked whether we might see the inside of their house. "It's just a poor man's house," the old man objected with dignity. "There's a sick person in there." We apologized. The old lady said, "Are things going to get better for black folks?" and later, "I hope we're not going to have a war over there in China." It turned out that she was the only person, black or white, who asked us about the Far Eastern crisis in our three days in Arkansas.

The March on Washington

On August 28, 1963, Martin Luther King, Jr., delivered the most famous and frequently-quoted oration of modern times, his "I have a dream" speech, before a massive throng of civil rights marchers on the Mall in Washington, D.C. Stone wasn't impressed by King's speech or by any other he heard that day. Instead, he chose to highlight a Socialist Party gathering at which A. Philip Randolph called for economic justice for the poor, black and white alike.

.   .   .

September 16, 1963

THE MARCH IS OVER, but it will never be forgotten. Every one who was there had his own special moment. Mine was to stand in the early morning inside the Union Terminal and watch the thousands pouring in from New York and Pittsburgh and Chicago, and suddenly to feel no longer alone in this hot-house capital but as if out in the country people did care. Of the Marchers themselves, I along with almost every other observer was impressed with their gentle sweetness, a tribute to the Negro people, who have managed by humor and faith, amid so much suffering, not to be soured.

For me the heroes of the March, or heroines, were the gnarled old colored ladies on tired feet and comfortably broken shoes, the kind who walked into history in Montgomery. Amid the well dressed middle class Negroes and their white sympathizers were many black folk misshapen by malnutrition and hard work. They carried upon them a story more plainly writ than any banner. These were, literally, the downtrodden and the tread-marks of oppression were visible upon their faces. They sang, "We shall not be moved." But those who saw them—and what life had done to them—were moved.

Then it was a pleasure to see amid the Marchers so many old-time radicals, the unquenchables of so many vanished movements, many of them long ago forced out of jobs and pulpits, now joyously turning up again, with the feeling that they were at last part of a mass upsurge, no longer lonely relics.

With Lincoln behind them, and those eager thousands before them, the speakers at the Memorial were inevitably dwarfed and on the whole disappointing. None—not even Martin Luther King, who is a little too saccharine for my taste—broke through to the kind of simple purity of utterance the place and the occasion called for. The price of having so many respectables on the bandwagon was to mute Negro militancy—John Lewis of SNCC had to tone down his speech under pressure from Archbishop O'Boyle—and the rally turned into one of support for the Kennedy civil rights program. Somehow on that lovely day, in that picnic atmosphere, the Negro's anguish never found full expression.

Far superior to anything at the Monument were the discussions I heard next day at a civil rights conference called by the Socialist Party. On that dismal rainy morning-after, in a dark union hall in the Negro section, I heard A. Philip Randolph speak with an eloquence and a humanity few can achieve. When he spoke of the abolitionists, and of the heroes of the Reconstruction, it was with a filial piety and an immediacy that made them live again. One felt the presence of a great American. He reminded the black nationalists gently that "we must not forget that the civil rights revolution was begun by white people as well as black at a time when the winds of hate were sweeping the country." He reminded the moderates that political equality was not enough. "The white sharecroppers of the South," he pointed out, "have full civil rights but live in bleakest poverty." One began to understand what was meant by a march for "*jobs* and freedom." For most Negroes, civil rights alone will only be the right to join the underprivileged whites. "We must liberate not only ourselves," Mr. Randolph said, "but our white brothers and sisters."

The direction in which full emancipation lies was indicated when Mr. Randolph spoke of the need to extend the public sector of the economy. His brilliant assistant on the March, Bayard Rustin, urged an economic Master Plan to deal with the technological unemployment that weighs so heavily on the Negro and threatens to create a permanently depressed class of whites and blacks living precariously on the edges of an otherwise affluent society. It was clear from the discussion that neither tax cuts nor public works nor job training (for what jobs?) would solve the problem while automation with giant steps made so many workers obsolete. The civil rights movement, Mr. Rustin said, could not get beyond a certain level unless it merged into a broader plan of social change.

In that ill-lighted hall, amid the assorted young students and venerables like Norman Thomas, socialism took on fresh meaning and revived urgency. It was not accidental that so many of those who ran the March turned out to be members or fellow travellers of the Socialist Party. One saw that for the lower third of our society, white as well as black, the search for answers must lead them back—though Americans still start nervously at the very word—toward socialism.

The Fire Has Only Just Begun

This condemnation of national hypocrisy in response to the murder of Martin Luther King on April 4, 1968, is surely one of the bitterest essays I. F. Stone ever wrote. From today's perspective, it's a valuable reminder of how progressive—and therefore dangerous—the thinking of Dr. King really was, and a useful corrective to the warm-and-fuzzy mythologizing of him as a universally beloved hero.

.   .   .

April 15, 1968

THE ASSASSINATION OF DR. MARTIN LUTHER KING, JR., was the occasion for one of those massive outpourings of hypocrisy characteristic of the human race. He stood in that line of saints which goes back from Gandhi to Jesus; his violent end, like theirs, reflects the hostility of mankind to those who annoy it by trying hard to pull it one more painful step further up the ladder from ape to angel.

The President and the Washington establishment had been working desperately up until the very moment of Dr. King's killing to keep him and his Poor People's March out of the capital; his death, at first, promised to let them rest in peace. The masses they sang were not so much of requiem as of thanksgiving, that the nation's No. 1 Agitator had been laid to rest at last. Then a minority of his own people, and not all of them the ignorant and the hungry, celebrated his memory with an orgy of looting while black radicals and New Leftists hailed the mindless carnival as a popular uprising. Since the liquor stores were the No. 1 target, it might sourly be termed the debut of Marxism-Liquorism in revolutionary annals. Those among his own people who sneered at his nonviolent teaching as obsolete now seized upon his death as a new excuse for the violence he hated. Thus all sides firmly united in paying him homage.

191

Dr. King was a victim of white racism. Its record encourages such murders. Dr. King was only the most eminent in a long series of civil rights victims. The killers are rarely caught, even more rarely convicted; the penalties are light. The complicity, in this case, may go further. It is strange that the killer was so easily able to escape when the motel in which he was killed was ringed with police; some came within a few moments from the very direction of the fatal shot. Violent anti-Negro organizations like the Klan have their cells in many police forces. The Memphis police had shown their hatred in the indiscriminate violence with which they broke up Dr. King's march a week earlier. The Attorney General should be pressed to include the Memphis police in his investigation of the slaying.

Though Dr. King was the greatest Southerner of our time, few Southern political leaders expressed any sorrow over his passing. Most, like Stennis of Mississippi, ventured no more than antiseptic and ambivalent condemnation of *all* violence. In the House on April 8 the few Southerners who spoke deplored the riots more than the killing. The one exception was Representative Bob Eckhardt of Texas, who dared call Dr. King "my black brother." Privately many white Southerners rejoiced, and their influence was reflected in the scandalous failure to declare a holiday in the District the day Dr. King was buried. Though stores closed, government offices were open and Negro mailmen delivered the mail as usual. This is still, despite its black majority, a Southern-ruled town; it shuts down on Washington's birthday, but not Lincoln's.

The most powerful of the District's absentee rulers, Senator Robert C. Byrd (D. W. Va.), went so far as to imply in a Senate speech April 5, that Dr. King was to blame for his own death. Byrd said those who organize mass demonstrations may "in the end . . . become themselves the victims of the forces they set in motion." While Dr. King "usually spoke of nonviolence," Byrd went on smugly, "violence all too often attended his action and, at the last, he himself met a violent end." This should make Byrd the South's favorite criminologist.

Byrd is the Senator to whom the blacks of Washington must come for school and welfare money. As chairman of the Senate Appropriations subcommittee on the District of Columbia budget, Byrd wields far more power than the city's figurehead Negro "Mayor." He has used this key position to block liberalization of welfare rules not only in the District but in the country, since the federal government can hardly apply elsewhere rules more liberal than those he will allow in the District. Byrd has become the national pillar of the "man in the house" rule. This, as the report of the Commission on Civil Disorders protested, makes it necessary for the unemployed father to "abandon his family or see them go hungry." In this sense not a few of the child looters in our gutted ghettoes can trace their delinquency straight back to Robert C. Byrd.

For whites who live like myself in almost lily-white Northwest Washington on the very edge of suburbia, the ghetto disorders might have taken place in a distant country, viewed on TV like Vietnam (which it begins to resemble), or as a tourist attraction on a visit in the bright spring sunshine before curfew to the sullen and ruined ghetto business districts. It was not until five days after the trouble started that two young soldiers turned up for the first time to guard our own neighboring shopping center—"as a precautionary measure," they explained—and tape appeared on its liquor-store windows. Even sympathetic and radical whites found themselves insulated from what was going on not just by the military cordons but even more by an indiscriminate black hostility. Even some liberal and leftist families with children moved out of integrated neighborhoods on the edge of the ghetto in apprehension. These were our first refugees from black power.

Nothing could be more deceptive than the nationwide mourning. Beneath the surface nothing has changed, except perhaps for the worst. The President has called off his address to a joint session indefinitely. His Senate Majority Leader, Mansfield, warns the Congress not to be "impetuous" in reacting to the disorders. How fortunate we should be if all our dangers were as remote as this one! The new civil rights bill, if it passes, is more likely to bring new evils in its anti-riot provisions than reform in housing.

In Washington, as in most cities hit by black violence, the police and the troops have been on their best behavior to the point where business spokesmen are complaining that there has been too much leniency in dealing with looters. For once, to the Administration's credit, lives have been put ahead of property. Had police and soldiers begun to shoot, the killings would have become a massacre and the riots a black revolution. As it is, in Washington at least, the black community has been grateful for the protection afforded it. But this leniency is unlikely to survive when and if white rather than black areas begin to go up in smoke. There is little time left for the big multi-billion-dollar program which alone can rehabilitate the hopeless and bitter generation of blacks that racial discrimination and the slums have bred. Whites still think they can escape the problem by moving to the suburbs, and as long as they think so, nothing will be done. There are already 55,000 troops in our 110 scarred cities—more than we had in Vietnam three years ago. Already the police talk of guerrilla war. If it comes, a half million troops will not be enough to contain it. A looting suspect told one reporter at a police station here, "We're going to burn this whole place. It might take years but we'll do it." This is the agony of a lost race speaking. If we cannot respond with swift compassion, this is the beginning of our decline and fall.

The Mason-Dixon Line
Moves to New York

Journalist James Traub has labeled the 1968 school crisis centered on the Ocean Hill–Brownsville neighborhood of Brooklyn as "one of the great, agonizing racial psychodramas in New York history," and the following dispatch from its front lines suggests many of the swirling, conflicting emotions that helped make it so. At any time, the challenges of educating poor children within a vast, bureaucratic system would tend to make a battle over control of neighborhood schools a complex and emotional issue; in 1968, at the height of a national debate over race relations and with an anti–civil rights backlash among many whites being led by presidential candidate George Wallace, the conflict was sharply intensified. After a two-month strike by the United Federation of Teachers, the power of the local Ocean Hill–Brownsville school board was effectively shattered—and so was the long-standing Black-Jewish alliance that had long played a progressive role in New York City politics.

.   .   .

November 4, 1968

ON MY WAY INTO NEW YORK CITY from La Guardia, the taxi-driver told me that his daughter, after a first year as teacher in a black ghetto, had transferred out to Long Island in despair. "The children were wonderful," he said. "The trouble was the parents." An hour later at lunch a Jewish schoolteacher from Brooklyn complained of the black children in her mathematics class for slow learners, but said the black parents, when she called on them for help, were without exception not only cooperative but grateful. But teacher and taxi-driver agreed in blaming Mayor Lindsay, though just for what was not clear. Indeed very little in New York's crisis is clear, perhaps because the real motivations are kept hidden as shameful. More and more people, particularly among the striking teachers, and in the

Jewish community, are flailing about in hysteria. A sample: I asked the Brooklyn schoolteacher just what was the issue in the strike. She replied with appalling simplicity, "Anti-Semitism." How do you win a strike against anti-Semitism? By circumcising all gentiles and turning Black Muslims into Black Jews? "What does Mr. Shanker want?" the mayor asked in a similar vein in a radio interview next day. "For the police vans to come into the [Ocean Hill–Brownsville] community, arrest them and send them to New Jersey?" Is the Exodus to be re-enacted, this time with a black cast?

The plain truth is that John V. Lindsay is in trouble because he suddenly finds himself the Mayor of a Southern town. The Mason-Dixon line has moved north, and the Old Confederacy has expanded to the outer reaches of the Bronx. Even without this tide of racism, it would take a genius with two heads to govern the city successfully. Some of its basic problems are universal. One is size. Another is bureaucracy; the educational bureaucracy has entrenched itself in a maze of regulations beyond effective public control. A third is poverty; by next year one of every eight New Yorkers will be on relief. The city is choked with automobiles and people. Even if all eight million were a multiple birth from the same mamma, they would aggravate the hell out of each other. But in New York, as elsewhere, those of a different color, whether black or Puerto Rican, are no longer willing to accept second- or third-class citizenship submissively. They are pushing upwards into the better jobs and the sunnier places. In New York, the world's biggest Jewish city, this has created a special problem—a confrontation between blacks and Jews. This is rapidly turning Lindsay into the world's most down-trodden WASP.

The defeat two years ago of his proposal for a civilian review board to hear complaints against the police was the first disturbing signal in what had been the most liberal city in the country. New York's lower-middle-class whites were reacting like their counterparts elsewhere. In the struggle over schools the fears have now spread to liberal teachers hitherto sympathetic to the civil rights movement. Conflicts in the ghetto with Jewish landlords and storekeepers were relatively easy to contain. But the teachers' strike has churned up fears in an educational establishment that Jewish teachers and principals have dominated for a generation. Now that black unrest seems to threaten union standards and their jobs they are reacting like less liberal and less intellectual "ethnic" groups. The teachers' union is moving closer to the benighted old-line A.F.L. craft unions. A formidable anti-black coalition is shaping up. One of its victims may be the good name of the Jewish community.

If this great city is to be saved from race war, more Jewish intellectuals are going to have to speak up in ways that their own people will resent, just as white Southerners resented those who spoke up for the Negro. The teachers' union is exaggerating, amplifying and circulating any bit of anti-Semitic drivel it can pick up from any far-out black extremist, however unrepresentative, and using this to drive the Jewish community of New York into a panic. Albert Shanker and the teachers' union are exploiting natural Jewish fears of anti-Semitism in order to win the community's support for the strike and for its major objective, which is to prevent effective decentralization and community control of the school system. Unless more Jewish leaders speak up in public and say what they do in private, this manufactured hysteria may prove a disaster for both the black and the Jewish communities. Peoples, like generals, tend to be obsessed by their last war. To hear some New York Jews talk one would think the America of 1968 was the Germany of 1932. They do not see that they themselves are caught up in the backlash which is creating in Wallace the nearest American counterpart to Der Fuehrer, that they are joining the rednecks, that the danger lies in white racism not black. The latter is despairing and defensive; the former holds the potential of a new Nazism in its effort to maintain white supremacy. It would be eternally disgraceful were Jews this time to be among the Brown Shirts.

To visit the black-controlled schools which have stirred such forebodings on both sides of the controversy is like waking from a nightmare. I spent Friday, October 25, in the Ocean Hill–Brownsville district, observing classes and talking with teachers and principals in JHS 271 and its intermediate school neighbor, IS 55, and the visit was therapeutic. It was a day without pickets and I saw only one policeman. The atmosphere was incredibly different from what I had been led to expect. I found black and white teachers, Jewish and gentile, working together not just peacefully but with zest and comradeship. The cleanliness and the neat clothing of the children reflected well on the homes from which they came. The classes were orderly.

There was none of that screaming by teacher against pupil, and among the children, which is common in most New York schools. I felt at the end of the day that the racial and union issues were terribly overblown and that the real concern within the embattled district was simply to create effective schools. I saw no reason why this could not be reconciled with proper union standards and I felt it would be a tragedy if this experiment in community control were shut down.

I watched Mrs. Naomi Levinson teach an English class full of eager black children. I read some of the touching poems and essays they had produced. "It's the first time in my eight years as a teacher," she told us proudly, "that I have been allowed to use unconventional teaching methods." I talked with another teacher, Leon Goodman, whose face lit up with pleasure when he explained the new methods of teaching science he was allowed to apply. "We get them to think rather than simply to copy down abstractions from the blackboard." Both impatiently denied that they had encountered any anti-Semitism.* I sat in on a teacher-team conference of five English teachers, three black, two white, one of the whites a delicate-featured blonde WASP, the other an intense and dark-eyed Jew. The two whites were volunteers. One of them had brought a bongo drum into the classroom to use with the reading of Vachel Lindsay's incomparably rhythmic "Congo" as a way to awaken the children to the wonders of poetry. The atmosphere of this mixed group was wholly devoid of any racial self-consciousness or tension. One felt their pleasure in working together. In the corner of one classroom we watched a young black teacher with a group of children who took turns at reading "The Prince and the Pauper." On the blackboard was the assignment, "Write a story about something that went wrong in a person's life" and next to it in a row there were the helpful hints, "No money. Sickness. No food. No light. No home. No friends. No job." The words telescoped the familiar annals of the ghetto.

The only racialism, if it can be called that, was in the evidence of efforts to awaken black pride. There were some vivid watercolors produced in a new painting class and exhibited in a hallway as "Soul on Paper." Another

---

*About three-fourths of the non-striking teachers in Ocean Hill–Brownsville are white and about one half of these are Jewish.

hallway blackboard had "Black Is Beautiful" written not only in French and Spanish but in Greek, Hebrew, Punjabi, Swahili, Arabic and Esperanto. One room's walls were covered with pictures and clippings variously headed "Religion, Statesmen, Musicians, Scientists, Inventors, Diplomats" showing black achievement in these fields.

In the classroom where Leslie Campbell, an African gown over his normal clothes, teaches Afro-American Studies, there were posters showing "Our Homeland" and "Our Proud and Glorious Past." They reminded me of Zionist posters in many Jewish Sabbath schools. There were also posters of "The Proud Look" and "Black Pictures of Christ." Campbell after class was friendly and open. He described himself as a black nationalist revolutionary but said he found himself very much in a minority on the faculty. "Most of my black colleagues," he said, "are simply educationists," though they agree on African studies for its psychological value. The other teacher of Afro-American Studies at JHS 271, Alan Kellock, turned out to be a young white man who has studied in Egypt and Ghana and is finishing a doctorate in African history for the University of Wisconsin. He said he had encountered no racial prejudice in Ocean Hill–Brownsville. What purpose did he see in Afro-American history courses? "To get the black children to feel they are worthwhile people. To give them a sense of identity and dignity." Kellock obtained his teaching license last summer. He feels JHS 271 is the most promising place to teach in the entire city.

David Rogers, in his blockbuster of a new book, *110 Livingston Street: Politics and Bureaucracy in the New York City School System,* quotes an authoritative earlier professional study of the city's schools by Strayer and Yavner. "The greatest failing of the schools today," they found as he did, "is the failure to use the creative ability of teachers." When I read this afterwards, I understood the enthusiasm I had found in the two schools I visited. I had thought of community control as a kind of lesser evil, a way of appeasing black dissatisfaction. I did not realize what a dead hand the bureaucracy has fastened on the schools and how much could be done just by lifting it. "Not many teachers come into the system sour," said Percy Jenkins, the Virginia-born Negro who is now principal of IS 55, "but they don't stay long without becoming sour. The kids come in with lively minds but by the fourth grade they too have lost interest." Jenkins himself, a graduate of West Virginia State College, had been in "the system" 15 years and risen to assistant principal before he was chosen to head IS 55 in this community-control experiment. "What you see here," one white teacher explained later, "is a function of the principal, of the fresh directions he maps out and of the commitment brought to this experiment by young liberal arts college volunteers with new ideas."

I spoke with Rhody McCoy, the head of the district; with his assistant, Lloyd Hunter; with the principal of JHS 271, William H. Harris, and with his white assistant principal, John Mandracchia. I have never met a more devoted group of people. All of them are harassed and overworked but sustained by a combination of desperation and joy, desperation because they fear the experiment may soon be wiped out under union pressure, joy in a chance to demonstrate in the little time they have what community control could accomplish. They are enlightened men; one forgets all the nonsense of black and white in talking with them; color vanishes. They fear black extremism as much as white misunderstanding. *And their focus is on the child.*

That cannot be said of their opponents. The child, whether black or white, seems to be the forgotten bystander in the teachers' strike. The union's rallying cry is "due process," i.e., for teachers, and its concern is their tenure. Its alliance is not with the parents for better education but with the employing bureaucracy for the maintenance of their common privileges. The "due process" issue they have raised is a monumental bit of hypocrisy. The best analysis of it may be found in the report by the New York Civil Liberties Union, *The Burden of Blame.* The unsatisfactory teachers were *transferred,* not discharged, and transfers normally are made without hearing or charges; the teachers prefer it that way, to keep their records free from blemish.

The real problem is how to keep teachers *in* ghetto schools. The Board of Education regulations are designed to discourage teachers from fleeing them. The contractual procedures between the Board and the union limit the teacher's freedom to transfer. "Yet," the civil liberties union reported, "in Ocean Hill–Brownsville, the UFT sought to ignore all these procedures and claimed the right for unlimited numbers of teachers to transfer out at will for the duration of the experiment, to abandon the experiment for as long as it continues and then to be free to return, presumably when 'normal' conditions had been reinstated. . . . Significant numbers of teachers did leave. . . . Months later, when the Ocean Hill–Brownsville Local Governing Board attempted to exercise a similar unilateral right of transfer, the UFT cried foul."

The Board of Education's notions of "due process" are as one-sided. I have read the full text of the decision handed down by Judge Francis E. Rivers as trial examiner in the case of the transferred teachers. It is by no stretch of the imagination the vindication it appears to be in the headlines.

The hearing, by screening out all but professional witnesses, and barring not only parent testimony but that of para-professional school aides, and by applying strict rules of evidence unsuited to administrative procedures, managed to acquit the teachers without any real exploration of the charges against them.

The Board of Education is past master at manipulating regulations and procedures to achieve the ends it seeks. The Rogers book shows how hard it is even for teachers and principals to find out how it operates. Only a Kafka could do justice to the murk it generates. In a column on due process in the *New York Post* October 24, Murray Kempton provided an incisive glimpse of these operations in the proceedings now underway against four JHS 271 teachers accused of threats, or acts of terror, against attempts to reinstate the transferred teachers. Their attorneys were forbidden to see the reports on which the charges were based. When one attorney asked, "Do you proceed under any rules and regulations?" the reply was "We do not." After all this talk about due process, Kempton commented, "we suddenly discover that in this system there is no protection for anybody except the conscience and good-will of the Superintendent."

All bureaucracies are secretive, none more so than the New York Board of Education. The Rogers book is an eye-opener, particularly in its account of how desegregation was sabotaged by the Board. It did not work, Rogers concludes, "because the bureaucracy and the staff made them fail." It was out of the frustration created by the failure of integration that black and Puerto Rican parents turned to community control. This, too, is being sabotaged by the Board and by the union. They fear the loss of power and privilege if democracy is substituted for bureaucracy. They have the support of all the unions which do business with the educational system, a billion-dollar business. The New York trade union movement, like its educational establishment, has been a stronghold of white supremacy. This is where and how the racial issue arises, and the Jewish community is being enlisted because teaching has been a Jewish preserve in New York as it was once an Irish Catholic preserve. If community control is crushed, the racial struggle will take on more violent and hateful forms to the detriment of both the black and Jewish communities.

The Jews, as the more favored and privileged group, owe the underprivileged a duty of patience, charity and compassion. It will not hurt us to swallow a few insults from overwrought blacks. It is as right to invoke the better Jewish tradition against Jewish bigotry as to invoke the better American tradition against white racism. The genocidal threat, if any, in this situation lies in the slow death and degradation to which so many blacks and Puerto Ricans are doomed in our slums. To wipe out the slums and help save their occupants would be the truest memorial to those who died in Auschwitz. When an idealistic young Mayor and the Rabbi who tried to defend him are howled down in a synagogue, it is time for the slap that can alone bring hysterics to their senses. Lindsay was saying "a Jewish philosopher—" when he was forced to leave. The philosopher he was about to quote was Spinoza. He, too, was thrown out of the synagogue in his time. We ought to have better sense today.

Part Five

A PROMISED LAND?

For the Jews—Life or Death?

This article is an urgent appeal for help from the United States on behalf of the millions of Jews facing destruction in the Nazi death camps—an appeal that went tragically unanswered. What follows is the brief introductory note written when the article was first reprinted in the collection: *The War Years, 1939–1945.*

At his press conference on June 2, after this article was written, the President indicated that he was considering the conversion of an army camp in this country into a "free port" for refugees. Unfortunately, as the New York Post *has pointed out, "his statement was conditional, indefinite. The check is still on paper and we don't even know what the amount is." In these circumstances Mr. Stone's analysis of the urgency of the situation and his plea for public pressure to secure action from the Administration are no less valid than they were before Mr. Roosevelt spoke.*

.   .   .

June 10, 1944

THIS LETTER, ADDRESSED SPECIFICALLY to fellow-newspapermen and to editors the country over, is an appeal for help. The establishment of temporary internment camps for refugees in the United States, vividly named "free ports" by Samuel Grafton of the New York *Post,* is in danger of bogging down. Every similar proposal here has bogged down until it was too late to save any lives. I have been over a mass of material, some of it confidential, dealing with the plight of the fast-disappearing Jews of Europe and with the fate of suggestions for aiding them, and it is a dreadful story.

Anything newspapermen can write about this in their own papers will help. It will help to save lives, the lives of people like ourselves. I wish I were eloquent, I wish I could put down on paper the picture that comes to me from the restrained and diplomatic language of the documents. As I write, the morning papers carry a dispatch from Lisbon, reporting that the "deadline"—the idiom was never more literal—has passed for the Jews of Hungary. It is approaching for the Jews of Bulgaria, where the Nazis yesterday set up a puppet regime.

I need not dwell upon the authenticated horrors of the Nazi internment camps and death chambers for Jews. That is not tragic but a kind of insane horror. It is our part in this which is tragic. The essence of tragedy is not the doing of evil by evil men but the doing of evil by good men, out of weakness, indecision, sloth, inability to act in accordance with what they know to be right. The tragic element in the fate of the Jews of Europe lies in the failure of their friends in the West to shake loose from customary ways and bureaucratic habit, to risk inexpediency and defy prejudice, to be whole-hearted, to care as deeply and fight as hard for the big words we use, for justice and for humanity, as the fanatic Nazi does for his master race or the fanatic Jap for his Emperor. A reporter in Washington cannot help seeing this weakness all about him. We are half-hearted about what little we could do to help the Jews of Europe as we are half-hearted about our economic warfare, about blacklisting those who help our enemies, about almost everything in the war except the actual fighting.

There is much we could have done to save the Jews of Europe before the war. There is much we could have done since the war began. There are still things we could do today which would give new lives to a few and hope to many. The hope that all is not black in the world for his children can be strong sustenance for a man starving in a camp or entering a gas chamber. But to feel that your friends and allies are wishy-washy folk who mean what they say but haven't got the gumption to live up to it must brew a poisonous despair. When Mr. Roosevelt established the War Refugee Board in January, he said it was "the policy of this government to take all measures within its power . . . consistent with the successful prosecution of the war . . . to rescue the victims of enemy oppression."

The facts are simple. Thanks to the International Red Cross and those good folk the Quakers, thanks to courageous non-Jewish friends in the occupied countries themselves and to intrepid Jews who run a kind of underground railway under Nazi noses, something can still be done to alleviate the suffering of the Jews in Europe and some Jews can still be got out. Even under the White Paper there are still 22,000 immigration visas available for entry into Palestine. The main problem is to get Jews over the Turkish border without a passport for transit to Palestine. "Free ports" in Turkey are needed, but the Turks, irritated by other pressures from England and the United States, are unwilling to do for Jewish refugees what we ourselves are still unwilling to do, that is, give them a temporary haven. Only an executive order by the President establishing "free ports" in this country can prove to the Turks that we are dealing with them in a good faith; under present circumstances they cannot but feel contemptuous of our pleas. And the longer we delay the fewer Jews there will be left to rescue, the slimmer the chances to get them out. Between 4,000,000 and 5,000,000 European Jews have been killed since August, 1942, when the Nazi extermination campaign began.

There are people here who say the President cannot risk a move of this kind before election. I believe that an insult to the American public. I do not believe any but a few unworthy bigots would object to giving a few thousand refugees a temporary breathing spell in their flight from oppression. It is a question of Mr. Roosevelt's courage and good faith. All he is called upon to do, after all, is what Franco did months ago, yes, *Franco*. Franco established "free ports," internment camps, months ago for refugees who fled across his border, refugees, let us remember, from his own ally and patron, Hitler. Knowing the Führer's maniacal hatred for Jews, that kindness on Franco's part took considerably more courage than Mr. Roosevelt needs to face a few sneering editorials, perhaps, from the Chicago *Tribune*. I say "perhaps" because I do not know that even Colonel McCormick would in fact be hostile.

Official Washington's capacity for finding excuses for inaction is endless, and many people in the State and War departments who play a part in this matter can spend months sucking their legalistic thumbs over any problem. So many things that might have been done were attempted too late. A little more than a year ago Sweden offered to take 20,000 Jewish children from occupied Europe if Britain and the United States guaranteed their feeding and after the war their repatriation. The British were fairly rapid in this case, but it took three or four months to get these assurances from the American government, and by that time the situation had worsened to a point that seems to have blocked the whole project. In another case the

Bulgarian government offered visas for 1,000 Jews if arrangements could be made within a certain time for their departure. A ship was obtained at once, but it took weeks for British officials to get clearance for the project from London, and by that time the time limit had been passed. The records, when they can be published, will show many similar incidents.

The news that the United States had established "free ports" would bring hope to people who have now no hope. It would encourage neutrals to let in more refugees because we could take out some of those they have already admitted. Most important, it would provide the argument of example and the evidence of sincerity in the negotiations for "free ports" in Turkey, last hope of the Balkan Jews. I ask fellow-newspapermen to show the President by their expression of opinion in their own papers that if he hesitates for fear of an unpleasant political reaction he badly misconstrues the real feelings of the American people.

Jewry in a Blind Alley

A son of Jewish immigrants from Russia, I. F. Stone supported the creation of a Jewish homeland, while also being troubled by the plight of the Palestinian Arabs and strongly backing a peaceful solution to the conflict between the Jews and the Arabs over control of the land once known as Palestine. In this essay, Stone describes early efforts to find some form of accommodation between the two communities, while warning his fellow Jews that "political agreement will be impossible so long as a single Jewish state in Palestine is demanded." The "Bevin statement" Stone refers to was issued on November 13, 1945, by British Foreign Secretary Ernest Bevin; it temporized over the Arab-Jewish conflict over Palestine, suggesting that an Anglo-American Committee of Inquiry might be able to forge a solution. Of course, today, six decades later, the conflict continues unabated, in forms that Stone would probably find depressingly familiar.

·   ·   ·

November 24, 1945

I CAME TO PALESTINE UNHAPPY, and during the first few days I became even unhappier trying to figure out solutions of the problems involved; but the longer I have been here the happier I have come to feel despite all that has happened and may happen in the next few days.

I stayed five days in Egypt visiting with many Egyptians and spending some time in a village near Cairo. I was able to see the sharp contrast in cleanliness and health between the Egyptian villager and urban poor and the Arab villager and urban poor in Palestine. I felt happy that the coming of the Jews had helped rather than hurt the Arabs.

I was deeply moved by my visits to the colonies here. From Gevulot, in the far south of the Negev desert wastes, to glorious Minara, 3,000 feet above the Upper Jordan on the far northern edge, I saw young Jews from every clime and country reclaiming the land and making something for themselves and their children under conditions which are truly heroic. This sense of consecration and common effort in the Jewish community most powerfully attract all who prize human courage, devotion, and idealism. I was not at all surprised to hear of two cases of non-Jewish demobilized British soldiers, formerly in service here, applying for admission to membership in the Jewish Kibbutzim, or communal settlements.

I felt happy to see that despite difficulties which from abroad appear insuperable there was a great and growing community here, and in visits both to Arab villages and neighboring Jewish colonies, I feel a huge reservoir of good-will between the Arab and Jew which can be tapped; and I have not sensed in talks with Arabs either in Palestine or in Egypt, despite their differences, any feeling of race hatred or dislike of Jews as a people.

But at the cost of unpopularity perhaps in the Jewish community of America I wish to say as strongly as I know how that the new Bevin statement is only the latest indication of the blind alley into which Palestinian Jewry is being led by the failure to achieve any political understanding with the Arabs. And I wish to say just as strongly that political agreement will be impossible so long as a single Jewish state in Palestine is demanded.

We have been carrying on a campaign in America on the basis of half-truths, and on this basis no effective politics can be waged and no secure life built for Yishuv.* It is true that the Arabs have benefited by the Jews coming to Palestine, and it is true that there is plenty of room here for several millions more, but I cannot find a single Jew who can find a single Arab who favors a Jewish state in Palestine! It should not be hard to understand the natural dislike of any human being for being ruled by another people or his unwillingness to trust himself to such rule.

There is only one way in which a Jewish state here could be sold to the Arab world and that would be as part of a general settlement of Anglo-Egyptian and other Arab problems which would satisfy the aspiration of the Arabs for self-development and federation. That was what made Zionism acceptable in earlier days to the wise and far-seeing Feisal and other Arab leaders, but Britain's failure really to keep the promises given to the Arabs has made the Arabs naturally hostile to the promises given to the Jews. The Bevin statement is only another chapter in the record of broken promises to both.

*The Jewish community in Palestine.

The most significant point to be noted in the Bevin statement is that while consultation is assured the Arabs concerning any further Jewish immigration in accordance with the White Paper, not a single solitary word is said about a promise to consult with the Jews on the other major item in the White Paper—the undertaking to the Arabs that a start would be made in setting up self-governing institutions in Palestine within five years. I could not help noting also that in Egypt, if it were not for anti-Zionist political agitation, the British would be confronted immediately with a demand for a basic settlement of Anglo-Egyptian problems, including the Sudan, Suez, and British occupation.

It is true that the Jews are in a terrible position, on the one hand asking to be beneficiaries of British imperialism and on the other serving as its lightning rod. Two political axioms seem to be completely forgotten by Jewish world leadership. One is that politics cannot be played unless one has alternatives; one cannot bargain unless one can obtain similar wares elsewhere. The other is that in politics one saves favors for those one must win over and does not waste them on elements already in one's pocket. So long as the Jews are dependent on Britain with no alternative policy for an agreement with the Arabs, the Jews are helpless. Incidentally the Arabs are also helpless until they reach some agreement with the Jews, because just enough will be given both sides, as by Bevin, to keep both dissatisfied and embroiled. Let us remember that as long as there is no solution of the Arab-Jewish problem, Britain has an excuse to keep ample troops near the Suez Canal. I realize this does an injustice to the subjective intent of many British leaders, but it is politically true none the less.

I understand, after being in this part of the world, why the Jews must fight against the conversion of the Yishuv into what the Royal Commission of 1937 called "one more cramped and dangerous ghetto." Consignment to minority status in an Arab state is a violation of pledges made to the Jews, fulfilment of which they have a moral right to demand. But I understand too why the Arabs in Palestine, who are also human beings and who also have historic rights here, are prepared to fight against any subjection to a Jewish state.

I know there are other Arab states, while there is only one possibility for a Jewish state; I know that proposals to divide Palestine into two national states, put forward several times by Jewish sources, have fallen on stony ground. Nevertheless, despite present public utterances by the leadership on both sides, I think that a division on these lines, with two national states created on a parity principle, is ethically right and politically feasible and would be acceptable to a great majority of Jews and Arabs if it were imposed from above by Anglo-American or United Nations decision. Certainly only on this basis can Arab-Jewish political understanding be reached.

I heard much talk in London against partition. I think it ducks the fundamental and inescapable question of the Middle East. For the Arabs, the removal of the Jews would be a calamity. I am convinced that the Jews have already contributed much and can in the future contribute even more toward the development of the Arab world. The Arabs are a great people with great potentialities. For the Jews, conversely, the basic problem here is to get along with the Arabs, to win them by helping them and by demonstrating a sincere desire to live together on an equal basis. This is a nobler and politically sounder goal than any narrow Jewish nationalism. If Britain and America wish peace with justice in this part of the world, with the Jew and Arab both here, I am convinced the solution lies in this, the only escape route from *divide et impera*.

Palestine Pilgrimage

Another dispatch from I. F. Stone's very first trip abroad, which focused primarily on Palestine and the Middle East and helped lead to two books: *Underground to Palestine* (1946), dealing with the migration of European Jews to the Middle East in the wake of World War II, and *This Is Israel* (1948), a dramatic account of the founding of the new Jewish state, which combined text by Stone with photographs by Robert Capa, Jerry Cooke, and Tim Gidal. In this essay, based on his observations in Palestine and elsewhere, Stone advocates a "bi-national settlement" that would give both Jews and Arabs a homeland in Palestine.

.　　.　　.

December 8, 1945

I FEEL A LITTLE LIKE THE HERO of Jules Verne's "Around the World in Eighty Days," though he was a slowpoke by comparison. Last Tuesday I had tea in England and dinner in Ireland. I breakfasted the next day in Newfoundland and lunched in New York. I have just returned from a six weeks' trip abroad, a typical bit of American blitz journalism. My primary concern was Palestine, and the largest part of my time was spent there. But I had five days in London on my way and two days in Paris. I saw St. Peter's from the skies over Rome, and I climbed the Acropolis in awe during an overnight stop in Athens. I had five days in and around Cairo before I reached Palestine, and I saw every part of the Holy Land except the Dead Sea during my stay there. I spent two days and a night in the Lebanon, and stayed three days each in Cairo and London on my way back, with short descents from lonely night skies over Cyrenaica and Malta, and a breakfast near Marseilles.

It was my first trip abroad, and if a wandering newspaperman may be forgiven his enthusiasm, I came back drunk on the beauties of the world: that last look at Manhattan's heady towers on the way out; the infinite variety of sea and sky on the boat trip over; St. Paul's, mighty and melancholy amid the bomb ruins in a London dusk; Paris, as one had dreamed of it, miraculously unscathed by the war; a savage sunset over the wild Balkan headlands flying into Greece; the green delta stretching from horizon to horizon as one enters the Egyptian skies; the minarets and the stars over the Citadel in Cairo; dawn over the Negev from the watch tower at Gevulot, with Sinai far in the distance; Minara, my favorite colony, which shoulders the sky 3,000 feet above the Jordan across from the enormous Harmon, where Pan dwelt; and Jerusalem, clean, white, and lovely on its ancient hills. I was moved to tears twice on my trip, once when I walked for the first time into Notre Dame in Paris, and again when I came through the narrow winding streets of the Old City to the Wailing Wall in Jerusalem, and saw the few stones to which cling so many filial memories for a Jew.

I went over neither to uncover sensations nor to bolster preconceptions but to understand the British and the Arab as well as the Jewish point of view, to get the atmosphere of London and the flavor of Arab nationalism, and to see for myself what had been accomplished in Palestine. I dined with a Cabinet minister in London and had a two-hour off-the-record talk with Azzam Bey, head of the Arab League, in Cairo. My assignment, to achieve some grasp of the complexities and the tragedies involved in Britain's position, Arab aspirations, and urgent Jewish needs, was an assignment that called for an Isaiah, not a mere reporter. Perhaps I learned most from chance contact and talks with humbler folk—a devout English Catholic returning on the *Queen Elizabeth* from captivity in Japan, a cockney Jewish mother bombed out of her home in the East End of London, a Coptic doctor struggling against the disease and squalor of an Egyptian village, a young Sephardic Jew homeless in Athens whose Spanish passport had saved him in a German death camp, a brilliant Christian Arab leader in Beirut whose sympathetic understanding of Zionism surpassed that of any Zionist I encountered, a veteran English civil servant in Haifa, and above all the young men and women of the Jewish colonies I visited, the grandest young folk I have ever met.

I hated Egypt. I have never seen such poverty. There are wise and farseeing men in the Egyptian upper class, and I had the good fortune to speak with several. But there are also a whole horde of self-serving phonies, and some Egyptian officials seem to treat their own people with an arrogance and contempt beyond that of the worst foreign imperialist. The gap between rich and poor is unbelievably wide. Of all the villages in Egypt some fourteen now have health centers, and of these fourteen, five have doctors. It was to one of these show villages, near Gizeh, with the Pyramids visible not far away, that I was taken. The filth and squalor were beyond conception, and there, as in the Muski, the ancient quarter of Cairo, I saw a sight one cannot forget—flies feasting on the corrupted eyelids of little children. In the West one speaks of exploitation, but in the West the exploiting capitalist builds, constructs, produces; his activity adds as much as if not more than it subtracts. But in Egypt exploitation is of a different and almost one-sided character. The fellah lives on the Nile and the pasha lives on the fellah. In the West when we think of colonial nationalism, we think of Gandhi and Nehru. Egypt once had a Zaglul Pasha, responsive to his people's needs, but today one catches few if any overtones of idealism in the Wafdist movement he founded.

Egypt provides perspective on Palestine. There is the sharpest contrast between the markets of Egypt and the Arab markets in Palestine, as I saw them in the all-Arab town of Gaza or in the Arab sections of Jerusalem and Haifa. The Arab markets of Palestine are clean. The town and village Arab of Palestine is better dressed, healthier looking by far, than the Arab in Egypt, whose usual dress is a dirty, old-fashioned, single-piece garment which is almost an exact replica of the nightshirt grandpa in America used to wear. Passing from Egypt to Palestine one can see for oneself what is testified to in the Peel Royal Commission report on Palestine—that the coming of the Jews has not degraded the Arab but lifted his living standards.

I found myself immensely attracted by the life of the Yishuv, the Jewish community of Palestine. It is the one place in the world where Jews seem completely unafraid. I did not see the displaced persons' camps in Germany, but even in such free countries as England and France—and at home, in the United States—there are premonitory tremors in the Jewish communities, conscious or subconscious fears of the future. In Palestine a Jew can be a Jew. Period. Without apologies, and without any lengthy arguments as to whether Jews are a race, a religion, a myth, or an accident. He need explain to no one, and he feels profoundly at home; I am quite willing to attribute this to historic sentimentality, but it remains none the less a tremendous and inescapable fact.

In the desert, on the barren mountains, in the once malarial marshes of the Emek, the Jew has done and is doing what seemed to reasonable men the impossible. Nowhere in the world have human beings surpassed what the Jewish colonists have accomplished in Palestine, and the consciousness of achievement, the sense of things growing, the exhilarating atmosphere of a great common effort infuses the daily life of the Yishuv. I came away feeling that no obstacles, no setbacks, nothing but perhaps a Third World War and atomic bombs in the Middle East, could stop this people.

It happens that I felt myself painfully impelled to disagree with majority opinion in the Yishuv. I am not in favor of a Jewish state in Palestine. But it would be foolish, and it would be completely to misunderstand how history and human beings work, to disparage Zionism. Only a passionate, narrow, and mystical national faith made it possible for Jews to colonize areas the goats despised. Without the Zionist movement, what has been achieved in Palestine would never have come to pass. The closest parallel in American experience is Puritanism, and Palestine is indeed much like the frontier in our own country, both in colonial times and in the West. But the strength associated with such a movement also has its corresponding defects, and the defects of Zionism are reflected in its failure to take into account the feelings and aspirations of the Palestinian Arab. The Arab has benefited from the Jewish influx, but only indirectly. The Zionist has not hurt him, but the Zionist has made him feel shut out. This exclusiveness is natural and understandable, but it needs to be corrected if the Jews are to build for themselves a secure life in the Middle East.

I understood after seeing Egypt and talking with Christian Arabs in the Lebanon—many of them anti-Zionist only in public—why the Yishuv will fight and has a right to fight against permanent minority status under present conditions in an Arab state. But I also understand why the Palestinian Arabs, to whom Palestine is also home, who has fully as much right there as the Jew, does not wish to live as a minority in a Jewish state. No one likes to be ruled by an alien people, and though I, a Jew, found the friendliest sort of welcome visiting the Arabs, I found no Palestinian Arab in favor of a Jewish state. Relations on the day-to-day level between the two peoples are friendly and quite unlike what one expects. There is no sense of race tension as one feels it in our South or in encounters with anti-Semites in the

Western world. The Arab does not hate the Jew, but he fears being dominated by him, and this fear must be allayed.

In a visit to Amir on the upper Jordan, where the Hadassah was opening
a new health center for Jews and Arabs, I encountered a feeling among the
Arabs that they somehow risked the displeasure of the British governing authorities if they were friendly with the Jews. I found no evidence to support
this suspicion, but I believe that there is much the British could do to improve relations between leaders of the two peoples. I was told that at Haifa
the chief engineer, the leading British civil servant of the municipality, had
done much in a quiet unobtrusive way toward the success of the local government. Haifa's population—and its City Council—is equally divided between Jews and Arabs. The mayoralty was long held by a respected Arab,
succeeded since his death by his deputy, a Jew of Turkish origin. The chief
engineer told me that he could remember no occasion on which a split vote
in the council had not found Jews and Arabs on both sides. Admittedly it is
easier to run a municipality than a nation, but Haifa nevertheless illustrates
the fact that the two races can get along in equal partnership.

The earlier day when Arab nationalist and Zionist could work together,
as they did in the first honeymoon period after the war, came to an end for
two reasons. One was Britain's failure to fulfil the promises made the Arabs
on the basis of which their leaders accepted Zionism for Palestine. The
other was the Jewish demand, first by implication and then explicitly, for a
Jewish state in Palestine. The Jewish State slogan has made political cooperation between Jew and Arab impossible, and left the Jewish homeland completely dependent on British support. The British, feeling that the Jews had
to support the Empire under any circumstances, have more and more made
their concessions to the Arabs. These concessions have been at the expense
of the Yishuv, of French interests, and of the minorities in the Middle East
generally. It is because the Jews understand this and feel deeply the needs of
their homeless brethren in Europe that they have launched the present civil-
disobedience campaign. They scent an attempt to liquidate the Yishuv, and
they scent another cruel Evian farce beneath Bevin's fine talk of finding a
world solution for the Jewish problem. And I must confess that after being
in London, and with all due respect for the good intentions of British Labor, I agree with Palestinian Jewry.

I came away with a great liking and respect for the English people but a great distrust of their officials. I understand the average Englishman's resentment over American interference, and I favor not only American sharing of responsibility but an international solution for the Middle East. British fears of an Arab uprising largely reflect a hobgoblin of their own making; the great powers can impose any solution they choose. I think the equitable solution would be a bi-national state for Palestine and international trusteeship until population parity has been reached between Jews and Arabs. I think the powers must recognize the Arab aspiration for some kind of league or federation and put bi-national Palestine into it, and I think they must then provide some form of international guaranty for the Christian Lebanon, the Jewish community in Palestine, and other minorities in the East, but a guaranty free from the taint of "capitulations" in Egypt, a system of protection much abused both by the imperialist powers and the minorities themselves. A settlement of this kind depends, of course, on whether London and Washington are sincerely concerned with stability in the Middle East or merely with appeasing the Arabs in preparation for a new war against the Soviet Union. I do not speak from surmise when I report that from Ernest Bevin down, the British Foreign Office and the Colonial Office seem to be suffering from an obsession on this score, and the Jews are its principle victims.

A bi-national settlement would provide enough immigration certificates over, say, the next five or ten years—about 650,000—to take care of all Jews who must be given a refuge in Palestine. It would establish a Jewish community strong enough to hold its own in the Arab world. It would end Palestinian Arab fears of a Jewish state. It would genuinely fulfil Britain's obligations to both peoples, and it would lay the basis for a stable and developing order in the Middle East, in which British and world interests in communications and oil could be adequately safeguarded without infringing Arab independence. In that context, if the Jews give one-tenth the devotion to Arab relations that they have given to the land, they can build a secure homeland for themselves among their Semitic brethren. This way, I am deeply convinced, lies the only lasting and equitable solution for Palestine and the Middle East.

The Racist Challenge in Israel

By 1964, the fledgling state of Israel had grown and developed enormously, with a thriving economy and a strong security apparatus. In this travel dispatch, Stone reports the signs of progress—and warns of the seeds of future conflicts in the continuing animosity between Jewish and Arab inhabitants of Israel.

. . .

June 1, 1964

TO SEE ISRAEL AGAIN after eight years is to be struck at every turn by the triumphant evidence of progress. The flood of new immigrants, which has more than tripled its population since the achievement of independence eighteen years ago, is reflected in a continuous building boom. The dismal acres of shanty towns (*ma'abarôth*) hastily erected for new immigrants were still distressingly visible in 1956. Today they have given way (except for a hard-core of 3,000 which still clings to the old hovels) before whole new neighborhoods—and cities—of towering apartment houses. The roads have widened, the traffic jams grown worse. The country throbs with expansive vitality. Israel has become an affluent society. Even in the once Spartan kibbutzim, the outhouse and the cold outside shower have been replaced by private lavatories and running hot water, provided by individual solar heaters. Everywhere there are flowers. Even in Tel Aviv the whole new northern extension of that rather grubby city has become downright pretty with tree-lined boulevards and flower gardens. Not all the changes are to the taste of those who loved the old Palestine. The Dan Hotel in Tel Aviv has become as oversumptuous as its counterparts in Miami. The Desert Inn outside Beer Sheva, no longer a sleepy Bedouin town, might be in luxurious Palm Springs, except for the *mezuzoth* beside every door and the Arab-with-camel on duty at the entrance. The *dolce vita* has arrived, as the old-timers complain, complete with juvenile delinquents and call girls.

The other big change since the spring of 1956 is in the sense of security. Then infiltrating *fedayeen* from Egyptian training centers in the Gaza strip and Sinai were shooting up settlements at night and making travel after dark hazardous. The Sinai campaign later that year may have been a humiliating setback for England and France, but for Israel it put a stop to these terrorist raids, smashed Czech and Soviet arms dumps across the Egyptian border and established a UN force at the narrow straits where Elath's access to the Red Sea had been shut off by Nasser. This much was accomplished, whatever the wisdom of the retaliatory spiral which led up to the Sinai campaign, and its cost in the alienation of Afro-Asian sympathy from Israel.* Today one can travel everywhere with assurance. Unusually heavy rains had turned the country greener and lovelier than we had ever seen it in seven previous trips. Our visit was a succession of unforgettable scenes: Haifa's gleaming harbor from the top of Mt. Carmel, the wide lawns of Mishmar Ha-Emek, the rich green vistas of the once malarial Valley of Israel, the holy places of Nazareth, Tiberius and Safad, lunch on the eastern shores of Lake Galilee at Ein Gev within the shadow of the Syrian border, the mauve hills at twilight which look down on the fertile collectives in that narrow "finger" of Israel which stretches northward between Lebanon and Syria. Later we saw Ashdod, Israel's biggest seaport rising on the dunes where the Philistines once dwelt, and Kiryat Dan, a new complex of factories and farms to the north of Beer Sheva. We saw old friends in kibbutzim like Shoval and Hatzor nearby which were once lonely military outposts and are now thriving centers of rural industry as well as agriculture. Since 1959 the industrial byproducts of the collective settlements equal or surpass their agricultural output. The climax was our climb up those venerable hills to Jerusalem. There one can still step backward in time, and savor ways of life centuries apart. A fashionable crowd takes tea on the veranda of the King David overlooking the walls of the Old City and a few blocks away little boys in ear curls and suspenders rock back and forth over their pious

---

*See Michael Bar-Zohar's *Suez: Ultra Secret,* newly published in Paris, and Simha Flapan's critical article on it in the May issue of *The New Outlook,* a Middle East monthly devoted to Arab-Jewish reconciliation.

schoolbooks in the back-alley yeshivahs of Mea Shearim, keeping alive a medieval universe of orthodox Jewry.

Beneath the prosperous and picturesque surface there are problems grave enough to threaten Israel's future. But for those who have seen the crises of its earlier years it is impossible not to be optimistic. I first saw Palestine November 2, 1945, the day the Haganah began the war against the British by blowing up the watch towers from which they laid in wait for illegal immigrant ships; it seemed hopeless for so small a force to challenge so great an empire. In the spring of 1946 I traveled from Poland to Palestine through the British blockade with illegal immigrants on one of these Jewish Mayflowers. In 1947 I saw the British impose martial law on Tel Aviv in an effort to wipe out the terrorist campaign against them. In 1948 I was a witness to the joint attack of the Arab States on what was then an ill-prepared tiny community of 650,000 Jews.* In 1949 and 1950 I saw the lack of food and the letdown in morale which followed the war and the onset of the Arab blockade. To have seen such odds overcome makes it hard to take too pessimistically the problems of the dynamic, confident and expanding Israel of today.

They are nonetheless serious. The first is fiscal: Israel is living beyond its means. Its rate of economic growth is topped only by Japan's and few countries can match its steep rate of increase in exports. But in 1963 its adverse surplus of imports over exports was still $420 million and in the first quarter of 1964 its trade deficit rose to three times that in the first quarter of 1963. Capital imports have been running ahead of the trade deficit so that the government's cash reserves have been growing. But of total capital imports in 1963 of $500 million, $162 million was in German reparations and restitution payments which will now decline sharply. Israel will soon have to meet the challenge of austerity and better distribution of income. Its affluent society, like America's, has little-seen but wide fringes of poverty. An ostentatious luxury by the rich does not make this more bearable. And there, as in America, the problem of poverty is intensified by color and

---

*In *Underground to Palestine* (1946) I told the story of the illegal trip and in *This Is Israel* (1948) the story of how Israel won its war of independence.

"race." Israel has a double "Negro" problem. The darker Jews from the Orient and North Africa, as well as the Arab minority, suffer from prejudice.

The usual Jewish attitude toward the Arabs is one of contemptuous superiority. Our driver northward was a Jew who had fled from the Nazi advance into Hungary but that did not save him from racist habits. When I suggested that we give a boy a lift, he refused, saying the boy was an Arab. When I asked what was the difference, he said Arabs smelled bad. I said that is what anti-Semites said of us Jews in the outside world but this made no impression. His attitude, it is painful to report, is typical. Israel is a country not only of full employment but of labor shortages. Thousands of Arabs do the menial tasks of Tel Aviv. They find it as hard to obtain decent lodgings as Negroes do in America and for the same reasons; many "pass" as Jews to circumvent prejudice. In Haifa I visited the only secondary school attended by both Jews and Arabs but even there the classes turned out to be separate. The State of Israel has done much in a material way for the Arabs but the sense of humiliation outweighs any improvement. The spectacle fills one with despair. For if Jews, after all their experience of suffering, prove no better once in the majority than the rest of mankind, what hope for a world as torn apart as ours is by tribalism and hate?

More progress is being made in dealing with Israel's other integration problem—that of the Jews from the Orient and Africa. For these—unlike the Arabs—are people Israel wants. That does not save them from being looked down upon. Half the people of Israel are now from countries where Yiddish is unknown. In Israel, for the first time, the tender language of East European ghettoes has become an upper class tongue. The Ashkenazi, the Yiddish-speaking Jews, hold the commanding positions in the community. The Sephardi, or Oriental Jews, speaking Arabic, French or the Old Castilian of the Spain from which they were driven five centuries ago, are the hewers of wood and drawers of water. They make up half the population but their children are only 15 per cent of those in secondary schools and only 5 per cent of those in the university. Their cultural level is lower. They cannot afford to send their children to the higher schools. Discrimination has given them solidarity. "Communal" tickets have begun to appear in local elections, pitting Sephardi against Ashkenazi. The right wing parties are making demagogic appeals to the Oriental Jews. On the other side one Yiddish speaking *meshuganah* has just published a book to prove that the Yiddish-speaking from the West are the only true Jews! The government is trying its best to give preferences to the Orientals where equally qualified. It fears lest Israel run into a situation like that of Belgium where after 150 years the conflict between Walloon and Fleming divides the nation. Fortunately the common language of Hebrew, and the melting pot of school and Army, are available to ease Israel's divisions. Education is seen as the key to amalgamation but education costs money and here we come to Israel's other big headache, that of defense.

The amount spent on defense is a secret but some notion of its magnitude may be gathered from a veiled figure in the budget. This shows that about a third goes for an item called "Security, special budget and reserve." This has been rising. It was less than $300 million or 28.3 per cent of the 1963/64 budget and close to $400 million or 30.9 per cent of the 1964/65 budget. The next largest item was education, but this is less than 8 per cent of the budget. Were the arms race in the Middle East to end, Israel could afford to make secondary education free, too, as elementary education is now. Nothing could do more to develop her human resources and end the rankling inferiority of Oriental Jew and Arab. Another way to measure the impact of the arms race is to notice that "security, special budget and reserve" amounts to more than German reparations, UJA, private gifts and donations of food surpluses put together. If Israel enjoyed real peace, she would no longer be dependent on the bread of charity.

However one looks at it, peace is Israel's overriding problem. It's hard for a poor country to keep up with the Joneses in armament. "In the war for independence," said one of those tireless old-timers who make Israel the dynamic community that it is, "a Spitfire was hot stuff. We could buy one secondhand for £2,000. Now the Mystère costs us $750,000; the Mirage, $1,000,000; the super-Mirage, $1,250,000. But planes and tanks are given to Egypt by the Russians for very little. They gave Nasser fifteen submarines and a flotilla of Komars, swift mosquito boats armed with missiles which can shoot from thirty kilometers offshore. Now we're afraid Egypt may get enriched uranium from Moscow, too." Between Russian aid and German scientists there is a real fear that Egypt may some day be the instrument for a second go at Hitler's "final solution." Khrushchev's visit stirred deep anxiety.

"The Government of Israel regrets," Prime Minister Eshkol told the Knesset pointedly May 20, "that in spite of the Egyptian ruler's aggressive declarations against Israel he receives political support and supplies of arms from sources that generally advocate peace and coexistence." It is tragic that Israel could not have joined its neighbor in rejoicing over so fruitful and historic an achievement as the Aswan Dam. And it was mischief-making demagogy for Khrushchev to join the Arab States in stigmatizing as an imperialist plot the beginnings of the Jordan water scheme which could benefit the whole area. It does no more than put to use millions of precious gallons otherwise wasted in the Dead Sea.

To inflame the Arab-Israeli quarrel is to risk no small conflagration. Eshkol's statement on the eve of his visit to the United States reiterated previous denials that atomic development in Israel was designed for other than peaceful purposes. But doubts persist. There are circles in Israel which see nuclear arms as a necessity for survival. They fear that neo-Nazi German scientists are using Egypt as a proving ground for "unconventional" weapons. The arms race between Egypt and Israel can become the next hot spot in the proliferation of nuclear arms. A committee of distinguished scholars and scientists in Israel have began to agitate for a denuclearized Arab-Israeli area but there is no echo from Egypt, where a police state represses free opinion. Behind the quarrel which is dividing Israel's ruling party, the Mapai—the quarrel between Ben-Gurion and Eshkol over the irrepressible Lavon affair—is a struggle between younger military men who put their faith in force and an Old Guard which wishes to steer a course of moderation away from the apocalyptic adventurism of Ben-Gurion. The Suez affair showed that B.G. and the military were able to carry on secretly behind the back of civilian government. They might do so again. Now is the time to prevent Egypt and Israel from wasting their substance and endangering the world in the blind alley of a nuclear arms race.

Holy War

In the Six-Day War of June, 1967, Israel dealt a dramatic blow to Arab dreams of destroying the country by routing Egyptian, Jordanian, and Syrian armies and tripling their own territory through the seizure of the Gaza Strip, the Sinai Peninsula, the West Bank, and the Golan Heights. In the wake of this Israeli victory, Stone calls for "a reexamination of Zionist ideology" in search of a lasting *modus vivendi* for Jews and Arabs in Palestine—while sardonically acknowledging the seeming hopelessness of the conflict: "If God as some say now is dead, He no doubt died of trying to find an equitable solution to the Arab-Jewish problem."

.   .   .

August 3, 1967

STRIPPED OF PROPAGANDA AND SENTIMENT, the Palestine problem is, simply, the struggle of two different peoples for the same strip of land. For the Jews, the establishment of Israel was a Return, with all the mystical significance the capital R implies. For the Arabs it was another invasion. This has led to three wars between them in twenty years. Each has been a victory for the Jews. With each victory the size of Israel has grown. So has the number of Arab homeless.

Now to find a solution which will satisfy both peoples is like trying to square a circle. In the language of mathematics, the aspirations of the Jews and the Arabs are incommensurable. Their conflicting ambitions cannot be fitted into the confines of any ethical system which transcends the tribalistic. This is what frustrates the benevolent outsider, anxious to satisfy both peoples. For two years Jean-Paul Sartre has been trying to draw Israelis and Arabs into a confrontation in a special number of his review, *Les Temps Modernes*. The third war between them broke out while it was on the press.

This long-awaited special issue on *Le conflit israéloarabe* is the first confrontation in print of Arab and Israeli intellectuals. But it turns out to be

991 pages not so much of dialogue as of dual monologue. The two sets of contributors sit not just in separate rooms, like employers and strikers in a bitter labor dispute, but in separate universes where the simplest fact often turns out to have diametrically opposite meanings. Physics has begun to uncover a new conundrum in the worlds of matter and anti-matter, occupying the same space and time but locked off from each other by their obverse natures, forever twin yet forever sundered. The Israeli-Arab quarrel is the closest analogue in the realm of international politics.

The conditions exacted for the joint appearance of Israelis and Arabs in the same issue of *Les Temps Modernes* excluded not only collaboration but normal editorial mediation or midwifery. Claude Lanzmann, who edited this special issue, explains in his Introduction that the choice of authors and of subjects had to be left "in full sovereignty" (*en toute souveraineté*) to each of the two parties. The Arabs threatened to withdraw if an article was included by A. Razak Abdel-Kader, an Algerian who is an advocate of Israeli-Arab reconciliation. When the Israelis objected that *Les Temps Modernes* at least allow Abdel-Kader to express himself as an individual, the Arabs insisted on an absolute veto: there would be no issue if Abdel-Kader were in it.

In his Preface Jean-Paul Sartre lays bare the conflicting emotions which led him to embark on so difficult a task as to attempt the role—in some degree—of peacemaker between Arab and Israeli. They awaken the memories of his finest hours. One was that of the Resistance. "For all those who went through this experience," M. Sartre writes, "it is unbearable to imagine that another Jewish community, wherever it may be, whatever it may be, should endure this Calvary anew and furnish martyrs to a new massacre." The other was Sartre's aid to the Arabs in their struggle for Algerian independence. These memories bind him to both peoples, and give him the respect of both, as the welcome he received in both Egypt and Israel last year attests. His aim in presenting their views is, he says wistfully, merely to *inform*. His hope is that information in itself will prove pacifying "because it tends more or less slowly to replace passion by knowledge." But the roots of this struggle lie deeper than reason. It is not at all certain that information will replace passion with knowledge.

THE EXPERIENCES FROM WHICH M. Sartre draws his emotional ties are irrelevant to this new struggle. Both sides draw from them conclusions which must horrify the man of rationalist tradition and universalist ideals. The bulk of the Jews and the Israelis draw from the Hitler period the conviction that, in this world, when threatened one must be prepared to kill or be killed. The Arabs draw from the Algerian conflict the conviction that, even in dealing with so rational and civilized a people as the French, liberation was made possible only by resorting to the gun and the knife. Both Israeli and Arabs in other words feel that only force can assure justice. In this they agree, and this sets them on a collision course. For the Jews believe justice requires the recognition of Israel as a fact; for the Arabs, to recognize the fact is to acquiesce in the wrong done them by the conquest of Palestine. If God as some now say is dead, He no doubt died of trying to find an equitable solution to the Arab-Jewish problem.

The argument between them begins with the Bible. "I give this country to your posterity," God said to Abraham (Gen. XV:18) "from the river of Egypt up to the great river, Euphrates." Among the Jews, whether religious or secular mystics, this is the origin of their right to the Promised Land. The opening article in the Arab section of *Les Temps Modernes* retorts that the "posterity" referred to in Genesis includes the descendants of Ishmael since he was the son of Abraham by his concubine Ketirah, and the ancestor of all the Arabs, Christian or Muslim.

All this may seem anachronistic nonsense, but this is an anachronistic quarrel. The Bible is still the best guide to it. Nowhere else can one find a parallel for its enthnocentric fury. Nowhere that I know of is there a word of pity in the Bible for the Canaanites whom the Hebrews slaughtered in taking possession. Of all the nonsense which marks the Jewish-Arab quarrel none is more nonsensical than the talk from both sides about the Holy Land as a symbol of peace. No bit of territory on earth has been soaked in the blood of more battles. Nowhere has religion been so zestful an excuse for fratricidal strife. The Hebrew *shalom* and the Arabic *salaam* are equally shams, relics of a common past as Bedouins. To this day inter-tribal war is the favorite sport of the Bedouins; to announce "peace" in the very first word is a necessity if any chance encounter is not to precipitate bloodshed.

IN BIBLICAL PERSPECTIVE the Jews have been going in and out of Palestine for 3,000 years. They came down from the Euphrates under Abraham;
returned from Egypt under Moses and Joshua; came back again from the
Babylonian captivity and were dispersed again after Jerusalem fell to the
Romans in 70 A.D. This is the third return. The Arabs feel they have a superior claim because they stayed put. This appearance side by side in *Les
Temps Modernes* provides less than the full and undiluted flavor of an ancient sibling rivalry. Both sides have put their better foot forward. The Arab
section includes no sample of the bloodcurdling broadcasts in which the
Arab radios indulge; the Israeli, no contribution from the right-wing Zionists who dream of a greater Israel from the Nile to the Euphrates (as promised in Genesis) with complete indifference to the fate of the Arab
inhabitants. On neither side is there a frank exposition of the *Realpolitik*
which led Arab nationalists like Nasser to see war on Israel as the one way
to achieve Arab unity, and leads Jewish nationalists like Ben Gurion and
Dayan to see Arab disunity and backwardness as essential elements for Israeli security and growth. No voice on the Arab side preaches a Holy War in
which all Israel would be massacred, while no voice on the Israeli side expresses the cheerfully cynical view one may hear in private that Israel has no
realistic alternative but to hand the Arabs a bloody nose every five or ten
years until they accept the loss of Palestine as irreversible.

The picture, however, is not wholly symmetrical. There is first of all the
asymmetry of the victorious and the defeated. The victor is ready to talk
with the defeated if the latter will acquiesce in defeat. The defeated, naturally, is less inclined to this kind of objectivity. The editor, Claude Lanzmann, speaks of an "asymmetry between the two collections of articles
which derives at one and the same time from a radical difference in their
way of looking at the conflict and from the difference in the nature of the
political regimes in the countries involved." Even if not expressly authorized by their governments or organizations to participate, M. Lanzmann explains, all the Arabs except the North Africans wrote only after consultation
and defend a common position, while the Israelis, "as is normal in a West-
ern-style democracy," speak either for themselves or for one of their numerous parties. But this diversity may be exaggerated. On the fundamental
issue which divides the two sides, no Arab contributor is prepared to advo-

cate recognition of the state of Israel, while only one Israeli contributor is prepared to advocate its transformation into something other than a basically Jewish state.

The depth of this nationalistic difference may be measured by what happened to Israel's Communist party. Elsewhere national centrifugal tendencies have made their appearance in the once monolithic world of communism. In Israel the same nationalist tendencies split the Communist party into two, one Jewish, the other Arab. The days when Arab Communists faithfully followed Moscow's line straight into the jails of Egypt, Iraq, Syria, and Jordan by supporting the 1947 partition plan have long passed away. Today Arab and Jewish Communists no longer find common ground.* It would be hard to find an Arab who would agree with Moshe Sneh, head of the Jewish Communist party (Maki) in Israel, when he told *L'Express* (June 19–25), "Our war is just and legitimate. What united the 13 Arab States against us, irrespective of their regime, was not anti-imperialism but pan-Arabism and anti-Jewish chauvinism." He added boldly that Moscow in supporting the Arabs had "turned its back on the politics of the international left and on the spirit of Tashkent." But even Sneh's bitter rival, Meir Vilner, the Jewish leader of, and one of the few Jews left in, the Arab Communist party (Rakka) expresses himself in *Les Temps Modernes* in terms with which no Arab contributor to it agrees. M. Vilner is for the return of all the refugees who wish it, for full equality to Arabs in Israel and for a neutralist policy, but he defends the existence of Israel as a legitimate fact and denies that "one can in any way compare the people (of Israel) to Algerian colons or the Crusaders." The comparisons rejected by the leader of the Arab Communist party in Israel are the favorite comparisons of the Arabs outside Israel. The diversity of viewpoint on the Israeli side thus ends with the basic agreement on its right to exist, and to exist as a Jewish state. This is precisely where the Arab disagreement begins.

The gulf between Arab and Jewish views becomes even clearer when one reads two supplementary pieces contributed by two French Jews, Maxime

*The relative strength of the two since the split may be seen from the fact that the Jewish branch was able to elect only one deputy while the Arab branch, which draws the largest vote among the Arab minority, elected three, two Arabs and one Jew.

Rodinson, a distinguished sociologist and Orientalist, and Robert Misrahi, a well-known writer of the left. The former takes the Arab and the latter the Zionist side. But while M. Misrahi's article appears with the Israelis, M. Rodinson's contribution—by far the most brilliant in the whole volume—appears alone. He refused, for reasons of principle, to appear in the Arab ensemble. It is not hard to see why. For while M. Rodinson gives strong support to every basic Arab historical contention, he is too much the humanist (and in the last analysis no doubt the Jew) to welcome an apocalyptic solution at the expense of Israel's existence. There is still a gulf between M. Rodinson's pro-Arab position and the most moderate view any Arab statesman has yet dared express, that of Tunisia's President Bourguiba. Bourguiba's famous speech in Jericho, March 3, 1965, is reprinted in an appendix by *Les Temps Modernes,* along with an interview he gave *Le Nouvel Observateur* (April 15) a month later. But Bourguiba's speech, though it created a sensation by its relative moderation, merely suggested that the Arabs proceed to regain Palestine as they did Tunisia, by a series of more or less peaceful compromises. When *Le Nouvel Observateur* asked him whether this did not imply the progressive disappearance of the State of Israel, he would not go beyond the cryptic reply, "That is not certain."

The Arab section of the symposium is nevertheless far from being uniform. A Moroccan, Abdallah Larouia, professor of literature in Rabat, not only ends by saying that the possibilities of peaceful settlement must be kept open because a war would settle nothing, but even goes so far as to express the hope that the time may come when a settlement is possible without making a new exile, i.e., of the Israelis, pay for the end of another exile, i.e. of the Arabs from Palestine. He even suggests that under certain conditions, a Jewish community "with or without political authority"—a most daring remark—may prove compatible with Arab progress and development.

WHEN WE EXAMINE THESE CONDITIONS, we come to the heart of the fears expressed by the Arabs in this symposium. The Palestinian Arabs, from the first beginnings of Zionism, foresaw the danger of being swamped and dislodged by Jewish immigration. Neighboring Arab states feared that this immigration would stimulate a continuous territorial expansion at their expense and create a Jewish state powerful enough to dominate the area. The relative size and population of Israel when compared to its Arab neighbors are deceptive and may make these fears seem foolish, but historically the Middle East has often been conquered and dominated by relatively small bands of determined intruders. Even now, as the recent fighting showed, tiny Israel could without difficulty have occupied Damascus, Amman, and Cairo, and—were it not for the big powers and the UN—dictated terms to its Arab neighbors.

It was the attempt of the British to allay Arab apprehension by setting limits on Jewish immigration that precipitated the struggle between the British and the Jews. The 1917 Balfour Declaration, when it promised a "Jewish National Home" in Palestine, also said—in a passage Zionists have always preferred to forget—"that nothing shall be done which may prejudice the civil and religious rights of the existing non-Jewish communities in Palestine." British White Papers in 1922, in 1930, and again in 1939 tried to fulfill this companion pledge by steps which would have kept the Jews a permanent minority. It is this persistent and—as events have shown—justifiable Arab fear which is reflected in M. Laroui's article. In calling the Palestine problem "A Problem of the Occident" his basic point is that if the Occident wipes out anti-Semitism, or keeps it within harmless proportions, making refuge in Israel unnecessary for the bulk of Jewry, and Israel divorces its politics from the Zionist dream of gathering in all the Jews from Exile, this will end the danger of an inexorable expansion in search of "*lebensraum*" at the expense of the Palestinian Arabs, and finally make peace possible between the two peoples. Since immigration into Israel has dwindled in recent years, this Arab fear seems at the moment less a matter of reality than of Zionist theory and of a past experience which leads them to take it seriously.

The suggestion that Israel abandon its supra-nationalist dream finds its only echo on the other side of this collection of essays in Israel's No. 1 maverick and champion of Arab rights, Uri Avnery. Avnery was born in Germany in 1923 and went to Palestine at the age of ten, the year Hitler took power. He began his political career on the far nationalist right, as a member of the Irgun terrorist group in the struggle against the British, but has since swung over to the far left of Israeli opinion, to the point where he is considered anti-nationalist. In the wake of the first Suez war, he supported the Egyptian demand for evacuation of the Canal Zone and in 1959 he formed an Israeli committee to aid the Algerian rebels. At one time he organized a movement which asserted that the Israelis were no longer Jews but "Canaanites" and therefore one with the Arabs, forcibly converted remnants of the same indigenous stock. When this far-out conception attracted few Jews and even fewer Canaanites, he formed a "Semitic Action" movement which has now become "the Movement of New Forces." This polled 1.2 percent of the vote in the 1965 elections and by virtue of proportional representation put Avnery into Parliament. Avnery has been more successful as a publisher. He has made his weekly *Haolam Hazeh* ("This World") the largest in Israel by combining non-conformist politics with what the rather puritanical Israelis call pornography, though that weekly's girlie pictures would seem as old-fashioned as the *Police Gazette* in America.

Avnery writes in *Les Temps Modernes* that he would turn Israel into a secular, pluralist, and multi-national state. He would abolish the Law of Return which gives every Jew the right to enter Israel and automatically become a citizen. Avnery says this pan-Judaism of Zionism feeds the anti-Zionism of pan-Arabism by keeping alive "the myth of an Israel submerged by millions of immigrants who, finding no place to settle, would oblige the government to expand the country by force of arms."

Yet Avnery, who asks Israel to give up its Zionist essence, turns out to be a Jewish nationalist, too. After sketching out a plan for an Arab Palestinian state west of the Jordan, Avnery writes, "The Arabic reader will justly ask at this point, 'And the return of Israel to the limits of the UN plan of 1947?'" Since Israel in the 1947–48 fighting seized about 23 percent more territory than was allotted to it in the 1947 partition plan, this implies a modification of frontiers in favor of the Arab state which was supposed to be linked with it in an economically united Palestine. But to this natural Arab question Avnery replies,* "Frankly we see no possibility of this kind. The Arab armies are already 15 kilometers from Israel's most populous city (Tel Aviv) and at Nathanya are even closer to the sea." The Arabs may feel that Avnery is as unwilling to give up the fruits of conquest as any non-"Canaanite."

---

*Avnery was writing, of course, before the new outbreak of warfare had again changed these borders to Israel's advantage.

Avnery is as reluctant as any conventional Zionist to see his fellow Canaanite too close to Tel Aviv.

It is easy to understand why neither side trusts the other. In any case M.
Sartre's symposium is a confrontation largely of moderates and leftists, and
on neither side do these elements command majority support. Another
complexity is that while in settled societies the left tends to be less nationalistic than the right, in colonial societies the revolutionary left is often more
nationalistic than the native conservative and propertied classes.

THE OVERWHELMING MAJORITY opinion on both sides, even as expressed in a symposium as skewed leftward as this one, shows little tendency
to compromise. The Arabs argue that Israel is a colonialist implantation in
the Middle East, supported from the beginning by imperialist powers; that it
is an enemy of Arab union and progress; that the sufferings of the Jews in the
West were the consequence of an anti-Semitism the Arabs have never shared;
and that there is no reason why the Arabs of Palestine should be displaced
from their homes in recompense for wrongs committed by Hitler Germany.
M. Laroui alone is sympathetic enough to say that if the Jewish National
Home had been established in Uganda, the Arabs who felt compassion for
the sufferings of the Jews of Europe would have shown themselves as uncomprehending of the rights of the Ugandans as the West has been in Palestine. At the other end of the Arab spectrum a fellow Moroccan, a journalist,
Tahar Benziane, ends up in classic anti-Semitism, blaming the Jews themselves, their separatism and their sense of superiority, for the prejudice
against them. Benziane sees the only solution not just in the liquidation of
Israel but in the disappearance of world Jewry through assimilation. His
would indeed be a Final Solution. This bitter and hateful opinion, widespread in the Arab world, explains why Nazism found so ready an echo before the war in the Middle East and Nazi criminals so welcome a refuge in
Egypt. It also disposes of the semantic nonsense that Arabs being Semite
cannot be anti-Semitic!

The Zionist argument is that the Jewish immigration was a return to
the Jewish homeland. Robert Misrahi even goes so far as to argue that the
Jews had an older claim to Palestine than the Arabs since the Jews had
lived there in the ancient kingdom of the Hebrews long before the Hegira

of Mohammed! Misrahi argues the familiar Zionist thesis that their struggle against Britain proves them to be anti-imperialist, that their colonies
are socialist, that their enemies are the feudal elements in the Arab world,
and that the Arab refugees are the moral responsibility of the Arab leaders
since it was on their urging that the Arabs ran away.

There is a good deal of simplistic sophistry in the Zionist case. The whole
earth would have to be reshuffled if claims 2,000 years old to *irredenta* were
suddenly to be allowed. Zionism from its beginning tried to gain its aims by
offering to serve as outpost in the Arab world for one of the great empires.
Herzl sought to win first the Sultan and then the Kaiser by such arguments.
Considerations of imperial strategy finally won the Balfour Declaration from
Britain. The fact that the Jewish community in Palestine afterward fought
the British is no more evidence of its not being a colonial implantation than
similar wars of British colonists against the mother country, from the American Revolution to Rhodesia. In the case of Palestine, as of other such struggles, the Mother Country was assailed because it showed more concern for
the native majority than was palatable to the colonist minority. The argument that the refugees ran away "voluntarily" or because their leaders urged
them to do so until after the fighting was over not only rests on a myth but is
irrelevant. Have refugees no right to return? Have German Jews no right to
recover their properties because they too fled?

THE MYTH THAT THE ARAB REFUGEES fled because the Arab radios
urged them to do so was analyzed by Erskine B. Childers in the London
Spectator May 12, 1961. An examination of British and U.S. radio monitor-
ing records turned up no such appeals; on the contrary there were appeals
and "even orders to the civilians of Palestine, *to stay put.*" The most balanced and humane discussion of the question may be found in Christopher
Sykes's book *Crossroads to Israel: 1917–48* (at pages 350–5). "It can be said
with a high degree of certainty," Mr. Sykes wrote, "that most of the time in
the first half of 1948 the mass exodus was the natural, thoughtless, pitiful
movement of ignorant people who had been badly led and who in the day
of trial found themselves forsaken by their leaders. . . . But if the exodus
was by and large an accident of war in the first stage, in the later stages it
was consciously and mercilessly helped on by Jewish threats and aggression

toward Arab populations. . . . It is to be noted, however, that where the Arabs had leaders who refused to be stampeded into panic flight, the people came to no harm." Jewish terrorism, not only by the Irgun, in such savage massacres as Deir Yassin, but in milder form by the Haganah, itself "encouraged" Arabs to leave areas the Jews wished to take over for strategic or demographic reasons. They tried to make as much of Israel as free of Arabs as possible.

The effort to equate the expulsion of the Arabs from Palestine with the new Jewish immigration out of the Arab countries is not so simple nor so equitable as it is made to appear in Zionist propaganda. The Palestinian Arabs feel about this "swap" as German Jews would if denied restitution on the grounds that they had been "swapped" for German refugees from the Sudetenland. In a sanely conceived settlement, some allowance should equitably be made for Jewish properties left behind in Arab countries. What is objectionable in the simplified version of this question is the idea that Palestinian Arabs whom Israel didn't want should have no objection to being "exchanged" for Arabic Jews it did want. One uprooting cannot morally be equated with the other.

A certain moral imbecility marks all ethnocentric movements. The Others are always either less than human, and thus their interests may be ignored, or more than human, and therefore so dangerous that it is right to destroy them. The latter is the underlying pan-Arab attitude toward the Jews; the former is Zionism's basic attitude toward the Arabs. M. Avnery notes that Herzl in his book *The Jewish State,* which launched the modern Zionist movement, dealt with working hours, housing for workers, and even the national flag but had not one word to say about the Arabs! For the Zionists the Arab was the Invisible Man. Psychologically he was not there. Achad Ha-Am, the Russian Jew who became a great Hebrew philosopher, tried to draw attention as early as 1891 to the fact that Palestine was not an empty territory and that this posed problems. But as little attention was paid to him as was later accorded his successors in "spiritual Zionism," men like Buber and Judah Magnes, who tried to preach *Ichud,* "unity," i.e., with the Arabs. Of all the formulas with which Zionism comforted itself none was more false and more enduring than Israel Zangwill's phrase about "a land without people for a people without a land." Buber related that Max

Nordau, hearing for the first time that there was an Arab population in Palestine, ran to Herzl crying, "I didn't know that—but then we are committing an injustice." R. J. Zwi Werblowsky, dean of the faculty of letters at the Hebrew University, in the first article of this anthology's Israeli section, writes with admirable objectivity, "There can be no doubt that if Nordau's reaction had been more general, it would seriously have paralyzed the *élan* of the Zionist movement." It took refuge, he writes, in "a moral myopia."

This moral myopia makes it possible for Zionists to dwell on the 1,900 years of Exile in which Jews have longed for Palestine but dismiss as nugatory the nineteen years in which Arab refugees have also longed for it. "Homelessness" is the major theme of Zionism, but this pathetic passion is denied to Arab refugees. Even Meir Yaari, the head of Mapam, the leader of the "Marxist" Zionists of Hashomer Hatzair, who long preached bi-nationalism, says Israel can only accept a minority of the Arab refugees because the essential reason for the creation of Israel was to "welcome the mass of immigrant Jews returning to their historic fatherland!" If there is not room enough for both, the Jews must have precedence. This is what leads Gabran Majdalany, a Baath Socialist, to write that Israel is "a racist state founded from its start on discrimination between Jew and non-Jew." He compares the Zionists to the Muslim Brotherhood who "dream of a Muslim Israel in which the non-Muslims will be the gentiles, second-class citizens sometimes tolerated but more often repressed." It is painful to hear his bitter reproach—

> Some people admit the inevitably racist character of Israel but justify it by the continual persecutions to which the Jews have been subjected during the history of Europe and by the massacres of the Second World War. We consider that, far from serving as justification, these facts constitute an aggravating circumstance; for those who have known the effects of racism and of discrimination in their own flesh and human dignity, are less excusably racist than those who can only imagine the negative effects of prejudice.

When Israel's Defense Minister, Moshe Dayan, was on *Face the Nation* June 11, after Israel's latest victories, this colloquy occurred:

SYDNEY GRUSON (*New York Times*): Is there any possible way that Israel could absorb the huge number of Arabs whose territory it has gained control of now?

GEN. DAYAN: Economically we can; but I think that is not in accord with our aims in the future. It would turn Israel into either a bi-national or poly-Arab-Jewish state instead of the Jewish state, and we want to have a Jewish state. We can absorb them, but then it won't be the same country.

MR. GRUSON: And it is necessary in your opinion to maintain this as a Jewish state and purely a Jewish state?

GEN. DAYAN: Absolutely—absolutely. We want a Jewish state like the French have a French state.

This must deeply disturb the thoughtful Jewish reader. Ferdinand and Isabella in expelling the Jews and Moors from Spain were in the same way saying they wanted a Spain as "Spanish," (i.e., Christian) as France was French. It is not hard to recall more recent parallels.

It is a pity the editors of *Les Temps Modernes* didn't widen their symposium to include a Jewish as distinct from an Israeli point of view. For Israel is creating a kind of moral schizophrenia in world Jewry. In the outside world the welfare of Jewry depends on the maintenance of secular, non-racial, pluralistic societies. In Israel, Jewry finds itself defending a society in which mixed marriages cannot be legalized, in which non-Jews have a lesser status than Jews, and in which the ideal is racial and exclusionist. Jews must fight elsewhere for their very security and existence—against principles and practices they find themselves defending in Israel. Those from the outside world, even in their moments of greatest enthusiasm amid Israel's accomplishments, feel twinges of claustrophobia, not just geographical but spiritual. Those caught up in Prophetic fervor soon begin to feel that the light they hoped to see out of Zion is only that of another narrow nationalism.

Such moments lead to a reexamination of Zionist ideology. That longing for Zion on which it is predicated may be exaggerated. Its reality is indisputable but its strength can easily be overestimated. Not until after World War II was it ever strong enough to attract more than a trickle of Jews to the Holy Land. By the tragic dialectic of history, Israel would not have been born without Hitler. It took the murder of six million in his human ovens to awaken sufficient nationalist zeal in Jewry and sufficient humanitarian compassion in the West to bring a Jewish state to birth in Palestine. Even then humanitarian compassion was not strong enough to open the gates of the West to Jewish immigration in contrition. The capitalist West and the Communist East preferred to displace Arabs rather than to welcome the Jewish "displaced persons" in Europe's postwar refugee camps.

It must also be recognized, despite Zionist ideology, that the periods of greatest Jewish creative accomplishment have been associated with pluralistic civilizations in their time of expansion and tolerance: in the Hellenistic period, in the Arab civilization of North Africa and Spain, and in Western Europe and America. Universal values can only be the fruit of a universal vision; the greatness of the Prophets lay in their overcoming of ethnocentricity. A Lilliputian nationalism cannot distill truths for all mankind. Here lie the roots of a growing divergence between Jew and Israeli; the former with a sense of mission as a Witness in the human wilderness, the latter concerned only with his own tribe's welfare.

But Jewry can no more turn its back on Israel than Israel on Jewry. The ideal solution would allow the Jews to make their contributions as citizens in the diverse societies and nations which are their homes while Israel finds acceptance as a Jewish State in a renascent Arab civilization. This would end Arab fears of a huge inflow to Israel. The Jews have as much reason to be apprehensive about that prospect as the Arabs.

It can only come as the result of a sharp recrudescence in persecution elsewhere in the world. Zionism grows on Jewish catastrophe. Even now it casts longing eyes on Russian Jewry. But would it not be better, more humanizing, and more just, were the Soviet Union to wipe out anti-Semitism and to accord its Jews the same rights of cultural autonomy and expression it gives all its other nationalities? The Russian Jews have fought for Russia, bled for the Revolution, made no small contribution to Russian literature and thought; why should they be cast out? This would be a spiritual catastrophe for Russia as well as Jewry even though it would supply another flow of desperate refugees to an Israel already short of Jews if it is to expand as the Zionist militants hope to expand it.

ISRAEL HAS DEPRIVED anti-Semitism of its mystique. For the visitor to Israel, anti-Semitism no longer seems a mysterious anomaly but only another variant of minority-majority friction. *Es is schwer zu sein eid Yid* ("It's hard to be a Jew") was the title of Sholom Aleichem's most famous story. Now we see that it's hard to be a goy in Tel Aviv, especially an Arab goy. Mohammad Watad, a Muslim Israeli, one of the five Arabic contributors to the Israeli side of this symposium, begins his essay with words which startingly resemble the hostile dialogue Jews encounter elsewhere. "I am often asked," he writes, "about my 'double' life which is at one and the same time that of an Arab and that of an Israeli citizen." Another Arab contributor from Israel, Ibrahim Shabath, a Christian who teaches Hebrew in Arabic schools and is editor-in-chief of *Al Mirsad,* the Mapam paper in Arabic, deplores the fact that nineteen years after the creation of Israel "the Arabs are still considered strangers by the Jews." He relates a recent conversation with Ben Gurion. "You must know," Ben Gurion told him, "that Israel is the country of the Jews and only of the Jews. Every Arab who lives here has the same rights as any minority citizen in any country of the world, but he must admit the fact that he lives in a Jewish country." The implications must chill Jews in the outside world.

The Arab citizen of Israel, Shabath complains, "is the victim today of the same prejudices and the same generalizations as the Jewish people elsewhere." The bitterest account of what they undergo may be found in an anonymous report sent to the United Nations in 1964 by a group of Arabs who tried unsuccessfully to found an independent Socialist Arab movement and publication. Military authorities, despite a Supreme Court order, refused to permit this, and the courts declined to overrule the military. Their petition is reprinted in the Israeli section of this symposium. Though the military rule complained of was abolished last year, and police regulations substituted, it is too soon—especially because of the new outbreak of warfare—to determine what the effect will be on Arab civil liberties. Israelis admit with pleasure that neither in the Christian villages of Central Galilee nor in the Muslim villages of the so-called "Triangle" was there the slightest evidence of any Fifth Column activity. Those Israelis who have fought for an end of all discrimination against the Arabs argue that they have demonstrated their loyalty and deserve fully to be trusted.

IT IS TO ISRAEL'S CREDIT that the Arab minority is given place in its section to voice these complaints while no similar place is opened for ethnic minority opinion in the Arabic section. Indeed except for Lebanon and to some degree Tunisia there is no place in the Arab world where the dissident of any kind enjoys freedom of the press. There is no frank discussion of this in the Arab section. One of the most vigorous and acute expositions of the Arab point of view, for example, is an article by an Egyptian writer, Lotfallah Soliman, who has played a distinguished role in bringing modern ideas to the young intellectuals of his country since World War II. His autobiographical sketch says cryptically, if discreetly, "He lives presently in Paris." I stumbled on a more candid explanation. In preparing for this review, I read an earlier article in *Les Temps Modernes* (August–September 1960) by Adel Montasser on *La répression anti-démocratique en Égypte*. Appended to it was a list of intellectuals imprisoned by Nasser. Among them was Lotfallah Soliman. Obviously it's hard to be a free Egyptian intellectual in Nasser's Egypt. Many of those then imprisoned have since been freed, but it is significant that a writer as trenchant and devoted as Soliman has to work in exile.

It is true that the full roster of Arab minority complaints in Israel had to be presented anonymously for fear of the authorities. But in the Arab section of this book no place was allowed even anonymously for the Jewish and the various Christian minorities to voice their complaints. As a result the Arab contributors were able to write as if their countries, unlike Europe, were models of tolerance. They hark back to the great days of Arabic Spain where (except for certain interludes not mentioned) Christian and Jew enjoyed full equality, religious, cultural, and political, with the Muslim: Spain did not become synonymous with intolerance, Inquisition, and obscurantism until the Christian Reconquest. But today no Arab country except, precariously, Lebanon, dimly resembles Moorish Spain. As a result the Jews from the Arabic countries tend to hate the Arab far more than Jews from Europe who have never lived under his rule, which often recalls medieval Christiandom. A glimpse of these realities may be found in the most moving article in this whole symposium. This is by Attalah Mansour, a young

Christian Arabic Israeli novelist of peasant origin who has published two novels, one in Arabic and the other in Hebrew, and worked as a journalist on Avnery's paper *Haolam Hazeh* and on the staff of *Haaretz,* Israel's best and most objective daily paper. M. Mansour knows doubly what it is to be a "Jew." He is as an Arab a "Jew" to the Israelis and as a Christian a "Jew" to the Muslims. He tells a touching story of an accidental encounter in (of all places) the Paris Metro with a young man who turned out like him to be Greek-rite Christian though from Egypt. They exchanged stories of their troubles, like two Jews in the Diaspora. "We in Egypt," the young stranger told him, "have the same feelings as you. There is no law discriminating between us and the Muslims. But the governmental administration, at least on the everyday level, prefers Mahmoud to Boulos and Achmed to Samaan"—i.e. the man with the Muslim name to the man with the Christian. "Omar Sharif, the well-known movie actor," the Egyptian Christian added, "is Christian in origin. But he had to change his Christian name for a Muslim to please the public." In Israel, similarly, Ibrahim often becomes Abraham to pass as a Jew and to avoid widespread housing discrimination.

If in this account I have given more space to the Arab than the Israeli side it is because as a Jew, closely bound emotionally with the birth of Israel,* I feel honor bound to report the Arab side, especially since the U.S. press is so overwhelmingly pro-Zionist. For me, the Arab-Jewish struggle is a tragedy. The essence of tragedy is a struggle of right against right. Its catharsis is the cleansing pity of seeing how good men do evil despite themselves out of unavoidable circumstance and irresistible compulsion. When evil men do evil, their deeds belong to the realm of pathology. But when good men do evil, we confront the essence of human tragedy. In a tragic struggle, the victors become the guilty and must make amends to the defeated. For me the Arab problem is also the No. 1 Jewish problem. How we

---

*I first arrived in Palestine on Balfour Day Nov. 2, 1945, the day the Haganah blew up bridges and watch towers to begin its struggle against the British and immigration restrictions. The following spring I was the first newspaperman to travel with illegal Jewish immigrants from the Polish-Czech border through the British blockade. In 1947 I celebrated Passover in the British detention camps in Cyprus and in 1948 I covered the Arab-Jewish war. See my *Underground to Palestine* (1946) and *This is Israel* (1948). I was back in 1949, 1950, 1951, 1956, and 1964.

act toward the Arabs will determine what kind of people we become: either oppressors and racists in our turn like those from whom we have suffered, or a nobler race able to transcend the tribal xenophobias that afflict mankind.*

Israel's swift and extraordinary victories have suddenly transmuted this ideal from the realm of impractical sentiment to urgent necessity. The new frontiers of military conquest have gathered in most of the Arab refugees. Zionism's dream, the "ingathering of the exiles," has been achieved, though in an ironic form; it is the Arab exiles who are back. They cannot be gotten rid of as easily as in 1948. Something in the order of 100,000 have again been "encouraged" to leave, but the impact on public opinion abroad and in Israel has forced the state to declare that it will allow them to return. While the UN proves impotent to settle the conflict and the Arab powers are unwilling to negotiate from a situation of weakness, Israel can to some degree determine its future by the way in which it treats its new Arab subjects or citizens. The wrangles of the powers will go on for months, but these people must be fed, clothed, and housed. How they are treated will change the world's picture of Israel and of Jewry, soften or intensify Arab anger, build a bridge to peace or make new war certain. To establish an Arab state on the West Bank and to link it with Israel, perhaps also with Jordan, in a Confederation would turn these Arab neighbors, if fraternally treated, from enemies into a buffer, and give Israel the protection of strategic frontiers. But it would be better to give the West Bank back to Jordan than to try to create a puppet state—a kind of Arab Bantustan—consigning the Arabs to second-class status under Israel's control. This would only foster Arab resentment. To avoid giving the Arabs first-

---

*In September [1967], Black Star will publish a vigorous little book *The Aryanization of the Jewish State,* by Michael Selzer, a young Pakistani Jew who lived in Israel. It may help Jewry and Israel to understand that the way to a fraternal life with the Arabs inside and outside Israel must begin with the eradication of the prejudices that greet the Oriental and Arabic-speaking Jews in Israel who now make up over half the population of the country. The bias against the Arab extends to a bias against the Jews from the Arab countries. In this, as in so many other respects, Israel presents in miniature all the problems of the outside world. Were the rest of the planet to disappear, Israel could regenerate from itself—as from a new Ark—all the bigotries, follies, and feuds of a vanished mankind (as well as some of its most splended accomplishments).

class citizenship by putting them in the reservation of a second-class state is too transparently clever.

What is required in the treatment of the Arab refugees Israel has gathered in is the conquest both of Jewish exclusivism and the resentful hostility of the Arabs. Even the malarial marshes of the Emek and the sandy wastes of the Negev could not have looked more bleakly forbidding to earlier generations of Zionist pioneers than these steep and arid mountains of prejudice. But I for one have a glimmer of hope. Every year I have gone to Palestine and later Israel I have found situations which seemed impossible. Yet Zionist zeal and intelligence overcame them. Perhaps this extraordinarily dynamic, progressive, and devoted community can even if need be transcend its essential self.

I WAS ENCOURAGED TO FIND in this volume that the most objective view of the Arab question on the Israeli side was written by Yehudah Harkabi, a Haifa-born professional soldier, a brigadier general, but a general who holds a diploma in philosophy and Arabic studies from the Hebrew University and from Harvard. He has written a book on *Nuclear War and Nuclear Peace.* His article "Hawks or Doves" is extraordinary in its ability to rise above prejudice and sentiment. He does not shut his eyes at all to the Arab case. He feels peace can come only if we have the strength to confront its full human reality. "Marx affirms," he concludes, "that knowledge of the truth frees man from the determinism of history." It is only, General Harkabi says, when Israel is prepared "to accept the truth in its entirety that it will find the new strength necessary to maintain and consolidate its existence." The path to safety and the path to greatness lies in reconciliation. The other route, now that the West Bank and Gaza are under Israeli jurisdiction, leads to two new perils. The Arab populations now in the conquered territories make guerrilla war possible within Israel's own boundaries. And externally, if enmity deepens and tension rises between Israel and the Arab states, both sides will by one means or another obtain nuclear weapons for the next round.

This will change the whole situation. No longer will Israeli and Arab be able to play the game of war in anachronistic fashion as an extension of politics by other means. Neither will they be able to depend on a mutual balance of terror like the great powers with their "second-strike" capacity. In this pygmy struggle the first strike will determine the outcome and leave nothing behind. Nor will the great powers be able to stand aside and let their satellites play out their little war, as in 1948, 1956, and 1967. I have not dwelt here on the responsibility of the great powers, because if they did not exist the essential differences in the Arab-Israeli quarrel would still remain, and because both sides use the great power question as an excuse to ignore their own responsibilities. The problem for the new generation of Arabs is the social reconstruction of their decayed societies; the problem will not go away if Israel disappears. Indeed their task is made more difficult by the failure to recognize Israel, since that means a continued emphasis on militarization, diversion of resources, and domination by military men. For Israel, the problem is reconciliation with the Arabs; the problem will not go away even if Moscow and Washington lie down together like the lion and the lamb or blow each other to bits. But the great powers for their part cannot continue the cynical game of arming both sides in a struggle for influence when the nuclear stage is reached. It is significant that the one place where the Israeli and Arab contributors to this symposium tend to common conclusions is in the essays discussing the common nuclear danger. To denuclearize the Middle East, to defuse it, will require some kind of neutralization. Otherwise the Arab-Israeli conflict may some day set off a wider final solution. That irascible Old Testament God of Vengeance is fully capable, if provoked, of turning the whole planet into a crematorium.

Part Six

A WAR MADE OF LIES

What Few Know About the
Tonkin Bay Incidents

On August 4, 1964, President Lyndon Johnson spoke on national television, asking Congress for authorization to use force in Vietnam in response to a claimed
"unprovoked attack" against a U.S. destroyer on "routine patrol" in the Tonkin
Gulf on August 2, followed by a "deliberate attack" by North Vietnamese PT
boats on a pair of U.S. ships two days later. Three days later, the Gulf of Tonkin
Resolution was passed by Congress, unanimously by the House (416–0), and by
the Senate 88–2, with Senators Wayne Morse of Oregon and Ernest Gruening of
Alaska casting the only dissenting votes. That resolution was the slender reed on
which the subsequent vast escalation of the war was built. Here I. F. Stone offers
one of the first investigative reports into the omissions and deceptions in mainstream reporting of the Tonkin Gulf incidents.

.   .   .

August 24, 1964

THE AMERICAN GOVERNMENT and the American press have kept the
full truth about the Tonkin Bay incidents from the American public. Let us
begin with the retaliatory bombing raids on North Vietnam. When I went to
New York to cover the UN Security Council debate on the affair, UN correspondents at lunch recalled cynically that four months earlier Adlai Stevenson
told the Security Council the U.S. had "repeatedly expressed" its emphatic
disapproval "of retaliatory raids, wherever they occur and by whomever they
are committed." But none mentioned this in their dispatches.

On that occasion, last April, the complaint was brought by Yemen
against Britain. The British, in retaliation for attacks from Yemen into the
British protectorate of Aden, decided to strike at the "privileged sanctuary"
from which the raids were coming. The debate then might have been a preview of the Vietnamese affair. The British argued that their reprisal raid was

247

justified because the fort they attacked at Harib was "a center for subversive and aggressive activities across the border." The Yemeni Republicans in turn accused the British of supporting raids into Yemen by the Yemeni Royalists. "Obviously," Stevenson said, "it is most difficult to determine precisely what has been happening on the remote frontiers of Southern Arabia." But he thought all UN members could "join in expressing our disapproval of the use of force by either side as a means of solving disputes, a principle that is enshrined in the Charter," especially when such "attacks across borders" could "quickly escalate into full-scale wars." The outcome was a resolution condemning "reprisals as incompatible with the purposes and principles of the United Nations." That resolution and Stevenson's words are as applicable to Southeast Asia as to Southern Arabia. Though the Czech delegate cited them in his speech to the Council on August 7 about the Vietnamese affair, no word of this appeared in the papers next day.

In the August 7 debate, only Nationalist China and Britain supported the U.S. reprisal raids. The French privately recalled the international uproar over the raid they had made under similar circumstances in February, 1958, into the "privileged sanctuary" afforded the Algerian rebels by Tunisia. They struck at the Sakiet-Sidi-Youssef camp just across the border. Senators Kennedy, Humphrey, Morse and Knowland denounced the raid and Eisenhower warned the French the U.S. would not be able to defend their action in the Security Council.

Reprisals in peacetime were supposed to have been outlawed by the League of Nations Covenant, the Kellogg Pact and the United Nations Charter. All of them pledged peaceful settlement of disputes. Between nations, as between men, reprisals are lynch law. Some White House ghost writer deserves a literary booby prize for the mindless jingle he turned out to defend ours in Vietnam. "The world remembers, the world must never forget," were the words he supplied for Johnson's speech at Syracuse, "that aggression unchallenged is aggression unleashed." This gem of prose is a pretty babble. What the world (and particularly the White House) needs to remember is that aggression is unleashed and escalated when one party to a dispute decides for itself who is guilty and how he is to be punished. This is what is happening in Cyprus, where we have been begging Greeks and Turks to desist from the murderous escalation of reprisal and counter-reprisal. Johnson practices in Southeast Asia what he deplores in the Mediterranean.

Public awareness of this is essential because the tide is running strongly toward more reprisal raids in the Far East. The first was the raid by U.S. Navy planes in June on Pathet Lao headquarters in Laos in retaliation for shooting down two reconnaissance planes. We would not hesitate to shoot down reconnaissance planes over our own territory; such overflights are a clear violation of international law. But the U.S. now seems to operate on the principle that invasion of other people's skies is our right, and efforts to interfere with it (at least by weaker powers) punishable by reprisal. This is pure "might is right" doctrine.

The very day we took the Vietnamese affair to the Security Council, Cambodia illustrated a sardonic point to be found in Schwarzenberger's *Manual of International Law*—"military reprisals are open only to the strong against the weak." The UN distributed to Security Council members the latest in a series of complaints from Cambodia that U.S. and South Vietnamese forces had been violating its borders. It alleged that at dawn on July 31 "elements of the armed forces of the Republic of Vietnam, among them Americans in uniform," opened fire "with automatic weapons and mortars," seriously wounding a peasant and killing a bull. If Cambodia could only afford a fleet large enough, we suppose it would be justified by Johnsonian standards in lobbing a few shells into the U.S.A.

Even in wartime, reprisals are supposed to be kept within narrow limits. Hackworth's *Digest*, the State Department's huge Talmud of international law, quotes an old War Department manual, *Rules of Land Warfare*, as authoritative on the subject. This says reprisals are never to be taken "merely for revenge" but "only as an unavoidable last resort" to "enforce the recognized rules of civilized warfare." Even then reprisals "should not be excessive or exceed the degree of violence committed by the enemy." These were the principles we applied at the Nuremberg trials. Our reprisal raids on North Vietnam hardly conformed to these standards. By our own account, in self-defense, we had already sunk three or four attacking torpedo boats in two incidents. In neither were our ships damaged nor any of our men hurt; indeed, one bullet imbedded in one destroyer hull is the only proof we have been able to muster that the second of the attacks even took place. To fly sixty-four bombing sorties in reprisal over four North Vietnamese bases and an oil depot, destroying or damaging twenty-five North Vietnamese PT boats, a major part of that tiny navy, was hardly punishment to fit the crime. What was our hurry? Why did we have to shoot from the hip and then go to the Security Council? Who was Johnson trying to impress? Ho Chi Minh? Or Barry Goldwater?

This is how it looks on the basis of our own public accounts. It looks worse if one probes behind them. Here we come to the questions raised by Morse of Oregon on the Senate floor August 5 and 6 during debate on the resolution giving Johnson a pre-dated declaration of war in Southeast Asia. Morse was speaking on the basis of information given in executive session by Secretaries Rusk and McNamara to a joint session of the Senate Committee on Foreign Relations and Armed Services. Morse said he was not justifying the attacks on U.S. ships in the Bay of Tonkin but "as in domestic criminal law," he added, "crimes are sometimes committed under provocation" and this "is taken into account by a wise judge in imposing sentence."

Morse revealed that U.S. warships were on patrol in Tonkin Bay nearby during the shelling of two islands off the North Vietnamese coast on Friday, July 31, by South Vietnamese vessels. Morse said our warships were within three to eleven miles of North Vietnamese territory, at the time, although North Vietnam claims a twelve-mile limit. Morse declared that the U.S. "knew that the bombing was going to take place." He noted that General Khanh had been demanding escalation of the war to the North and said that with this shelling of the islands it was escalated. Morse declared the attack was made "by South Vietnamese naval vessels—not by junks but by armed vessels of the PT boat type" given to South Vietnam as part of U.S. military aid. Morse said it was not just another attempt to infiltrate agents but "a well thought-out military operation." Morse charged that the presence of our warships in the proximity "where they could have given protection, if it became necessary" was "bound to be looked upon by our enemies as an act of provocation." The press, which dropped an Iron Curtain weeks ago on the anti-war speeches of Morse and Gruening, ignored this one, too.

Yet a reading of the debate will show that Fulbright and Russell, the chairmen of the two committees Rusk and McNamara had briefed in secret session, did not deny Morse's facts in their defense of the Administration and did not meet the issue he raised. Fulbright's replies to questions were hardly a model of frankness. When Ellender of Louisiana asked him at whose request we were patrolling in the Bay of Tonkin, Fulbright replied:

> These are international waters. Our assistance to South Vietnam is at the request of the South Vietnamese government. The particular measures we may take in connection with that request is our own responsibility.

Senator Nelson of Wisconsin wanted to know how close to the shore our ships had been patrolling:

> MR. FULBRIGHT: It was testified that they went in at least eleven miles in order to show that we do not recognize a twelve-mile limit, which I believe North Vietnam has asserted.
>
> MR. NELSON: The patrolling was for the purpose of demonstrating to the North Vietnamese that we did not recognize a twelve-mile limit?
>
> MR. FULBRIGHT: That was one reason given . . .
>
> MR. NELSON: It would be mighty risky if Cuban PT boats were firing on Florida, for Russian armed ships or destroyers to be patrolling between us and Cuba, eleven miles out.

When Ellender asked whether our warships were there to protect the South Vietnamese vessels shelling the islands, Fulbright replied:

> The ships were not assigned to protect anyone. They were conducting patrol duty. The question was asked specifically of the highest authority, the Secretary of Defense and the Secretary of State. They stated without equivocation that these ships, the *Maddox* and the *C. Turner Joy*, were not on convoy duty. They had no connection whatever with any Vietnamese ships that might have been operating in the same general area.

Fulbright did not deny that both destroyers were in the area at the time of the July 31 shelling and inside the territorial limits claimed by North Vietnam. He did not deny Morse's charge that the U.S. knew about the shelling of the islands before it took place. He merely denied that the warships were there to cover the operation in any way. Our warships, according to the official account, just happened to be hanging around. Morse's point—which neither Fulbright nor Russell challenged—was that they had no business to be in an area where an attack was about to take place, that this was bound to appear provocative. Indeed the only rational explanation for their presence at the time was that the Navy was looking for trouble, daring the North Vietnamese to do something about it.

Morse made another disclosure. "I think I violate no privilege or secrecy," he declared, "if I say that subsequent to the bombing, and apparently because there was some concern about the intelligence that we were getting, our ships took out to sea." Was this intelligence that the ships were about to be attacked within the territorial waters claimed by North Vietnam? Morse said our warships went out to sea and "finally, on Sunday, the PT boats were close enough for the first engagement to take place." This dovetails with a curious answer given by Senator Russell at another point in the debate to Senator Scott of Pennsylvania when the latter asked whether Communist China had not published a series of warnings (as required by international law) against violations of the twelve-mile limit. Russell confirmed this but said, "I might add that our vessels had turned away from the North Vietnamese shore and were making for the middle of the gulf, *where there could be no question,* at the time they were attacked."

The italics are ours and call attention to an evident uneasiness about our legal position. The uneasiness is justified. A great many questions of international law are raised by the presence of our warships within an area claimed by another country as its territorial waters while its shores were being shelled by ships we supplied to a satellite power. There is, first of all, some doubt as to whether warships have a right of "innocent passage" through territorial waters even under peaceful circumstances. There is, secondly, the whole question of territorial limits. The three-mile limit was set some centuries ago by the range of a cannon shot. It has long been obsolete but is favored by nations with large navies. We make the three-mile limit the norm when it suits our purposes but widen it when we need to. We claim another 9 miles as "contiguous waters" in which we can enforce our laws on foreign ships. While our planes on reconnaissance operate three miles off other people's shores, we enforce an Air Defense Identification Zone on our own coasts, requiring all planes to identify themselves when two hours out. In any case, defense actions may be taken beyond territorial limits. The law as cited in the U. S. Naval Academy's handbook, *International Law for Sea-Going Officers,* is that "the right of a nation to protect itself from injury" is "not restrained to territorial limits. . . . It may watch its coast and seize ships that are approaching it with an intention to violate its laws. It is not obliged to wait until the offense is consummated before it can act."

More important in this case is the doctrine of "hot pursuit." The North Vietnamese radio claims that in the first attack it chased the U.S. warships away from its shores. "The right of hot pursuit," says Schwarzenberger's *Manual of International Law,* "is the right to continue the pursuit of a ship from the territorial sea into the high sea." The logic of this, our Naval Academy handbook explains, is that "the offender should not go free simply because of the proximity of the high seas." It is easy to imagine how fully these questions would be aired if we spotted Russian ships hanging around in our waters while Cuban PT boats shelled Key West. Our actions hardly fit Johnson's description of himself to the American Bar Association as a champion of world law.

There are reasons to believe that the raids at the end of July marked a new step-up in the scale of South Vietnamese operations against the North. These have been going on for some time. In fact, a detailed account in *Le Monde* (August 7) says they began three years before the rebellion broke out in South Vietnam. Ever since January of this year the U.S. press has been full of reports that we were planning to move from infiltration and commando operations to overt attacks against the North. *Newsweek* (March 9) discussed a "Rostow Plan No. 6" for a naval blockade of Haiphong, North Vietnam's main port, to be followed by PT boat raids on North Vietnamese coastal installations and then by strategic bombing raids. In the middle of July the North Vietnamese radio reported that the U.S. had given South

Vietnam 500 "river landing ships" and four small warships from our mine sweeping fleet. A dispatch from Hong Kong in the *New York Times* (August 14) quoted an "informed source" as saying that the North Vietnamese had concealed the fact "that the shelling of the islands" on July 31 "had been directed at a sensitive radar installation." The shelling of radar installations would look from the other side like a prelude to a landing attempt.

These circumstances cast a very different light on the *Maddox* affair, but very few Americans are aware of them. The process of brain-washing the public starts with off-the-record briefings for newspapermen in which all sorts of far-fetched theories are suggested to explain why the tiny North Vietnamese navy would be mad enough to venture an attack on the Seventh Fleet, one of the world's most powerful. *Everything is discussed except the possibility that the attack might have been provoked.* In this case the "information agencies," i.e. the propaganda apparatus of the government, handed out two versions, one for domestic, the other for foreign consumption. The image created at home was that the U.S. had manfully hit back at an unprovoked attack—no paper tiger we. On the other hand, friendly foreign diplomats were told that the South Vietnamese had pulled a raid on the coast and we had been forced to back them up. As some of the truth began to trickle out, the information agencies fell back on the theory that maybe the North Vietnamese had "miscalculated." That our warships may have been providing cover for an escalation in raiding activities never got through to public consciousness at all.

The two attacks themselves are still shrouded in mystery. The *Maddox* claims to have fired three warning shots across the bow of her pursuers; three warning shots are used to make a merchantman heave-to for inspection. A warship would take this as the opening of fire, not as a warning signal. The North Vietnamese radio admitted the first encounter but claimed its patrol boats chased the *Maddox* out of territorial waters. The second alleged attack North Vietnam calls a fabrication. It is strange that though we claim three boats sunk, we picked up no flotsam and jetsam as proof from the wreckage. Nor have any pictures been provided. Whatever the true story, the second incident seems to have triggered off a long planned attack of our own. There are some reasons to doubt that it was merely that "measured response" against PT bases it was advertised to be. Bernard Fall, author of *The Two Viet-Nams,* who knows the area well, pointed out in the *Washington Post* August 9 that "none of the targets attacked" in the reprisal raids "was previously known as a regular port or base area. Hon-Gay, for example, was one of the largest open-pit coal mining operations in Asia, if not the world." Was this one of the strategic industrial targets in Rostow's "Plan No. 6"?

Lyndon Johnson Lets
the Office Boy Declare War

As I. F. Stone evidently surmised, it is probably not a good sign when U.S. involvement in a new ground war in Asia is announced apparently off-handedly during a routine briefing by a State Department press officer. Stone was unfortunately prescient when he penned the last two sentences of this article about Vietnam: "One thing alone is certain. The further we get in, the harder it will be to get out."

·　·　·

June 9, 1965

THERE SEEMS TO BE A PECULIAR DIVISION of labor here in Washington. The President makes peace speeches and the Pentagon makes foreign policy but the unpleasant task of declaring war is left to the poor State Department. The news that U.S. troops in Vietnam have been authorized to engage in full combat is the news that we are embarking on a new war. Article I, Section 8, of the Constitution, that half-forgotten document, put the power to declare war in the hands of Congress. Its members might insist at least that they have the right to hear declarations of war from some official higher up than the press officer of the State Department. It is hard to find any Constitutional or administrative reason to explain why Robert J. McCloskey, the press officer, should have been pushed suddenly into the pages of history by being assigned the task of announcing at his daily usually routine and almost always boring, noon press briefing that we were no longer advising or patrolling or defensively shooting back in Vietnam but going full-scale into war. As a major decision, it should have been announced at the White House. As a change in military orders, it might have been made public at the Pentagon. As a hot potato, both seem to have passed it on to the State Department. There in turn it was passed on down from the Secretary through the many Assistant Secretaries to the lowest echelon available. Maybe the higherups are hoping it will be called not Johnson's or McNamara's but Bob McCloskey's war.

Nothing better attests the slim popular support for the war than the care thus exercised by Lyndon Johnson not to be photographed marching at the head of the troops straight into it. The White House acted as if it couldn't be bothered by such trivial matters. "The White House," *The Washington Post* reported June 9, "declined to comment on the State Department announcement. Informed officials sought to play down the significance of the announcement, arguing that American forces already are patrolling vigorously and that the commander should not be inhibited in making the best use of his troops." This genius at obfuscation was evident in the very form of the announcement given McCloskey to read: the U.S. commander in Saigon had been authorized to commit U.S. troops to "combat support" of South Vietnam units *if* asked to do so by the South Vietnamese government. This would seem to put the power to declare America at war in the hands of whoever happened to be on top in Saigon's Ferris wheel changes of government and military command. This is quite a departure from the tight centralization of powers characteristic of the Johnson Administration. Here in Washington minor officials can hardly announce a new post office for Chilicothe, Ohio, without clearing it with the White House. But whether or not our troops move into full combat will be decided by someone 9000 miles away whose name the papers can't even spell properly. Delegation of powers has never been so distant. It looks as if while the rest of us may be plunged into war, Lyndon Johnson wants to keep as far away from it as possible. Maybe he can blame it on Dirksen, who was foolish enough to say plainly that he feared this new move would "transform this into a conventional war." That's the kind of candor that lost Republicans the last election.

The truth is that the South Vietnamese army is out of reserves, though the expected Viet Cong monsoon offensive is only just getting underway. The urgent problem at the moment is to supply from U.S. combat forces the extra 160,000 men McNamara was so confident a few months ago he could mobilize from among Saigon's idle but indifferent youth; the men who couldn't be drafted there will soon have to be drafted here. The political situation is as precarious as the military. The Quat government, which has no real popular base, is tottering under attack by Catholic extremists who will be satisfied by nothing short of an Asian anti-communist Armaggedon. The shaky government and its shakier military needed the shot in the arm of a public announcement that they were being given a blank check to draw as they pleased on American manpower. But worse is in the offing. Military planners here must be prepared to deal with the possibility that the Viet Cong may soon inflict so heavy a blow as to demoralize the South Vietnamese forces and make impossible the maintenance of any governmental façade in beleaguered Saigon. Very shortly the problem may be more serious than providing mobile reserves to rescue South Vietnamese forces from unexpected attacks. The problem soon may be that if resistance is to go on, the U.S. will have to take over the government and the war altogether.

So we will do what we swore after the Korean war we would never do again—commit American troops to an Asian land war. Militarily and politically, McCloskey's war is folly. It will tie down a major portion of U.S. military power in a minor theatre of conflict, and create an image made to order for hostile propaganda. White men will be fighting colored men in an effort to put down a rebellion so deeply rooted that it has gone on for two decades, and extended its power steadily during the four years in which we trained, directed and supplied a satellite native army. We are worse off politically than the French were a decade ago: they at least had a puppet Emperor, Bao Dai, to cover the nakedness of imperial rule. Once again, as against the Japanese and the French, the communists can muster wide support as leaders of a resistance to alien domination. We have again made Ho Chi Minh a national leader.

It would be hazardous to comfort ourselves by expecting no more than another Korea, a distant limited conflict, relatively minor in casualties and rich in business stimulation. Vietnam is not Korea. Korea was a civil war between North and South; there were few communist guerrillas behind South Korea's lines. South Korea had a real government and it was headed by a national hero. Syngman Rhee, for all his failings, was a man who had devoted his life to his country's liberation from Japanese rule. There is no such figure to head a South Vietnamese government; the guerrillas hold most of its territory and can at will shut off road and rail supply to the besieged cities. It is doubly a civil war, within the South as well as between South and North. It therefore does not lend itself to the kind of neat settlement arrived at in the Korean war. That war could be ended when Chinese "volunteers" pushed our forces back to the 38th parallel and reconstituted the status quo ante. It was also relatively easy to limit the Korean war on the understanding that our side would not bomb the privileged sanctuary in China from which the "volunteers" were supplied and their side would not bomb the privileged sanctuary in Japan from which our troops operated. It will be more difficult to keep this war contained.

If our troops meet serious reverses in the South, it will be hard to resist the clamor for a tougher bombing policy in the North. If Hanoi and Haiphong are bombed, the North will have nothing to lose and will escalate the war by moving its army south. Those elements in our military itching for a preventive war against China will press for bombing the roads and railroads which connect it with Vietnam. Whether and how China will react, what Russia will do, are unknowns, perhaps as much in Peking and Moscow as in Washington. To go to war is to leave oneself at the mercy of the unexpected. How far it will spread and how many lives it will cost depends on the capricious roulette of war. One thing alone is certain. The further we get in, the harder it will be to get out.

Time to Tell the Truth for a Change

Johnson's escalation of American involvement in the war in Vietnam was accompanied by repeated protestations of our strenuous behind-the-scenes diplomatic efforts to find a peaceful settlement. However, leaks undermined these claims, suggesting that U.S. intransigence had played a major role in expanding the conflict.

. . .

November 22, 1965

We are ready now, as we always have been, to move from the battlefield to the conference table. I have stated publicly, and many times, again and again, America's willingness to begin unconditional discussions with any government at any place at any time. Fifteen efforts have been made to start these discussions with the help of forty nations throughout the world, but there has been no answer.

   —LBJ announcing troop buildup in Vietnam July 28

As IN THE U-2 INCIDENT, our government has again been caught in falsehood. It owes the country an honest explanation before more of our sons die in Vietnam. The State Department's admissions in the wake of Eric Sevareid's revelations in *Look* explain a cryptic remark made by UN Secretary General U Thant last February and a mysterious leak at UN headquarters in New York last August. "I have been conducting private discussions on the question of Vietnam for a long time," U Thant told a press conference February 24, "I am sure that the great American people, if only they knew the true facts and the background to the developments in South Vietnam, will agree with me that further bloodshed is unnecessary." Then he added sadly, "As you know in times of war and of hostilities the first casualty is truth." He was slapped down the same day in a curt White House statement.

This brings us to the leak, which now falls into perspective. "In twenty months," Mr. Johnson said in a White House speech August 3, "we have agreed to fifteen different approaches to try to bring peace, and each of them has been turned down by the other side." This was too much for someone at UN headquarters. Someone called in two UN correspondents, Hella Pick of the *Manchester Guardian* and Darius S. Jhabvala of the *New York Herald-Tribune,* and leaked the story which the State Department has now confirmed, that only eleven months earlier, in September 1964, we turned down a chance for secret peace talks U Thant had arranged with the North Vietnamese.* It appeared in the *Herald-Tribune* August 8 and in the *Manchester Guardian* August 9. The account in the latter suggests that the source of the story was someone close to Adlai Stevenson and that he told it in such a way as to put the blame on the State Department and avoid direct criticism of Kennedy and Johnson.

The *Manchester Guardian* story said Washington had "cold-shouldered at least two opportunities for contacts with North Vietnam in the last two years." The first was after the fall of Diem in the autumn of 1963, when Hanoi "was willing to discuss the establishment of a coalition neutralist government in Saigon." Note that the reference was to a coalition neutralist government and not to a National Liberation Front government. This throws light on another cryptic remark by U Thant at his press conference last February. "In my view," he then said, "there was a very good possibility in 1963 of arriving at a satisfactory political solution." The second lost opportunity mentioned in the *Manchester Guardian* account was the secret meeting to which Ho Chi Minh had agreed in September, 1964, but which we rejected. The *Guardian* went on to say:

> Details of these peace moves have come from an unimpeachable source. The State Department, however, seems to be dismissing the report of Ho Chi Minh's willingness to talk last year as irrelevant. It says there was no indication that anything would come of it, and hints that President Johnson was not involved in the matter at all. Nor is it

*An earlier hint of this had appeared the previous April 18 in a dispatch to the *St. Louis Post-Dispatch* from its UN correspondent, Donald Grant.

clear whether the State Department ever informed President Kennedy
that Hanoi was willing to talk after the fall of Diem. *Mr. Adlai Stevenson certainly knew of these moves, and it appears to have been one of his
great regrets that Washington did not react positively.* [Emphasis added.]
The intermediaries who were involved in the effort to bring about a
meeting between Hanoi and Washington believe that the Communist
position hardened as a result of Washington's negative attitude.

Sevareid's account of his talk with Stevenson shortly before the latter's
death last July adds to the August leak. It reveals that U Thant made two
more attempts at peace. The September meeting was rejected for fear that it
might leak to the Goldwater forces during the election campaign. "When
the election was over," Sevareid relates, "U Thant again pursued the matter;
Hanoi was still willing to send its man. But Defense Secretary McNamara,
Adlai went on, flatly opposed the attempt." The argument against peace
talks was that "the South Vietnamese government would have to be informed and that this would have a demoralizing effect on them; that government was shaky enough as it was." McNamara denied this and the State
Department's spokesman last Monday said the Secretary of Defense "did
not participate in the U.S. government handling of this matter." But the
spokesman did not deny that a second Rangoon meeting with the North
Vietnamese was possible after the election. U Thant's next effort was a
cease-fire offer on U.S. terms. On this, the spokesman was evasive. He said
it was not true that U Thant "at any time said he would accept any formulation concerning a cease-fire that the U.S. might propose—although he did
advance his own suggestions." When pressed for clarification, the
spokesman would only say, it would be "highly inappropriate to disclose the
details." The Department always seems to consider candor inappropriate.
Through this bureaucratic fog we can see that the Department dares not
deny the second Rangoon meeting it turned down nor the offer of a cease-
fire. "Stevenson," Sevareid's account continues, "told me that U Thant was
furious over this failure of his patient efforts but said nothing publicly."
Apparently U Thant persevered in his efforts, however. For if one goes
back and rereads the transcript of the February 24 press conference one sees
that he said he had "presented concrete ideas and proposals" to the princi-

pal parties concerned, including the U.S., but that the results "have not been conclusive." Next day UN headquarters reported a message from Hanoi that it was sympathetic to the proposals U Thant had outlined.* But the same day at a press conference Secretary Rusk made clear U.S. rejection. He said the U.S. would not enter negotiations to end the Vietnamese war until North Vietnam gave some "indication" that it was "prepared to stop what it is doing and what it knows it is doing to its neighbors." This embodied the view that the war was a simple case of aggression from the North and implied that we would not negotiate until the other side laid down its arms.

What terms was Hanoi thinking of? In the *Weekly* last April 12, "Peace Feelers? Is the Truth about Them Being Withheld?" we reprinted a letter to the *Times* of London April 1 by William Warbey, a British Laborite M.P. back from talks in Hanoi with Ho Chi Minh and Prime Minister Pham Van Dong. Warbey outlined their terms for a settlement as told to him and previously "to others who passed their message on to Washington." This called for a neutralized North and South, with resumption of trade between them, but with autonomous regimes on both sides of the 17th parallel. "The people of the Southern zone" would have the right "to form and support a government which genuinely represents all the major sections of the Southern population" and each zone would have the right "to enjoy economic, cultural and 'fraternal' relations with the countries of its choice," i.e. South Vietnam could be linked economically and culturally with the West if it so chose while North Vietnam presumably would remain linked with the Soviet bloc. Warbey wrote that the only precondition on which the North was insisting was the cessation of bombing attacks upon it. Note that these terms did not call for a government based on the National Liberation Front but on "all the major sections of the Southern population," and that it was broad enough to envisage free elections. It was also suggested that eventual reunification might be based on a bi-federal system. This would seem to offer a solution which would be democratic and honorable and a face-saver for the U.S. This may make it easier to understand what U Thant meant when he told a luncheon last Tuesday, the day after the State Department's

---

**Facts on File for 1965, p. 74E3.

admissions, "If only bold steps had been taken as late as 1964 I feel that much of today's tragic development could have been avoided."

The day the Warbey letter appeared in the *Times* of London, Mr. Johnson was asked at press conference whether he had "any evidence of a willingness on the part of the Communists to negotiate" in Vietnam. We called attention in that same issue of April 12 to the curious wording of his reply. He said he had "no evidence that they are ready and willing to negotiate *under conditions that would be productive.*" Our italics. Last Monday's press conference at the State Department suggested that what we would consider "productive" would be restoration of an independent South Vietnam under our wing. The Department's spokesman insisted that the Johns Hopkins speech last April 7 did not mark any change in policy when it offered "unconditional discussions." To prove continuity of policy he read the reporters two previous Presidential statements. In one, at an AP lunch, April 20, 1964, Mr. Johnson said "Once war seems hopeless, then peace may be possible. The door is always open to any settlement which assures the independence of South Vietnam and its freedom to seek help for its protection." This implies (1) that peace can only come when the other side realizes war is hopeless and (2) that the settlement to which our door is open is one which assures an independent South Vietnam, which can call on the U.S. and SEATO for protection. The other quotation offered was from Johnson's message August 5, 1964, assuring Congress "that we shall continue readily to explore any avenues of political solution that will effectively guarantee the removal of Communist subversion."

Any compromise which would give the National Liberation Front some role in a coalition government would seem to be ruled out by that formulation. It implies their surrender or extermination. The fact that the State Department put these two quotations forward as embodiments of our policy foreshadows war to the bitter end rather than negotiation. When a reporter said, "Well, all that does not say that he [Johnson] is willing to have unconditional discussions," the Department's spokesman replied, "Well I think then that we are hung up on semantics." This makes sense only if "unconditional discussions" means something very different from unconditional negotiations. In negotiations we would still insist on winning at the bargaining table what we have yet to win either on the battlefield or in our dealings with the Vietnamese people. When reporters at the press confer-ence tried to elicit what standards the government imposes in determining whether peace feelers are "serious" or "sincere," the spokesman retreated be-hind a smoke-screen of double-talk. The truth I believe is that we wait for a signal that the other side is ready, not to negotiate, but to surrender.

I hope I am wrong because if this is the policy then it will take a good many years of fighting and a lot of American and Vietnamese lives. It will poison our relations with the Soviet Union and may end the hopes of pre-venting a new step-up in the arms race. The Soviets, as can be seen in the latest attack from Peking, are under fire for serving U.S. interests in trying to bring about peace. Peking discloses that Kosygin went to Hanoi last Feb-ruary 6 in an attempt to bring about a negotiated settlement. This was also the report carried by the *London Sunday Observer* February 7 from Hong Kong in a dispatch by Stanley Karnow which reflected the judgment of the U.S. intelligence community there. That was the day Johnson, under the impact of the Viet Cong attack on our barracks at Pleiku, ordered the bombing of the North in accordance with contingency plans drawn up months earlier and long urged upon him by the military. To bomb the North while Kosygin was there virtually as our emissary trying to bring about peace, and to continue the bombing indefinitely instead of limiting it to a reprisal raid, may turn out to have been the Big Mistake of the war. It hardly made the search for peace easier. On this, too, the Administration has been deceptive.

What It's Like to Be in Saigon

I. F. Stone reports from Saigon. The picture he paints of a well-intentioned American military and political establishment that is isolated in protected enclaves, oblivious to events in the surrounding country, and arrogantly convinced that it knows how best to bring peace and democracy to an alien people, helps to explain the nature of the Vietnam quagmire in which the U.S. would remain stuck for another eight years—and surely suggests an analogy to other, more recent, conflicts.

·　　·　　·

May 9, 1966

What I remember most of Saigon is the heat, the squalor and the despair. I began by being terribly frustrated and ended by being terribly fascinated. The frustration arose from trying to get things done in a country which seems engaged in a giant conspiracy to slow everything down; I'd hate to have to run a war in the vast snafu that is South Vietnam; only an Eagle Scout like Westmoreland could stand it without going off his rocker. Just what the fascination was I don't quite know, perhaps it was the ringside seat Saigon offers on the inexhaustible vitality and folly of the human race.

The heat lay like a suffocating blanket on the city, and it was hard to know which was worse, the sunny days or the cloudy when a blue haze of carbon monoxide lay low over the teeming streets. At night with the windows open in a cheap hotel which charged New York prices, one slept not just naked but with every pore alert for an occasional hint of breeze. After the midnight curfew one is awakened from time to time by the dull thud of mortars like a giant tapping on distant doors. One night the whole hotel shook, the doors went rat-tat-tat, as a huge armada passed overhead and dumped its deadly freight somewhere far off in the darkness. There were three waves of this miniature earthquake and one suddenly realized the meaning of the term privileged sanctuary, for Americans in Vietnam can sleep with the assurance that amid the heavy traffic overhead, there are no enemy planes. Goliath never had it so good.

Even on the quieter nights, sleep begins to be impossible around five. There is a constant roar of heavy trucks from the clogged waterfront nearby. The noise overhead surpasses that in the areas adjoining La Guardia airport, and starts much earlier; the decibel factor alone makes it easy to believe that Saigon's Tan Son Nhut is now the world's busiest airport. The guerrillas have cut the railroads and made the roads impassable everywhere—except for those who pay their fees and are granted passage. For Americans it is safe to travel only in the skies. In the morning one emerges early on streets from which the garbage is no longer carted away. This and the lax currency control on entry are the first signs of disintegration; the government is falling apart. The generals maneuver, no longer so much for power as for some political foothold. Their wives, so it is said, are the brains of the family and devote them to the business of selling export and import licenses. The coolies who used to collect the garbage probably make five times as much now on the docks or in construction, for labor is scarce in the war boom that has seized Saigon. One newspaper article I saw suggested that maybe garbage collection ought to be handed over to free enterprise, a touching testimonial to the spread of the American theology to these lands beyond the sea.

In the mornings, moving from air-conditioned U.S. offices to the hot bake-oven outside, one felt ninety-eight years old by 10 A.M. and ready to collapse in a pre-lunch siesta under an electric fan, those days electricity was available. After lunch, one hastened back to the darkened and sweaty refuge of one's hotel room. The once beautiful and broad avenues of the great city outside are filled with a mad tangle of vehicles. Here a tiny donkey cart carries a rustic family into town; it is loaded down with pots and pans and bags. From the interstices children look out big-eyed with wonder. There a two-seater cyclopus goes by with two soigné matrons, exquisitely kept in their privileged middle age, engaged in shrewd and vivacious conversation. The streets swarm with cyclopuses—the old rick-shaw raised to a higher technological level by being wedded to the bicycle, with which the driver pushes from behind. Next in the hierarchy of public transport is the motorized cyclopus, then tiny Renault taxis. They contest the streets with a constant flow of jeeps and military buses. Maneuvering dashingly amid this wildly tooting herd of vehicles is an occasional Vietnamese motorcycle "cowboy" with miniature Stetson and tight Western movie pants. The costume makes the slight, delicate-boned Vietnamese look more mannikin than man, a tiny caricature of a Texan. The scene is dominated from time to time by the passage, often under armed escort, of some Vietnamese VIP in a Peugot, Mercedes-Benz or Cadillac; these testify to how many people do quite well on the war.

Most of the people's daily life seems to be spent in the streets. On the crowded sidewalks, capitalism is in flower. Half the population of Saigon seems to have set itself up in business with items from the American PX. Everywhere there are tiny stalls selling Gillette razor blades, Spearmint chewing gum, Almond Joys, Colgate toothpaste, Chesterfield cigarettes and Hershey bars at a generous markup. So large an outflow from the PX indicates that military service has not stifled the Yankee trader spirit in our troops. Along the curb and under the stalls, mats are spread on which whole families lunch and dine; the food is cooked on a tiny brazier, and delicately served by the mothers. The meals, mostly seafood stews served on rice, are eaten with the gusto of a family picnic. Everybody seems to be having a good time, from the children begging in the streets to the shoeshine boys showing off to an admiring crowd how much they can overcharge the big barbarians from oversea. In the endless pageantry of the streets, I even encountered one patriotic demonstration. Just before 8 A.M. on Nguyen Hué street I was attracted by a crowd standing at attention while the South Vietnamese flag was raised and a loud speaker broadcast the national anthem. When the ceremony was finished the crowd filed into the building. It was the headquarters of the General Confederation of Employers. This evidence of a renaissance in national spirit may give Henry Cabot Lodge a lift.

The crew of the Air Vietnam plane on which I flew from Hong Kong to Saigon was entirely Vietnamese. Lunch was first rate French Asian cuisine with good French wines. The stewardess gave me my first glimpse of how demurely seductive the Vietnamese woman's costume can be: delectably feminine loose flowing pants as the undergarment, usually white, with a kind of split sari over it of contrasting color. It is the direct opposite of the strip tease. The girl is completely covered from throat to feet, not even the ankles are visible. Yet as the girl moves the flowing garments suddenly mold and reveal the figure for a fleeting intimate moment. The moving limbs provide a constant, spontaneous and luminous ballet.

The civilian arrival hall of the airport at Saigon was a huge shed of wood and tin, almost furnace-like in its suffocating heat. When I finally got away in an Air Vietnam bus, the sky was a luscious pale blue with tufts of white cloud but the scene below was hot and dusty. April, before the monsoon rains begin, is Saigon's hottest and driest month. I saw no signs of the mortar attack on the airport a few days earlier. It must have been in a distant corner of that huge airport. There was a big unpainted restaurant with a billboard in French advertising the first dentifrice of the Republic with "fluor." Other billboards as we sped by advertised the Lambretta scooter, GM's Cadillacs and Chevrolets, and Pan Am. We passed villas taken over by the military. Sandbag embankments were visible behind their low white walls. Some of the villas were as big as palaces. We went over a bridge and caught a glimpse of dark unpainted shacks high on stilts along a river bank as far as one could see. Near them, set back from the water, were white and pink stucco villas with gardens behind high white walls. The rich and the poor seemed to live almost side by side in this neighborhood.

At the hot dusty freight shed which is Saigon's air terminus, a taxi driver made a deal with me—the newly arrived sucker—for 200 piastres to the Hotel Caravelle, or ten times the normal price. Then he strode off in lordly satisfaction, leaving me to handle my bags. Several eager urchins seized them despite my effort to explain in French and English that I had no cash. When I got into the miniature cab and left them empty handed, I was treated to a pantomime of pained indignation and an outburst of grandiloquent Vietnamese by the budding entrepreneurs until my lordly driver handed out two five-piastre bills to quiet down the demonstration. At the Caravelle, only a few blocks away, I learned that my telegraphic confirmation of a reservation was worthless. I soon discovered that the Caravelle was inhabited by phantoms. I had the names of half a dozen persons to see, all presumably at the Caravelle, and all equally unknown to the management. I did not learn until later that every room there was acquired only by intricate bribery; the lucky few who have rooms are forced to treat the management as a pampered mistress; one day asked to bring expensive film from the PX, another day some choice foodstuff. The only exception was A. J. Muste and his CNVA* delegation which got a big room, perhaps because it was conveniently wired for sound by the police and they preferred to have the pacifists where they could keep a close watch on their comings and goings. I soon was sent off to what I was assured was a modern air-conditioned hotel. The room at the Federal turned out to have a broken down fan and a shower which never once in my eight day stay had hot water.

Saigon, as I emerged on it that Sunday afternoon, must have been a lovely French Asian capital before the war with its broad tree-lined boulevards, open squares and shady arcades. Now it seemed an Asiatic honky tonk. Though it was siesta time, here and there U.S. soldiers in pairs sauntered dolefully past the many bars looking like Bill Mauldin types in search of an ersatz Mama. Small boys were already out pimping in the hot afternoon, hinting in pidgin English at bizarre pleasures. The immemorial entrepreneurial spirit flourished in the world's oldest commodity, women, but the soldiers seemed too shy to close such deals in broad daylight. Warding off importunate pedicab drivers I made straight for the big white building at Nguyen Hué street and Le Loi boulevard which is the center of journalistic activity in Saigon—JUSPAO, the Joint U. S. Public Affairs Office, on a square adjoining the white walled palace of Saigon's City Hall. JUSPAO is surrounded by a barricade, with a guard house at either end. I got by one of them only to find the main entrance locked. As I walked from one locked door to another, alone behind that white-washed barricade, one lone American in full view of the promenading Sunday crowds, I felt conspicuously alone, an easy tempting target for any potshot from a VC sympathizer. That was my one moment of apprehension. Soon one treats the possibility of being hit by a bomb in Saigon as matter-of-factly as the chance of an auto accident in the States.

Fortunately one locked side door was soon opened for me by a lonesome duty officer. I was greeted inside by a huge picture of Lyndon Johnson, looking in that setting almost Orientally inscrutable. Next to the picture was a sign in English and Vietnamese saying peremptorily, "Clear your weapon before going topside." When I asked the duty officer what clearing

*Committee for Nonviolent Action.

one's weapon meant, he said it meant taking any live bullet out before going upstairs but that actually the order had been superseded by a later one simply requiring all weapons to be left below. I was heartened by this sign of progress.

Before being permanently accredited as an American correspondent, one has to obtain a press card from the South Vietnamese government. This is the sole act of deference to Vietnamese sovereignty required of the visiting American. The contrast between the two press HQs reflects the real balance of forces. JUSPAO has taken over a multi-storied elegant white building on one of the town's most important squares. The ARVN press office is housed in a nearby second story loft, dark, grimy and cooled only by an old-fashioned fan. A press card is issued without question, and for most U.S. correspondents that one visit to the loft is all they will make during their tour of duty. A formal military press briefing is held there at 4:30 P.M. each day, a half hour before the daily briefing at JUSPAO, but only a few wire service men, on days when they are hungry for news, turn up. The military briefing officer speaks in Vietnamese but often interrupts his interpreter to correct the latter's sometimes incomprehensible English.

Back across the street, in the air-conditioned realm of JUSPAO, with its snack bar, its PX and—like oases—its clean water fountains, the American finds himself, as the French say, *chez lui,* at home. The newcomer, even if a stray heretic like myself, encounters that unpretentious amiability which is the most attractive and democratic side of our American character. I had failed to bring the required letter from one's editor but after some good-humored joshing from a press officer who told the military I was chief cook and bottlewasher of my own publication, my card was issued. I was also asked to sign a form absolving the U.S. government from liability if anything happened to me while riding in a military plane. During the eight days I was in Saigon I met with nothing but courtesy from U.S. officers, civilian or military. The question in my mind was how so many well-meaning, friendly and intelligent people, with so much in the way of funds and Vietnamese informers at their disposal, could guess so consistently wrong about events in Vietnam. Honolulu, and its aftermath of anti-American riots, were only the latest examples of this incomprehension. I would like to sketch out a tentative answer on the basis of what I saw and heard.

The first thing that strikes one is the extent to which the Americans in Vietnam live in enclaves—not just military but psychological enclaves. JUSPAO, the Embassy, the various AID missions and the military HQs in Saigon are like miniature fortresses in a hostile land. They reminded me strongly of the sand-bagged and barricaded offices of the British in their conflict with Israel's Haganah and the terrorists in the three turbulent years before Britain withdrew from Palestine in 1948. But these fortresses are vulnerable from within; they depend on Vietnamese employes and there is no certain way to distinguish friend from foe. The situation must be apple pie for Viet Cong intelligence. Our press and our soldiers live in a world apart; few speak even such bad French as mine, much less Vietnamese. The mentality we develop is the "compound" complex which has always afflicted foreigners living as traders or soldiers in a foreign land. We bring America with us wherever we go, and live wrapped in a kind of cellophane which separates us from the people of the country. Our relations with them are almost entirely mercenary, and the women, the informers and the soldiers we buy are about as unsatisfactory as bought love is everywhere. They must secretly regard us with amusement or contempt.

To watch the young Ivy Leaguers arriving briskly at the Embassy of a morning is to feel oneself on the eve of the Harvard–Yale game. The team spirit is bursting out all over; it demands optimism; patriotism is equated with euphoria. All is for the best, albeit not in the best of all possible worlds. One day the official spokesman is enthusiastic about the firing of General Thi as a move against "war-lordism." When Thi's removal turns out to be a bad mistake, the same spokesman discovers that these are just the birth pangs in South Vietnam of "federalism," the problem of integrating each region into the national whole. He even touches on the U.S. Civil War until a tart newsman suggests there are enough civil wars going on in South Vietnam without rehashing the problem of the Gray and the Blue. Everything is public relations and public relations is make-believe. Every top official is more concerned with his "image" than with unpleasant realities. To mention these is to get off the team. Bright gimmicks are turned into speeches and proliferate into pamphlets long before anything has been accomplished or even after hopes have collapsed. The word is taken for the deed. As one moves from talking to the men who work in the field to those who work in Saigon and then think of the men in Washington, one sees that the further from the scene the more imaginary the picture we have created. The most confining enclave of all is this enclave in our heads.

Under the supposed benevolence of our policy one soon detects a deep animosity to the Vietnamese and a vast arrogance. We assume the right to remold them, whether they choose to be remolded or not. The war, like the cold war, has developed a vein of zealotry alien to the easy-going American character. An enthusiastic psychological warrior, anxious to impress me, took me out for a drink on the cool veranda of the Continental Palace; one could imagine how the French planters and civil servants must have gathered there in the afternoons for their aperitifs. My new found friend—he claimed to know all about me—told me that in working with captured VC he found that 95 per cent were "recoverable" human beings. It was my first evening and I did not dare repay his hospitality by asking what we did with the other 5 per cent—dispose of them like Kleenex? Directives go down from on high to treat the villagers with some discrimination. But the poor GI's one encounters are too full of rage at the fate which has brought them there. A boy from Mobile told me 50 per cent of the people in Saigon were VC, 45 per cent indifferent and 5 per cent with us; he thought we ought to go all-out to win the war—smash Hanoi—or go home. His buddy from Minnesota said at first he had been afraid all the time. He described the sleepless nights in the jungle, the stink of the water. Now he had become a fatalist; he felt he might get it anywhere, so why worry? Terrorism is hard to take, to see a buddy blown up by a mine or knocked off by a sniper hardly makes one benevolent to the natives. One hears frightful stories of troops in the field setting fire to villages or, on evacuating them, defecating in the cooking utensils, out of sheer hate and resentment.

In Saigon, on R and R (rest and recreation), the bar girls gyp the troops with the skill of their sisters in the clip joints of Greenwich Village. A soldier can spend a month's pay on "Saigon tea" and emerge as virgin as he entered. The soldiers feel that they are taken advantage of on every hand, and they are. I heard a burly sergeant explode one night at the Caravelle when he found, as usual, that advance reservations had been ignored. "We're out there in the jungle trying to hold this country together," he shouted angrily, "and this is what we get for it." There is hardly benevolence in the words one hears so frequently at the daily military briefing—"search and destroy"—as if we were an Old Testament God. In the cool panelled classroom in which the briefings are held, the only theory of the war which seems to emerge is implied by the "kill count" as if we were on an insect extermination mission and could go home when all the termites had been destroyed. It is significant that those like General Lansdale and Colonel John Paul Vann who would approach the Vietnamese as people soon find themselves sidetracked, suspect and frustrated. The machine instinctively reacts against the human, and what we are running, or what is running us, is a bureaucratic war machine.

Americans with cameras search out VC atrocities with indignation, but the use of napalm and saturation bombing is regarded merely as another form of technology. The machine is forgiven atrocities many-fold more terrible than those of the guerrillas. The Vietnamese are expendable. I came across cold warriors who had operated in Germany, in Bolivia, in Brazil and in Santo Domingo and now, in all innocence, commit similar follies in Vietnam. They place a very high value on the purity of their intentions and a very low estimate on the motivations of the Vietnamese. One old acquaintance gave me a briefing on all we were doing for the Vietnamese and then dropped remarks which revealed a very different attitude. The editors in Saigon, who have been asking for freedom of the press, called a one-day general strike to protest an attack on a pro-government editor (the military could hardly object to that) but appended to this a demand for greater press freedom. When I asked my friend about this, he said cynically, "they only wanted to save a day's newsprint." Yet he had been telling me we were there to protect democracy from communism. Every demand for democratic rights is regarded as perverse if not subversive; this is also the basic attitude toward elections. One often feels our people regard the Vietnamese as irrelevant to our worldwide holy war against communism. As my friend said, "After all it's only an accident that this war is being fought here. We have to smash the idea of wars of liberation." If Vietnam and the Vietnamese are badly battered in the process, it's too bad. The growing awareness of this essential indifference to their fate is giving the Vietnamese a common despair that might some day prove stronger even than fratricidal passion.

Our capacity for overlooking the obvious is enormous. Even one of the best and most independent reporters here was shocked by the anti-Americanism of recent demonstrations in Saigon and in Hué and Danang. He shares the naive view that we are there to help the Vietnamese and regards the demonstrations as sheer ingratitude. The simple fact that occupying armies, whether allied or enemy, always become unpopular hardly ever figures in official calculation. It would be too hard to reconcile it with the planned steady increase in the number of troops. This, in a country as fiercely nationalistic as Vietnam, spells more trouble of the same kind but to face the facts might force us to recast our policy. An experienced British correspondent told me that several months ago he raised the question with a U.S. official of the resentment and annoyance created by the influx of foreign troops, with the money to get first choice of everything from women to pedicabs. He predicted that urban unrest might prove worse than the trouble in the villages. He was told he ought to try and be more "constructive."

A group of Buddhist neutralists of whom I shall tell more in my next letter published a volume in French and English called *Dialogue.* In one of them Pham Cong Thien writes, "Here is my Nada prayer: Lead us not into Salvation, but deliver us from Deliverance." This is the true cry of the heart from a country torn apart.

Why We Fail as Revolutionaries

Another essay on Vietnam with relevance to other U.S. attempts to reshape foreign governments and cultures: "How often," Stone asks, "can intelligent and well-meaning Americans see glamorous 'revolutionary' programs collapse into the same old repression without noticing there is something fundamentally wrong?"

.   .   .

July 30, 1966

SOME THINGS CANNOT BE LEARNED. A man cannot learn *not* to breathe. There are limits on the adaptation of societies, as of organisms. An established order cannot run a social revolution. Nicholas I was so impressed with the Decembrists who tried to otherthrow him that he ordered a summary of their criticisms to be drawn up for the guidance of his government, though only after they had been exiled or executed. "It is necessary," this document said, "to improve the condition of the farmers, to end the humiliating sale of human beings." Nothing came of these proposed reforms. Instead the regime established, in the dreaded Third Section, a new type of political police. This is the inescapable pattern of counter-revolution when it tries—in the currently fashionable phrase—to win the hearts of the people. The regime may be aware of the need for social reform, but is unable by nature to bring it about. The failure of the Decembrists was the high water mark of the Holy Alliance, which sought to police Europe against the dangers of liberalism, as the U.S. since the Truman Doctrine has sought to police the world against the dangers of communism. Without overstressing historical parallels, it is instructive to go back and notice that the Holy Alliance, in intent, was not as bleakly reactionary as it was in practice. It, too, sought to combine progress with repression, as we do in Vietnam. Metternich's famous secret memorandum to Alexander I envisaged a stability which "will in no wise exclude the development of what is good, for stability is not immobility." A new pamphlet from Mr. McNamara's Defense Department, arguing the case for military assistance, uses almost identical phrases. It quotes with approval a study of the military in underdeveloped countries which says "The military . . . may be able to play a key role in promoting mobility while maintaining stability." The military dictators we supply nevertheless do turn out to be immobile, as did the Holy Alliance before them, though it too was not without social insight. The reactionary Catholic theologian Baader who helped frame the Holy Alliance "maintained," long before McNamara's computers came up with the same revelation at Montreal, "that revolutionary sentiments are due . . . to the poverty of the masses." These are distant branches of the same family tree which gave us the Honolulu Declaration.

This perspective is necessary if we are to understand why we have failed in twelve years to bring about the social revolution so often promised in Vietnam. Four Americans who took part in this effort record their experiences in a new book, *Men Without Guns: American Civilians in Rural Vietnam*. The editor, George K. Tanham, went to Vietnam in 1964 as Director of Provincial Operations for AID and is at present deputy to the Vice-President of the RAND Corporation. He was writing the book's concluding chapter when the Honolulu Declaration was made public. "It should be noted," he comments somberly, "that similar high-sounding declarations in the past have accomplished little. However," he concludes, with an obvious effort to sound a bit hopeful, "with the full backing of the Saigon government and with such high level American support, this new rural-development effort may succeed." Considering Mr. Tanham's experience and position, that is not a very hearty testimonial, though events since Honolulu already make it look too optimistic.

Mr. Tanham's three collaborators have each provided a close-up from firsthand experience of the AID program in three different types of provinces. Robert Warne covers Vinh Binh in the Mekong Delta. Earl Young tells of his work in Phu Boh, in the Central Highlands. William Nighswonger describes his work in the coastal province where the U.S. air base at Danang is located. Like so many Americans who have worked at the grass roots in Vietnam, their reports have an honesty and sobriety very different from the glossy version of events which figures in Saigon's pamphlets and Washington's speeches. But at a certain point even these men stop short, as if at a wall they dare not climb.

How often can intelligent and well-meaning Americans see glamorous "revolutionary" programs collapse into the same old repression without noticing there is something fundamentally wrong? In his preface, Mr. Tanham makes the familiar point that while the Viet Cong have exploited rural dissatisfaction, "the governments of South Vietnam from Diem to the present have not met this challenge . . . and shown the way toward real economic and social progress. In spite of frequent high sounding government declarations, there has been no real revolutionary effort." Why should this be surprising? Mr. Tanham has long been one of the government's experts in studying communist revolutionary warfare. These experts pore through communist literature but seem to miss the elementary and essential points, perhaps because to speak plainly in terms of class interests is regarded today as slightly subversive if no politically pornographic. How can you expect revolutionary changes from a government based on the possessing classes? We have been supporting a series of dictatorial regimes based on absentee landlords, military men and urban business type who can no more think in revolutionary terms than a horse can fly.

In a chapter on "Challenge and Response," Mr. Tanham demonstrates his own lack of adequate response to this challenge. The lack is characteristic of the U.S. counter-insurgency establishment. He writes of the Viet Cong, "Land is taken from the landowners, many of whom are in Saigon or other large cities and redistributed to the peasants." Naturally the peasants like this. Why don't we do the same? Because the government we support is based on the landlords. Mr. Tanham does not ask the question nor provide the answer. Both are obvious, but this is the kind of obvious that counter-revolutionary movements are incapable by their nature of recognizing. A related example is provided by Mr. Warne's account of Vinh Binh province. He relates that "land ownership in Vinh Binh is confused since most of the land records were destroyed by the Vietminh. It is estimated that 60 per cent of the farmers do not have title to the land they farm. Only about a third of these now pay rent because in the insecure areas the landowners are unable to collect rents." This is revealing, but Mr. Warne seems to miss its significance. If 60 per cent of the farmers do not have title to the land, 60 per cent of the farmers stand to lose the land they till if Saigon re-establishes control. If two-thirds of these farmers now pay no rent because these areas are "insecure," then the return of security means the return of the rent collector. From the peasant point of view the "pacification" drive thus looks like an attempt by the landlords to regain control of the land. It would be quite a feat to take a peasant's land and win his heart at the same time.

The most revealing thing about this book is that it says so little about land reform. Mr. Warne, who worked in the Mekong Delta, where this is a crucial problem, gives us only a passing glimpse of the land ownership situation. "Through the government's Land Reform Service," Mr. Warne writes, "some tenant farmers are making installment payments to purchase land confiscated from the French and from large Vietnamese landowners. However, the majority of these installment contracts are in arrears at present." The land reform forced many peasants to pay for land they had seized when the landlords fled during the French war. Wherever the area is "insecure," peasants take advantage of the fact to forget about the installments due.

"In 1958, as a land reform measure," Mr. Warne writes, "the government disallowed holdings in excess of 240 acres, but this regulation has not been well enforced." As a matter of fact, as I learned in talking with U.S. farm experts in Saigon only a few weeks ago, these maximums have been easily and widely evaded though they are fantastically high when compared with the land reforms in Japan (ten acres rice-land, family maximum) or Formosa (seven acres). Though an American farm adviser as early as 1955 began pressing for agrarian reform to "save the day in the coming battle for Vietnam," the reform when Diem finally enacted it was limited, belated and tricky. In a peasant country like Vietnam, this was politically fatal. Yet the whole subject gets only a few passing remarks in *Men Without Guns*.

The record shows more pressure for land reform in Vietnam during the Eisenhower Administration than since; as our military intervention has grown, our capacity for political maneuver has shrunk. In the Johnson years the subject has been soft-pedalled, though it still appears in our political litany about Vietnam and Latin America. There are several reasons for muffling talk of land reform. One is that in Vietnam, as in Brazil, it alienates the local upper classes with which we are allied. Another arises from the contrast between our preaching and our practice. Where U.S. lands have been seized for agrarian reform, we have either overthrown the government and forced return of the land, as in Guatemala, or tried by every means, fair or foul, to bring down the offending regime, as in Cuba. A third reason, apparent in congressional appropriation hearings, is the instinctive hostility of Southern Senators and Congressmen, often themselves *latifundistas,* to talk of breaking up big estates for the sake of the landless. Eastland, who so admired Trujillo, may fear this lest it give *nigras* bad ideas in his own delta. The main reason we drop the subject so easily is that our real concern in Vietnam, as in Latin America, is not with the people but with our anxiety to demonstrate that we can contain communism. This inevitably degenerates into a military operation. The military may indeed carry on some "civic action." This is no new departure. Our marines in Nicaragua and the Dominican Republic built wells and improved sanitation during the occupation of the 1920s. Then we handed these countries over to dictators we had trained. Our concern was to make them safe for the United Fruit Company. Somoza and Trujillo were our products in the twenties and thirties like Diem and Ky in the fifties and sixties. Though everybody from LBJ down constantly talks of social revolution, the record shows our real concern is with putting it down, not bringing it about. We like to talk about revolution, but we rush in helicopters and napalm when it threatens to break out. This is the real face of the *Pax Americana* we are trying to impose.

While Others Dodge the Draft, Bobby Dodges the War

By the fall of 1966, New York Senator Robert F. Kennedy, the shining hope of many liberal Democrats, had begun his *Hamlet* act over Vietnam and the presidency. While expressing misgivings over the gradual escalation of the war, he was loath to break with President Lyndon Johnson over the issue, once remarking that for him to try to bring down the administration over Vietnam would be like a priest in Bogotá trying to depose the Pope. Here, I. F. Stone shows little patience for Kennedy's equivocation.

·   ·   ·

October 24, 1966

ROBERT F. KENNEDY is not setting a good example for American youth. To be a trimmer, to put career ahead of duty, to be all but silent on the greatest moral and political issue of our time is to be no different from the other politicians. We are sure that if a young man went to the Senator and asked his advice on how best to dodge military service in Vietnam, Kennedy would regard him as a coward and unpatriotic. But we are also sure that if we had the Senator's confidence and asked him privately why he was not speaking out on the war, he would explain it was too risky, that he had already established a position slightly to the left of the Administration in his Vietnam speech of February 19, 1966, that this was sufficient to hold his liberal constituency and that anything more would be politically dangerous, and might put him in the isolated position of a Morse or Gruening. To die for your country is one thing. To put your political future in jeopardy for it is another.

These are roles we take for granted in the ancient dramaturgy of human conflict. Honor requires the soldier to kill or be killed, whatever his scruples. But it is not regarded as dishonorable for the politician to swallow his misgivings and allow the young to go out to die without protest. Kennedy in the U.S. Senate has at his disposal a forum second only to that of the Presidency. But he hasn't said a word about the war in the Senate since his one speech last February. A wistful committee has been organized for a Kennedy-Fulbright ticket in 1968 but Fulbright has been speaking out while Kennedy has been falling silent. Kennedy did not support his effort to rescind the Tonkin Bay resolution nor to alert the country on the danger in Thailand. He even achieved the feat of delivering a speech on peace in New York (October 11, 1966) without mentioning Vietnam!

Kennedy thinks of himself as a moral man. He proclaims it in South Africa and in Latin America but at home, where thousands are being drafted every month, he says as little as he can about the one issue that matters most. It is only in response to questions that he occasionally speaks of the war, often with a remarkable complacency. "We have to realize," he told a questioner in Iowa (*New York Times,* October 10, 1966), "that the casualties are going to continue to be large." Shouldn't he, who sees himself as the candidate of youth, do something to stop them? He has a small army of ghost writers turning out speeches and hunting up apt quotations. Why not on the war?

At Hunter College in New York recently he confined himself, as Brother Teddy does, to the safe topic of aid to Vietnamese refugees. He met "all questions on the propriety of the war in Vietnam," the *New York Times* reported October 8, 1966 "with an appeal for the students to acknowledge that was a subject separate from providing relief for noncombatants hurt by the war." It is indecent to talk of helping the refugees while keeping silent about the napalm and the saturation bombings that make a hell of their lives. He would go no further than to say, coyly, "You are aware that I have some reservations about our role in Vietnam." This drew the biggest applause of the evening, but it is time Kennedy stopped getting cheers for such tepid observations. The students cheered because they were hungry for a word against the war and because they had faith in Kennedy. But he betrays their faith, by playing skillful politics on the issue that may mean life or death for them. We are glad to see that he was heckled in Chicago and met with signs saying, "Kennedy and Douglas Support Mass Murderers in Vietnam." There, too, in the same equivocal vein as at Hunter, he said he "happened to have some disagreements with President Johnson on Vietnam" (*Washington Post,* October 16, 1966). Is he saving them for his memoirs?

William Shannon in *Harper's* for October (1966) says he is out for the Vice-Presidency in 1968. "With skillful publicity," Shannon writes, "this could be made to appear not as an act of bold usurpation and impatient ambition by Kennedy but a reluctant rescue mission to prop up an aging wartime President whose popularity is sagging." Just as Johnson moved left to outflank Goldwater, with whom he had been allied in the Senate, so Kennedy moved left to outflank Humphrey and take over the latter's liberal constituency. But he is careful not to get so far out as to break his ties with the White House.

We do not mean to imply that Kennedy is insincere. We only note that the liberal views he has adopted also serve his political purposes. Nor do we mean to say that he is not troubled by the war. We believe he is. But he is not troubled enough to risk a confrontation with Johnson. In a *Wall Street Journal* (October 17, 1966) survey of Bobby's campaign activities one can see how little he deals with any concrete issues in those tours which have the bobby-soxers squealing. As for the war, that paper noted, "Actually Mr. Kennedy has been careful of late to avoid sharp attacks on the President. When he expressed doubts about Vietnam policy, he always stresses that 'these are very complex problems, with no simple solutions.'" Johnson was for peace, too, before he won election. What guarantee that Kennedy would prove any better, under the enormous pressure of the military bureaucracy, if his convictions are already so feeble, his mind so divided?

The Mindless Momentum of a
Runaway Military Machine

Yet another analysis of Vietnam with sobering contemporary echoes. William Westmoreland, the general who commanded American military operations in the Vietnam War from 1964 to 1968 and served as Army Chief of Staff from 1968 to 1972, was dispatched in 1967 to offering reassuring reports on progress in Vietnam to an American public whose patience for the war was rapidly vanishing. Stone took a much more jaundiced view: "The United States can win this war in Vietnam *if* it is prepared to put in a million men, or more, and then to slug it out patiently year after year until the guerrillas are worn down." It was clear to President Johnson and to the policy-makers around him that Americans were prepared to do no such thing.

· · ·

May 1, 1967

THE CENTRAL THESIS of General Westmoreland's debut on the home front is the oldest alibi of frustrated generals—they could have won the war if it hadn't been for those unpatriotic civilians back home. This was how the Kaiser's ex-generals consoled themselves over their beers after World War I and this was the soothing syrup the French generals spooned up after Dienbienphu. But the former lost the war despite all their monocled splendor because they invited exactly what they had always told themselves they ought to avoid—a war on two fronts, against France and Russia at the same time. The latter lost because their perpetual talk of how they were really winning, when year after year they were losing the finest cadres of the French officer class in the Indochinese morass, finally made the French people realize their generals were first-class liars and their dirty little colonial war not worth the cost. Both cases provide obvious parallels to our own predicament, headed as we are for that major war on the Asian mainland we were always told to avoid, and led by generals who have claimed to be winning ever since 1961, and still claim it, though, as Westmoreland also said, they see no end in sight! We wonder what kind of logic they teach them at West Point.

The heart of General Westmoreland's opening speech at the AP luncheon came when he said the enemy was "discouraged by repeated military defeats" but hanging on because "encouraged by what he believes to be popular opposition to our efforts in Vietnam." One does not need to be a military expert to question this assessment. From the enemy point of view, they are doing far better than they had a right to expect. An undeveloped nation of 30 million people with little industry of its own has defied the world's greatest military power for six years. The rebels have grown from a handful to a formidable army despite (or perhaps because of) the constant step-up in our bombardment North and South. In recent months a whole series of enormously expensive and glamorously named U.S. military sweeps have done little but tear swaths in the jungle. While our casualties have risen sharply, the enemy has managed to elude us, and to strike back at times and places of his own choosing. We are switching troops from the Mekong Delta to handle a swiftly deteriorating military situation in the northern part of South Vietnam. It is no secret that Westmoreland wants more troops and that we are going to need a limited mobilization to get them. Add the billion-dollar losses of our air war, and the growing difficulties of the no longer almighty dollar, as the mounting costs of this "little war" undermine it, and ask yourself whether the other side may not feel downright exuberant, indeed overconfident.

Let us put the case in the most hard-boiled terms. The United States can win this war in Vietnam *if* it is prepared to put in a million men, or more, and then to slug it out patiently year after year until the guerrillas are worn down. It can win if it deliberately de-escalates the firepower and meets the guerrillas on their own terms, in close combat, instead of alienating the entire population with indiscriminate artillery and airpower. A nation of 30 million cannot defeat a nation of 200 million if the bigger nation cares enough to pay the price of victory and has the patience to pursue it. The key is *patience,* and patience is what the United States lacks. It is not just the signs of popular opposition to the war which encourage the other side. It is the visible impatience. Even our hawks don't like the war and want to get it over with as quickly as possible. For us the war is a nuisance. For them the war is a matter of life-and-death. They are prepared to die for their country. We are prepared to die for our country too—if it were attacked—but not for the mere pleasure of destroying theirs. This is why they have the advantage of morale, and for this General Dynamics cannot provide a substitute.

Self-deception has been the characteristic of our leadership in this war from its beginning. Self-deception is still the key to Westmoreland's presentation. Even after so many years he still refuses to recognize the popular roots of the Vietnamese rebellion. He prefers to see it as something essentially artificial and imposed, which Hanoi can turn off with some magic spigot. First we were going to end the war by bombing Hanoi, but now that we'll soon be running out of meaningful targets in the North, we are in effect promised a quick victory if only we can bomb Berkeley into submission. The general who couldn't defeat the enemy abroad now returns to take it out on the *peaceniks* at home. Our country, he says, is founded on debate. But now, though we may be blundering toward a world war, we are told that debate is treasonable. The greatest issue in our country's history must be decided by momentum and default. Our generals would like to suppress peace sentiment here as they do in Saigon. Free discussion is to be made suspect.

A "high government source" told an equally anonymous *Baltimore Sun* (April 21) reporter (we suspect it was Johnson himself talking to his friend Philip Potter) that the U.S. had to avoid the buildup of a war psychology at home and conduct the Vietnamese war "rather coldly" because our power is so "beyond comprehension" that we mustn't let it get out of hand "if the Northern Hemisphere is not to go up in smoke." This is the awful truth a solemn joint session of Congress ought to hear. Yet Johnson is doing what his better judgment tells him not to. Westmoreland is stepping up war fever at home while abroad the wraps are taken off Hanoi, Haiphong and the Mig air bases in a way which brings nearer that final confrontation with

China and perhaps also the Soviet Union. As Senator McGovern told a *Washington Post* reporter (April 26) after a brilliant and courageous Senate attack on the growing war madness, "They [i.e., Johnson and the generals] are really going for broke." As the fog of war closes in, and the drums beat louder, which is patriotism, which is love of country, to fall silent or to try and speak some sobering word?

Same Old Formulas,
Same Tired Rhetoric

By 1969, Johnson's war had been inherited by Richard Nixon, who had been elected president in part because of his vague promises to implement an un-specified "plan" to end the war. Here Stone analyzes a "blizzard of hints" from the Nixon White House concerning a new peace strategy, and finds them devoid of substance.

. . .

June 2, 1969

IN AN EXCHANGE OF TOASTS at the White House last month, the Australian Prime Minister drew an implied comparison between Lincoln and Nixon. Walt Rostow, too, used to get Lyndon Johnson's juices flowing in the morning by telling him he was just like Lincoln. The Australian got so carried away that he ended up by demonstrating his native talent with the boomerang. If Lincoln had not persevered against the Copperheads and the Horace Greeleys, Mr. Gorton explained, there would today be "a slave autocracy in the South. . . . But there would have been no United States." Since Lincoln and the North were trying to reunite the country by force of arms ("aggression") against the wishes of the Southern states for independence ("self-determination"), Mr. Gorton's flattery was clearly beginning to rebound. The more he went on the more it sounded like a toast to Ho Chi Minh.

Mr. Gorton's analogy invites elaboration. If John Brown had succeeded in raising a slave revolt, if the North had helped the rebels, and if England had intervened on the side of the slaveholders (as the Tories later wanted to), the situation would have been comparable to the Vietnamese war. Suppose further that England, tired of a costly distant conflict, had proposed that all "non-Southern" forces withdraw, thus putting Lincoln's Unionist armies in the same "foreign" category as Britain's. Suppose the slaves were asked to lay down their arms while the slaveholders kept their army intact, and trust to "free elections" under a vague promise of international supervision but with the slaveholder regime still in power. Suppose that regime in Richmond were filling the jails with spokesmen for poor white, non-slave-holding and pro-peace elements while Britain—heavily arming this regime in preparation for its own troop withdrawal—piously insisted that its only purpose was to give the South the right of self-determination. That is where Nixon stands today.

For those who wonder just what Nixon was up to in his May 14 peace proposals, the Nixon-Gorton visit offers another source of illumination. Except for New Zealand, with its 150 token soldiers, Australia is the only white country which has put troops beside our own in the effort to revive the white man's burden in Asia. The war is almost as unpopular in Australia as here, and Gorton's opposition—the Labor party—led the protest demonstrations which greeted Ky two years ago in Australia. The conservative coalition Gorton heads was Johnson's faithful junior partner. Gorton was here only a week before Nixon's Vietnam speech. If Nixon were contemplating any real departure in policy, he would be leaving Gorton out on a limb. It would be necessary to prepare Australian public opinion. But nothing in their exchanges reflected any change in policy; they spoke as simple-mindedly as Johnson of their joint effort "to help South Vietnam preserve its independence."

Those who are working themselves into euphoria by wishful exegesis of what Nixon did *not* say in his May 14 address would be wise to pause a moment over what Nixon and Gorton did not say in their exchanges a week earlier. These, as expected, attracted little attention in this country, and did not have to take American peace sentiment into account.* The Nixon farewell statement, which Gorton said was framed with his agreement and served as a final communiqué, spoke of their talks on "Vietnam and regional security." A continued U.S.-Australian protectorate over

*Indeed the only place the texts are available is in the *Weekly Compilation of Presidential Documents* for May 19.

Southeast Asia was implied. Nixon welcomed, and promised to support, Australia's decision to keep troops in Malaysia and Singapore when the British leave two years hence, forever ending the Kipling era east of Suez. But not a single word was said about the negotiations in Paris, or the hope of a turn toward peace.

Nixon, like Johnson, is playing for time. His May 14 address strongly recalls Johnson's at Johns Hopkins in April 1965. Johnson deluded many people into believing that he was moving toward peace at the very moment he was committing the first U.S. combat troops to the South. The only remarkable thing about the Nixon address is that at one point he seemed to be pulling his own leg. When Nixon said "repeating the old formulas and the tired rhetoric of the past is not enough," he seemed to be setting himself up for the cartoonists. If I were running the Secret Service I would find out who wrote that and take him down to the White House cellar for interrogation under the bright lights. For as Senator Gore showed in a devastating analysis on the Senate floor May 20, the speech was full of old formulas and tired rhetoric picked up almost verbatim from Johnson and Rusk. Even Nixon's titillating hints about free elections and a neutral South Vietnam were also uttered, as Gore found, in almost the same words by Rusk in 1966. The parallels with Johnson sound as if Nixon was down on the ranch. If this weren't politics, it would be plagiarism.

The speech is so tricky it has everybody confused except Henry Kissinger. "Proponents leak stories that the President is sending subtle signals to the Reds that he'd let them share in a new Saigon government as part of a peace package," the *Wall St. Journal* said May 23. "Opponents warn this would bring the 'disguised defeat' Nixon had vowed not to accept. White House aides insist no decision has been made." Never have there been so many hints with so little substance.

You can read in Chalmers Roberts in the *Washington Post* (May 18) that silence gives consent and that what Nixon didn't say May 14 really means he is ready to accept even an interim coalition government. This was "spelled out by persons in a position to know," Roberts wrote ecstatically. But gravitation being what it is, what goes up must come down, and he added a *but*—"The U.S. cannot accept settlement terms which would turn the South over to the Communists and make a mockery of the years of American and South Vietnamese bloodletting." The only sure nonmockery, it would seem, is to maintain in power the same oligarchy we have imposed on the South for 15 years.

On the other hand you may read in David Lawrence (May 21) that the Nixon Administration has "at last" decided that it will not tolerate the continuance of heavy attacks and is not ruling out drastic reprisals which "could mean the resumption at any moment of the bombing of North Vietnam and even a blockade of Haiphong harbor." Obviously the White House is handing out different lines of poop. Richard Wilson (Washington *Star,* May 21) reports jubilantly that before Nixon went on TV May 14 he gave an extemporaneous résumé to his top-level officials. They not only applauded but "there was no doubt what they were applauding." The main emphasis was on "not quitting" and on Nixon's "unpleasant options" if Hanoi does not accept mutual withdrawal. These include "a massive fire-bomb raid to destroy Hanoi." We'll put 'em back in the Stone Age yet. Senator Hugh Scott, the GOP whip, dropped hints of the same kind after Senator Kennedy—in the wake of "Hamburger Hill"—attacked the bloody nonsense of charging up any hill a well dug-in enemy baits for U.S. attack.

In the blizzard of hints, there is also a preview of what Nixon may say to Thieu on Midway June 8. It is hinted that if one reads the fine print closely one will see that Saigon holds a secure veto over the international supervisory body to verify withdrawals "and for any other purpose *agreed upon* between the two sides." The elections, too, would be held under "agreed procedures" and agreed means the agreement of the Thieu regime. While Nixon takes the high road, Thieu will have the low, and when domestic opinion gets tired of seeing the Reds reject Nixon's "generous" offers, the iron will be hot and the Pentagon hopes it can strike again.

Only the Bums Can
Save the Country Now

Although the phrase wasn't widely used at the time, by the early '70s a version of today's "culture war" was already in full swing, with leftist antiwar students, black advocates of civil rights, and nascent movements in support of a new feminism, gay rights, and other progressive causes ranged against a political and business establishment supported by a quasi-populist coalition of "white ethnics," southern conservatives, and anxious parents—Nixon's so-called "silent majority." When students around the country erupted in protests over Nixon's expansion of the war into Cambodia, the president responded with an angry attack, referring to "these bums . . . blowing up the campuses." Soon Ohio State National Guardsmen would kill four students and wound nine others during a mostly peaceful protest at Kent State University. In this angry article, Stone allies himself squarely with the "bums" in exposing the deceptive basis for the Cambodia policy. Later the same year, Stone would publish a book on the Ohio tragedy, *The Killings at Kent State: How Murder Went Unpunished.*

.   .   .

May 18, 1970

THE RACE IS ON between protest and disaster. Despite the first four martyr "bums" of Nixon-Agnewism at Kent State, the college shutdown their deaths precipitated, the outpouring of student and other protesters here last weekend, the campus lobbyists beginning to flood the halls of Congress, the Senate resolutions to limit or end Indochinese military operations, and the smoldering near-revolt within the Nixon Administration itself, we are still on the brink. We are in the first stages of a new and wider war from which withdrawal will be difficult. The military holds the reins and can precipitate new provocations and stage new alarms. The only hope is that the students can create such a Plague for Peace, swarming like locusts into the halls of Congress, that they stop all other business and make an end to the war the No. 1 concern it ought to be. Washington must no longer be the privileged sanctuary of the warmakers. The slogan of the striking students ought to be "Suspend Classes and Educate the Country." I see no other visible and adequate means to stop the slide into a conflict that may sweep very suddenly beyond the confines of Indochina if the man who gambled on Cambodia ends by gambling on the use of nuclear weapons.

In a dispatch from a landing zone in Cambodia, Jack Foisie of the *Washington Post* (May 8) described GIs jumping from helicopters under enemy fire with derisive denunciations of the war scrawled on their helmets. One of those he copied down sums up the situation of the whole country in this war. "We are the unwilling," it said, "led by the unqualified, doing the unnecessary, for the ungrateful." As usual the country is not being told the truth about why we went into Cambodia. In his war address of April 30 Nixon pictured the attack across the border as a preemptive exercise to hit an "enemy building up to launch massive attacks on our forces and those of South Vietnam." It was described as a swift preventive action from which we would soon withdraw and which was not part of any broader intervention in Cambodian affairs.

But thanks to the indiscretion of one Congressman, we now have the private—and more candid—version given members of Congress at special State Department briefings. This puts the origins and purpose of the Cambodian action in a very different light. The Congressman is Representative Hamilton Fish (R. N.Y.), a right-winger who has long questioned the logic of our heavy commitment in so peripheral an area as Southeast Asia. In a letter to constituents released May 13, Mr. Fish summarizes a private briefing by Under Secretary of State Richardson for selected members of Congress. Nixon said we moved across the border to nip enemy plans for an imminent attack. But from Richardson's briefing, Mr. Fish reports, "It was clear that the present military thrust into Cambodia hinged largely on the reportedly surprise overthrow of Prince Sihanouk." Nixon said in his April 30 speech that for five years "neither the U.S. nor South Vietnam moved against those enemy sanctuaries because we did not wish to violate the territory of a neutral nation." But Richardson gave the Congressmen a different story. He told them, "U.S. intelligence had known for years of those enclaves from which attacks on South Vietnam have been launched" but we had never attacked them before "because it was feared that Sihanouk would counter any invasion by allowing NVA [North Vietnamese Army] forces to enlarge their occupied areas."

Sihanouk was trying to maintain a precarious neutrality by playing one side against the other. Nixon was deceitful when he said in the April 30 speech that our policy since the Geneva Conference of 1954 "has been to scrupulously respect the neutrality of the Cambodian people" and added— as proof of our virtue—that since last August we have had a diplomatic mission in Pnom Penh "of fewer than 15" and that for the previous four years "we did not have any diplomatic mission whatever." The truth is that Sihanouk ousted our mission and broke relations in 1965 because he claimed the CIA had been plotting against him for years and even tried twice to kill him. Sihanouk was especially resentful of the Khmer Serei (Free Khmer) mercenaries the CIA and our Special Forces had enlisted from among Cambodians living in South Vietnam and Thailand to act as an anti-Sihanouk commando force. The CIA gave it facilities to broadcast anti-Sihanouk propaganda from Saigon.

"For the past five years," Nixon said with bland hypocrisy, "we have provided no military assistance and no economic assistance whatever to Cambodia." He did not explain that Sihanouk threw out our military mission because he said it had been trying to turn his armed forces against him, and gave up economic aid, too, rather than have it used as a cover for U.S. agents trying to overthrow him. This was not a figment of Sihanouk's imagination. As far back as 1958, in a police raid on the villa of one of his generals, Sihanouk found a letter from President Eisenhower pledging full support to a projected coup and to a reversal of Cambodian neutrality. This was part of a "Bangkok plan" worked out between the dictators of South Vietnam and Thailand (Diem and Marshal Sarit Thanarit) to dismember Cambodia and instigate civil war (see William Worthy's account in the York, Pa., *Gazette & Daily* of April 30). When Sihanouk resumed relations last August, in his desperate see-saw between the two sides, his condition was that the U.S. mission be kept small. He didn't want too many CIA agents roaming around.

That was poor Sihanouk's mistake. Cambodia neutrality was ended when the military we had long wooed finally overthrew Sihanouk on March 18. The most complete account yet published of the events leading up to the coup is to be found in *Le Monde Diplomatique* for April. It is by Daniel Roy, a Frenchman with 15 years' experience in Indochina who was for a time press attaché to Prince Sihanouk. He claims that funds for the coup were provided by a Cambodian adventurer turned banker in Bangkok who was associated in the enterprise with the notorious Son Ngoc Thanh, puppet President of Cambodia under the Japanese occupation. The latter fled to Thailand after the war and according to M. Roy is "today in the service of the CIA." M. Roy also charges that the coup was prepared by Khmer Serei forces who went over the border with their arms and wives and pretended that they were defecting to Sihanouk. They infiltrated the army and the police as a Trojan Horse for the CIA.

Let us now return to Congressman Fish's account of the private State Department briefing. "Following the fall of Sihanouk," the Congressmen were told, "the new anti-Communist government cut all supply lines [of the NVA and Viet Cong] except the Ho Chi Minh trail" which, of course, lies largely outside Cambodian territory. "*To resecure their severed supply routes,*" the account in the private briefing continued, "*VC and NVA began moving out of the enclaves, thereby threatening the overthrow of the Cambodian government*" (my italics). It is "against this background," Representative Fish's account of the briefing concludes, "that the American-South Vietnamese strikes into Cambodia were ordered."

The sequence is quite different from that given publicly by Mr. Nixon. Instead of preparing an attack on our forces in South Vietnam, the enemy was reacting to an attack on its supply lines. This upset the status quo, and risked a complete take-over of Cambodia by the other side. We intervened to save it from the consequences. Did our government give the new Lon Nol government of Cambodia assurances that we would defend it if its action in cutting all the supply routes precipitated an attack upon it?

It is true that at the State Department briefing "it was stressed that the present attacks were not aimed at either the confrontation of the estimated 40,000 to 50,000 VC and NVA believed operating in Cambodia or the defense of the present government of Cambodia. The raids were described as strictly 'spoiling actions,' aimed at supply, bunker and communication network destruction" and to give the South Vietnamese army additional time while the enemy rebuilds its supplies. But you have to be pretty feeble-minded to accept this at face value. What if Sihanouk, with NVA and Peking support, is restored to power, this time not as a precarious neutral but as an ally of the other side? What if we are then faced with the prospect, not just of restoring the old supply lines and bases but of Cambodia turning into one big enemy base? Who can believe that the Nixon Administration will stand by and let this happen?

This is the wider war which lies ahead. The overthrow of Sihanouk was a grave political mistake. It gave the other side a new ally with legitimacy and mass support, basic necessities for the Indochinese People's War which has already been proclaimed against us. The situation inside Cambodia was succinctly summed up in an interview which the pro-Nixon and pro-war *U.S. News & World Report* for May 18 held by cable with its correspondent, James N. Wallace, in Pnom Penh:

Q. Have the allied attacks in eastern Cambodia saved the rest of the country from a Communist take-over?

A. No. Unless the allied drive completely overwhelms the Communists, Cambodia's position remains about the same . . . the short-run result is even more chaos and confusion . . .

Q. Did the Cambodians welcome the Allied move?

A. Again, no. Cambodians do not like . . . the idea of South Vietnamese troops' rolling across Cambodia . . .

Q. What kind of reception would Sihanouk get?

A. Almost certainly he would receive more popular support than the Lon Nol government cares to admit. Sihanouk still is popular among a great many of Cambodia's 5.5 million peasants, who respected his traditional status as a god-king and liked his earthly personal relations with villagers.

The French journalist Max Clos, who has been covering Indochina for years during both the French and U.S. wars, foresees (*Le Figaro,* May 2–3) a Cambodian resistance based on peasant support, doing in their country what the Viet Cong have done in Vietnam and creating a "liberated zone" from which in time they will be able to take over Pnom Penh. "Mr. Nixon," M. Clos wrote, "hopes to withdraw his troops from Cambodia in a month and a half. Even if he succeeds, it is safe to predict he will have to send them back again."

The political folly of our latest move is not limited to Cambodia. The newly enlarged war must add to the shaky character of the Thieu regime, which has had to close down all the South Vietnamese schools in a rising student revolt much like our own. The idea of South Vietnamese troops being used to bolster a government which has been massacring Cambodian citizens of Vietnamese origin must add to Thieu's unpopularity. The bitterness between the Viets and the Khmers of Cambodia is incomparably older and more bitter than the recent animosities of the Russo-American cold war. It is only two centuries since the Viets seized the Mekong delta from the Khmers. Sihanouk, unlike his successors, never stirred up the mob against the Vietnamese and the VC and NVA intruders, unlike our forces, did not bomb and devastate Cambodian villages. This new shift strengthens the forces opposing our puppets on both sides.

This has been a political war from its very beginning against the French. We go on believing as they did that a political problem can be solved by military means. The annals of their war, like ours, is full of sensationally billed search-and-destroy operations which were finally going to cripple the rebels, like this latest "Operation Total Victory" across the Cambodian border. The Communists under Ho Chi Minh seized national leadership in the war against the French, as the adroit Sihanouk did in Cambodia. Now they both are allied against us. Sihanouk will now make it possible for the other side to implement the basic strategy of a People's War on a wider scale. The strategy is to force maximum dispersion upon the hated foreign invader to make him widen the area of his activity and stretch his lines of communication so that the guerrillas can pick and choose the most advantageous weak points for their concentrated attacks. We have picked up their treacherous

gambit by invading Cambodia and sooner or later unless we get out of Indochina altogether, we must send ground troops into Laos and Cambodia,
perhaps even into North Vietnam where a fresh army of 250,000 or more
awaits our landing. Nowhere has airpower, however overwhelming and unchallenged, been able to win a war.

What will happen when the country wakes up to find that instead of
withdrawing troops we are going to send in fresh divisions? What happens
to inflation, the budget and the stock market? To student and racial unrest?
Nixon, in a mood of self-pity, complained in his April 30 address that past
war Presidents did not have to face a nation "assailed by counsels of doubt
and defeat from some of the most widely known opinion leaders of the nation." He seems to attribute this to some perversity. He takes it as personal.
He does not stop to consider why this war has aroused so much more opposition than any past war, and done so in every class and every region and
every age-group, from Wall Street financiers to campus radicals. Even National Guardsmen give the V-sign to students, and soldiers go into battle
with peace amulets around their necks. He seems to think there is something wrong with the critics. He will not face up to the possibility that there
is something wrong with the war. Certainly this generation of Americans
would prove no less patriotic and brave than any other if our country were
really in danger.

It is a measure of our stupid leadership that the Cambodian war was
started on the phoney pretext that just across the border was a kind of enemy Pentagon and that we could cripple the enemy by smashing it. One
measure of the mendacity may be found in an intelligence briefing the *New
York Times* reported April 4, two weeks after Sihanouk's overthrow. It said
COSVN, the enemy HQ, had been moved from Cambodian to South
Vietnamese territory. The story even carried a map showing the old location at Mimot—which figures in recent accounts of the Cambodian operation—in the "fishhook" and the new location in a thick jungle area
described as "virtually inaccessible to ground troops" and "probably not seriously vulnerable to air attacks." It is difficult to believe that Nixon and his
aides are such idiots as not to be aware of this intelligence information.

The Eichmann trial taught the world the banality of evil. Nixon is
teaching the world the evil of banality. The man so foolish as to talk to

protesting students about football and surfing is the same man who (like Johnson) sees war in the puerile terms of "humiliation" and a challenge to his virility. He doesn't want us to be a "helpless giant" (which we are in Indochina) so he is plunging us into a wider quagmire where we will end up more helpless than ever.

The past week is the week in which the Nixon Administration began to come apart. Letters like Hickel's showed how isolated he is even from members of his own Cabinet, where there seems to be a silent majority against him. The antiwar round robin signed by more than 200 employes of the State Department shows how deeply the Cambodian affair has stirred even the most timid, conformist and conventional section of the bureaucracy. Nothing Nixon says can be taken at face value. Even when he said on April 20, in his troop withdrawal announcement, that a "just peace" was at last in sight, he must have been planning this expansion of the war. Indeed, General Westmoreland as Army Chief of Staff had already begun to lobby for a Cambodian invasion in off-the-record briefings.

There were two remarks of the deepest significance in the Nixon press conference of May 8. One was that if we withdraw from Vietnam "America is finished insofar as the peace-keeper in the Asian world is concerned." This revealed that he is still committed, despite that vague "low posture" talk on Guam, to a Pax Americana in Asia. If we are to police Asia we are in for many years of war and internal disruption. The folly is as great as if China were to try and become the "peace-keeper" of Latin America. The other remark was that unlike Johnson he would not escalate step by step but "move decisively." This is the Goldwater-LeMay thesis that we could have won the Vietnam war if we had smashed Hanoi and Haiphong in one great blow, perhaps with nuclear weapons. Hanoi, especially after the recent big bombing raids, expects something of the kind. Moscow and Peking are already trying to patch up their differences in expectation of it. If Nixon goes to nuclear weapons, the end result may well be World War III. Unless an army of students can fan out to the grass roots and make the country aware of these dangerous possibilities, terrible days may lie ahead.

Part Seven

HEROES AND OTHERS

Thomas E. Dewey

A caustic, entertaining sketch of New York Governor Thomas E. Dewey, Republican candidate for president in 1944 and a man who, in Stone's memorable phrase, "reeks of self-assurance . . . small stuff and cold fish."

.   .   .

May 20, 1944

ALBANY FASCINATES ME, but I can't say the same for Dewey. The capital of New York would inspire Dreiser and depress De Tocqueville, but its Governor is a Republican Presidential candidate, very standard model. I've waded through a foot-high pile of Dewey messages, speeches, and statements kindly supplied by his affable press secretary, James C. Hagerty. I listened to the Governor address the American Newspaper Publishers' meeting in New York and watched him being charming to the hopeful on the platform after it was over. I've read almost everything written about him, except the Rupert Hughes work, which seems to have confused him with George Washington and Lucky Luciano with a cherry tree. I've talked to people who work closely with him and to people who hate him, the latter being easy to find in Albany and New York where Dewey has been seen in close-up. And all I can report is that for the first time since becoming a Washington correspondent and on one of the few occasions since I became a newspaperman, I found myself with an assignment that bored me.

On international affairs, Dewey might be Warren G. Harding, an internationalist but—. On domestic affairs, where straight Hooverism is no longer possible even for a Republican, Dewey might be Alfred Landon, unalterably opposed to the New Deal, four square against its threat to the American way of life, but in agreement with its basic principles, though he thinks they are poorly administered. As a public figure, he is as familiar a type—the "clean government" reformer who is death on all crooks except the really big and respectable ones of our society. As a man, he is competent, courageous, hard-working, but extraordinary only in his drive, his singleness of purpose, the intensity of his ambition. I don't think he is wicked, sinister, dishonest, or fascist, though I suppose he will have such epithets thrown at him when the campaign gets heated; I think he is a good American, very far removed from anti-democratic crackpots, racial bigots, and Bertie McCormicks. But the man is uninteresting because he presents no complexities, deviates in no way from type. I can see nothing but the commonplace in his mind. I sense no lift of idealism in his spirit; his motivations seem to me wholly self-seeking. And the personality is completely lacking in human warmth.

This may sound harsh and it may be unjust, but it is said only after much thought and consideration, and it checks with the reactions of people who are his friends as well as with those of his enemies. Dewey has been called "a boy scout," and he is one in the sense that he sees the problems of our society purely in the obvious and elementary terms of personal morality; I say obvious and elementary because he would not see the profounder immoralities in our customary ways of living and doing business. But he is not a boy scout in the sense that he would let a naive but praiseworthy and wholesome sense of duty stand in the way of personal aggrandizement. He chose the law as a profession because he thought it offered the prospect of greater and more secure financial rewards than singing; none of those who have written of him or who know him claim that he was attracted to the law as a useful way to spend one's life, or because he was inspired by the example of some great judge or advocate. There is nothing in him of the Galahad or the Quixote. His sensational splurge as prosecutor in New York was a quick stepping-stone to the Governorship, not the beginning of a job that he felt had to be completed in the interest of civic duty or clean government, and the Governorship is a stepping-stone to the Presidency. He is a kind of Get-Rich-Quick Wallingford in politics, a man who plays for the quick rise and the big profit. That the profit is in personal advancement rather than money is a detail, not an essential. Dewey's eye has always been on the headlines, not the stars. The men who worked with him as D.A. will tell you that the press was as constantly in their thoughts as the jury.

A certain humility makes a man lovable and marks him wise. Dewey reeks of self-assurance. You look at him on the platform and think of Browning's line, "A man's reach should exceed his grasp," but only because the two spring from such different worlds. It is only in the most superficial sense that Dewey would ever think of himself as unfit; he is said to be busy boning up on American history now in preparation for the Presidency. He would never think of himself as unworthy. Big men usually have a sense of fun. Roosevelt has it, Churchill has it, Lenin had it, so saintly a figure as Gandhi jokes and frolics. Dewey would never dream of making a joke at his own expense. His humor, or what passed for it, is heavy-footed, as when he referred to newsboys at the publishers' dinner in New York as "purveyors of your products." (I was there; I heard it.) He is not what we call a regular guy. There is nothing in him of Willkie's rich curiosity, human interest, or careless vitality. Dewey is small stuff and cold fish, handsomer and physically robust but really a good deal like Coolidge, frugal spiritually, a man who does not give himself freely.

I saw Dewey for the first time at the publishers' dinner, a trying event for most of those present because so many long-winded speakers preceded him, a trying occasion for him because Eric Johnston of the United States Chamber of Commerce tried to steal the show, and almost succeeded. Johnston's speech was the improvisation of a shrewd highschool boy, and I remember it chiefly for its gorgeously mixed metaphors, but it went over big with the publishers. Dewey seemed restive until his moment came. He went forward like a singer, chest out, enormously self-possessed. He sounded like a man who had studied with a first-rate elocutionist in a smallish town. One could have written a musical score for the speech. His gestures, the modulation of his voice, the measured emphasis and stress, were too perfect to be pleasant; the manner was conceited. When he praised Secretary of State Hull, it was with the gracious condescension that he might have used in patting a small boy on the head. The speech was expertly prepared and made Johnston's seem as amateurish as it was. Dewey gave an orotund solemnity to such hollow stuff as "When we have ceased to wage war, we shall have to wage peace," with the air of a man delivering an epigram.

In Albany I found those close to Dewey devoted to him. Four investigations are going here full blast, and the town is overrun with racket-busters who used to work for Dewey in New York. They like him, irrespective of political differences, for Dewey is competent, a good executive, and the young lawyer's ideal of a prosecutor. The young men in his immediate entourage are capable rather than brilliant, and already envisage themselves as the Harry Hopkinses and Louis Howes of the next Administration. It is a giddy thing to be on a Presidential band-wagon, and those few of them who have New Dealish backgrounds are rapidly throwing earlier ideas overboard as excess baggage. Even in this innermost circle one has the feeling that Dewey inspires fear and respect rather than affection. "He's very self-centered and never seems interested in you personally," said one racket-buster reflectively in answer to a question. But outside the circle of Deweyites, one encounters only dislike of the Governor.

In part, this dislike is to Dewey's credit. The town is comfortably corrupt. So is the Legislature. The Governor's attack on the local O'Connell machine brought reprisal in the shape of an O'Connell investigation of the Republican Legislature. Dewey was forced to take the investigation over to protect his party, but the man he chose as special prosecutor, Hiram C. Todd, is forceful and independent, and there will be difficulty in keeping the investigation within safe bounds. Dewey started out to investigate favoritism in assessments in Albany, the payment of current expenses out of bond issues, and election frauds. He hoped to duplicate in Albany the success he had achieved as a gang-buster in New York and break the one important Democratic machine upstate. But an investigation of the Legislature, which has been Republican-controlled for many years, was not part of his original plan. The fears this investigation has aroused in his own party have served to make Republican legislators subservient to him, and he has ruled the Legislature like a little dictator. But the inquiry itself will not be allowed to go too far because it would hurt the Republicans more than the Democrats in an election year and would inevitably involve big money interests with which Dewey is himself allied.

To understand the political problems that confront Dewey in Albany, one must understand this old Dutch town at the head of navigation on the Hudson. It exhibits the slatternly side of the Democratic process. For the first twenty years of the century it was solidly Republican. During the past twenty years it has been as solidly Democratic. During both periods it has been corrupt, and during both the respectable elements have shared widely in the benefits of machine government. They resent these investigations. The Democratic era began with an alliance between Dan O'Connell, son of a saloon keeper, and the old-family owner of the Alleghany-Ludlum steel works. Albany's political revolutions have not been the result of uprisings by an outraged citizenry but of internal feuds in aging political machines. A legislative investigation before the last war plus some fiery attacks by Teddy Roosevelt upon the Barnes political machine only increased the Republican vote at the next election, and there are many people here who think local resentment will enable the O'Connells to pile up a larger majority than ever before. Dewey's unpopularity in Albany might cost him New York State and the Presidency.

From all I can see, the O'Connell machine is still united and vigorous. Unless Dewey can unearth evidence of some major crime, it is unlikely that he can shake its popular strength. But the O'Connell machine has been in power so long that it has been many years since any rough tactics were required to keep either its henchmen or the populace in line. Public standards are higher than they were a generation ago, and in some respects conditions under the O'Connell regime are better than under Barnes. The "Gut," Albany's old tenderloin, no longer flaunts its red-light section. The principal "crimes" Dewey has been able to lay at the door of the O'Connell machine are not of a kind to bring ordinary Albany citizens tumbling from their beds in alarm. "Bookmaking" establishments operate pretty openly. There are plenty of slot machines around. Saloons are open all night selling Hedrick beer, the O'Connell family brew. Election frauds seem to be common, but the O'Connells have so tight a grip on grand and petit jury lists that not much could be done about them.

Albany's city government seems to have been holding down its tax rate by paying current expenditures out of capital borrowings. Assessments seem to be adjusted to aid the deserving and teach the independents a lesson; Dan O'Connell's first political job was as tax assessor, a post he used to good advantage in building his machine. These are dishonest practices no one could wish to condone—except the property owners and lawyers who benefit by them, and their beneficiaries are many. We Americans are for clean government in theory and political favors in practice. This makes the Dewey type popular—at a distance. One of Dewey's advisers in Albany is a nice young Republican lawyer who represents large property interests through his father-in-law's estate, helps run a leading real-estate firm, and does a substantial volume of business representing the Republican minority which has to take its assessment appeals to the courts instead of to the district leader. Dewey assigned him to investigate assessments, and the investigation will make it easier for a time to be a Republican in Albany, but an assessments scandal will neither break the O'Connell machine nor make dramatic headlines elsewhere.

In part Albany's dislike for Dewey is a result of his shortcomings as a person. Other Governors were gracious and became part of the life of the town. Mrs. Roosevelt and Mrs. Lehman lived, shopped, and entertained in Albany. Both were a familiar sight downtown. "Albanians," as they call themselves, have the civic patriotism of a Greek city-state. "We never see Mrs. Dewey," they complain. Albany feels that Dewey is only a man on the make, hurrying through on his way somewhere else. It is contented in its corruption, thinks it civic misdeeds no worse than those of most cities, believes it is being smeared and sacrificed to provide a Dewey triumph, resents a certain ruthlessness and self-righteousness in the Governor's attitude toward it.

There are many complaints that Dewey is rude and standoffish in dealing with the townspeople. Lehman was chairman of Russian War Relief in Albany; as a matter of courtesy Dewey was invited to succeed him. The invitation went unanswered. The Inter-Racial Council runs a Booker T. Washington Center here. It held a musicale to raise funds. Tickets were sent the Governor. They were returned unacknowledged. The 4-H clubs held their annual meeting here. It is customary for Governors to address the meeting. Dewey refused because the Mayor of Albany had also been invited. He agreed to speak only when the Mayor withdrew. "He can't put his political ax aside for a moment," said one Albany newspaperman. Albany would agree with the irate Republican lady who once said, "You have to know Dewey to dislike him."

Farewell to F.D.R.

Not hagiography but a sober, appreciative assessment of Franklin D. Roosevelt a few days after his death on April 12, 1945, as well as a look back at his presidency—"for folk who scare easily . . . a series of scares"—and a cautiously optimistic look forward at the Truman era.

.   .   .

April 21, 1945

MR. ROOSEVELT'S BODY was brought back to Washington today for the last time. The crowds began to gather early in Lafayette Park opposite the White House, as they did all along the line of the procession from Union Station. I got down to the park early and stood with many others waiting. Some small boys climbed into a tree for a better view. The gray tip of the Washington Monument showed above the White House. The trees were in full green; tulips bloomed on the lawn. Outside on the sidewalk there were soldiers in helmets every few feet, and we could hear the harsh tones of command as the guard of honor lined up on the White House lawn. Florists' trucks pulled up at the door, and huge wreaths were taken inside. Cameras were set up on the front porch, and camera men were perched on high ladders on the sidewalks and among us in the park. Birds sang, but the crowd was silent.

In the park I recognized a group of girls from the C.I.O. offices in nearby Jackson Place, Walter Lippmann, and an Army and Navy Club bellboy with a sensitive Negro face. There were soldiers and sailors, Waves and Wacs. There were many Negroes, some of them quite obviously housemaids. There were well-dressed women and men in shirt sleeves. I noticed a small middle-aged priest, several grave and owlish Chinese, many service men with their wives or sweethearts, a tired man in overalls and blue-denim work cap. A tall gangling Negro boy in jitterbug jacket and pork-pie hat towered above the crowd in front of me. A man who seemed to be a hobo, unshaven and dirty, jarred the silence with a loud laugh at something a child behind him had said. There were close-mouthed New England faces, Jewish faces, Midwestern faces; workers and business men and housewives, all curiously alike in their patience and in the dumb stolidity that is often sorrow's aspect.

A truck sped by on Pennsylvania Avenue. On the roof of the truck two navy men operated a movie camera, taking pictures of the crowd. Far above us, twenty-four Flying Fortresses roared across the skies in proud forma-tion. One remembered the President's 50,000-plane speech, and choked. Motorcycle police heralded the procession's approach. The marching men, the solemn bands, the armored cars, the regiment of Negro soldiers, the uniformed women's detachments, the trucks filled with soldiers, and the black limousine carrying officials and the President's family went by slowly. They seemed part of an unreal pageant by comparison with the one glimpse of what we had come to see—the coffin covered with a flag. Many faces in the crowd puckered as it went past. In that one quick look thousands of us said our goodbye to a great and good man, and to an era.

I was at the *PM* office in New York Thursday when it happened. There was a commotion in the newsroom. A copyboy ran out of the wire-room with a piece of United Press copy in his hand. That first flash, "The Presi-dent died this afternoon," seemed incredible; like something in a night-mare, far down under the horror was the comfortable feeling that you would wake to find it was all a dream. The Romans must have felt this way when word came that Caesar Augustus was dead. Later, when work was done, I went to a meeting of liberals in an apartment on Washington Square. It was a gloomy gathering, much too gloomy to honor so buoyant a spirit as Mr. Roosevelt's. Some felt that with his passing the Big Three would split up, that hope of a new world organization was dim. One of those present reported, apropos, that an automobile-company official in Detroit had told a delegation of visiting French newspapermen, "Next we fight the Soviet Union." Some thought the Nazis would be encouraged to hold out, that the war had been lengthened by the President's passing. Everyone seemed to feel that trouble, serious trouble, lay ahead.

I don't want to sound like Pollyanna, but I can remember so many crepe-hanging sessions of this kind since 1932. The Roosevelt era, for folk who scare easily, was a series of scares. Just before he took office, when the bonus marchers were driven out of Washington, revolution seemed to be around the corner. There was the banking crisis. The NRA [National Recovery Administration] was suspected of being the beginning of fascism; one of my friends in New York cautiously erased his name from the volumes of Marx and Lenin he owned; he felt the men with the bludgeons might be in his apartment any day. The Supreme Court knocked one piece of reform legislation after another on the head, and Mr. Roosevelt, when he set out to fight back, showed a deplorable disrespect for the constitutional amenities. There were the Chicago massacre and the Little Steel strike. There was Hitler. France fell when our armed forces were in good shape for a war with Nicaragua. The Japs sank most of the fleet at Pearl Harbor. It was a lush era for Cassandras.

Somehow we pulled through before, and somehow we'll pull through again. In part it was luck. In part it was Mr. Roosevelt's leadership. In part it was the quality of the country and its people. I don't know about the rest of the four freedoms, but one thing Mr. Roosevelt gave the United States in one crisis after another, and that was freedom from fear. Perhaps his most important contribution was the example, the superlative example, of his personal courage. Perhaps some of us will feel less gloomy if we remember it. Perhaps some of us will be more effective politically if we also learn from Mr. Roosevelt's robust realism, his ability to keep his eye on the main issue and not worry too much about the minor details.

I found the mood of the intellectuals and New Dealers in Washington this week-end quite different from that in New York. There has been much swapping of information and sidelights, and there is a good deal of confidence in the new President. No one, least of all Mr. Truman, an impressively modest man, expects him fully to fill Mr. Roosevelt's shoes. But the general feeling among those who know Mr. Truman is that he will surprise the skeptical. I can only record my own impression for whatever it is worth. I talked with Mr. Truman several years ago and liked him immediately and instinctively. The Presidency is a terrific job, and it remains to be seen how he will stand up under its pressure. But he is a good man, an honest man, a devoted man. Our country could be far more poorly served. Mr. Truman is a hard worker, decisive, a good executive. He works well with people. He is at once humble about his own knowledge and capacities, as a wise man should be, and quietly confident about his ability to learn and to rise to the occasion.

I hate to confess it, but I think Mr. Roosevelt was astute and farsighted in picking Mr. Truman rather than Mr. Wallace as his successor. At this particular moment in our history, Mr. Truman can do a better job. Mr. Wallace's accession might have split the country wide open, not because of Mr. Wallace but because of the feeling against him on the right. Mr. Truman has the good-will of both sides and is in a position to capitalize on the sobering influence of Mr. Roosevelt's passing. The heaviest task of the President lies in the field of foreign relations, and the biggest obstacle to its accomplishment is in the Senate. It is fortunate that Mr. Truman's greatest and most obvious political assets are his relations with the Senate. He is a friendly person, and was well liked on both sides of the aisle. Isolationists like Wheeler and La Follette are among his friends, and he may be able to exert an influence with them that the circumstances and the momentum of past events denied to Mr. Roosevelt. The chances of a two-thirds' vote in the Senate for the new peace organization are improved by the shift in the Presidency. I say this with no disrespect to our great departed leader.

I think Mr. Truman will carry on Mr. Roosevelt's work. He had been very effective in support of Mr. Roosevelt in the Senate. I can authoritatively report that the famous B_2H_2 resolution* originated in Mr. Truman's office. Three of the sponsors, Senators Ball, Burton, and Hatch, were members of the Truman committee. Mr. Truman's closest personal friends in the Senate were Kilgore of West Virginia and Wallgren of Washington, both sturdy progressives and good New Dealers. There will be changes in the Cabinet, perhaps some for the better. On domestic policy Mr. Truman's record is an excellent one, and labor has nothing to fear from him. The shock of Mr. Roosevelt's death has created an atmosphere in which the new President may be able to unite the nation more closely than ever and carry it forward to that stable peace Mr. Roosevelt so deeply desired.

---

*The historic bipartisan Senate resolution of 1943, sponsored by Senators Ball, Burton, Hill, and Hatch (hence B_2H_2) urging U.S. initiative in forming a United Nations.

LaGuardia and UNRRA

Here is a rich evocation of the life and personality of Fiorello LaGuardia, the most beloved mayor of New York City, following his death after a long and painful battle against pancreatic cancer. UNRRA was the United Nations Relief and Rehabilitation Administration, founded in 1943 to provide relief to areas liberated from Axis powers. LaGuardia was their director general in 1946. UNRRA provided billions of U.S. dollars of rehabilitation aid and helped some eight million refugees.

.   .   .

September 22, 1947

THAT LONG AND LONELY FIGHT in the Bronx is ended. We have lost a great New Yorker and a great American. It is sad that the passing of Fiorello LaGuardia should have been pitiful. He was a man to provoke violent reactions—anger, hatred, enthusiasm, love, exasperation, devotion, anything but pity. He who loved combat, crowds, five-alarm fires, rough-and-tumble debate on street corners and on the floor of Congress, tumult and crisis, with all the ardor of a mischievous and exhibitionistic small boy, should not have had to wrestle unseen with a stealthy death. He should have died splendidly in battle, not slowly shrinking into skin and bone on a sickbed, restless, impatient, and frustrated, a giant spirit in a shrunken child's body, watching with dismay as the world moved through misery he had tried to alleviate toward a new tragedy his unheeded warnings foresaw. This, for the Little Flower, the Mayor, Butch, the Hat, was a cruel end.

LaGuardia's background was of that richly composite and polyglot kind that is America's glory, however much it may depress the anemic D.A.R. He was half Italian, half Jewish, and wholly American. He was born in New York but spent his childhood and youth in Arizona. From the Southwest he brought more than a fondness for sombrero-brimmed hats so broad they made the stout little fellow look like a perambulating mushroom; he brought something of the breezy independence of the frontier. No figure in American politics ever thumbed his nose so brashly at party regularity and got away with it. In the midst of the smug Coolidge era, when the party bosses tried to get rid of this maverick Republican, he defied them and was re-elected to Congress as a Socialist. He was a New Dealer before the New Deal; the leader of a rebel Republican faction which rode herd on the Hooverites in the early '30s, fought hard for relief, blocked the sales tax, and in 1932 triumphantly put through Congress the Norris-LaGuardia anti-injunction act, forerunner of the Wagner Act and LaGuardia's greatest legislative achievement.

What were the qualities and circumstances which enabled LaGuardia to serve fourteen years in Congress, to be elected Mayor of New York for three consecutive terms, to become a national and international figure, without that loyalty to party machine which is ordinarily an essential to success in American politics? He survived in Congress because his base was on the East Side, among the poor and the politically advanced. He succeeded without a machine in New York because Tammany mismanagement, a leftward tide, and a sense of civic responsibility made it possible for LaGuardia to muster a coalition which ranged from Wall Street bankers to Union Square labor leaders. He gave the city competent, honest, and reasonably progressive government for twelve years—the best mayor New York ever had. Though he was as temperamental as an operatic tenor, and as flamboyant as a prima donna, LaGuardia was a tireless and capable administrator. He was a natural-born popular leader for a democratic people: straightforward in speech, free from cant and hypocrisy, shrewdly and disarmingly candid in tight spots, with a flair for the direct and the dramatic.

To protest against Prohibition, LaGuardia brewed beer in his own office in Washington. To illustrate a speech on the high cost of living after World War I, he waved a lamb chop before a startled House of Representatives. To show his contempt for Hoover during the '30s, he gave his own White House invitations to street urchins. To make Midwestern farmers realize the need abroad, LaGuardia went on a personal tour as head of UNRRA; at one rally, in Minnesota, he mounted a farm wagon, held aloft a loaf of bread, and ripped off six slices to show assembled farmers an entire day's food allowance in some European countries—"And mark you, there's no

gravy goes with it." This was not demagogy. LaGuardia was not a dema-
gogue; he was not one to mouth irresponsible nonsense to inflame a crowd.
But he knew how to capture popular imagination. He knew how to translate abstractions into concrete and vivid realities. He could talk the ordinary man's language as no ordinary man could talk it—he had the gift of
plain, direct, and salty speech. Fiorello was no ivory-tower intellectual.

LaGuardia was never more earnest or more farsighted than in the efforts
he made during the last year of his life to prevent the drift toward a new
war. His proposal for a United Nations emergency food fund, last November, and his testimony against the Truman Doctrine, last March, were a plea
for the continuance of international cooperation, a warning against the
consequences if America tried to use its food and its money as instruments
of political domination. "It is reminiscent," he told a United Nations Assembly committee last November, "of the old days of politics here in my
town, when the poor in the district were given a basket of food on Christ-
mas and during the winter a bag of coal or two. Along came election time,
and they were . . . taken in hordes to vote the ticket." Before the Senate
Foreign Relations Committee, last March, on the Truman Doctrine, he
pleaded, "Let us not do anything that will create the impression that we
want to rule the whole world, that any government that does not please us
will be put out of business."

He urged another approach: "We can lick Communism in this world by
making democracy work, by proving to the world that people can live
properly and decently."

The Truman administration and the State Department had decided
otherwise. They had decided to abandon UNRRA for a system under
which we proposed to exact a political *quid pro quo* for feeding hungry
people; it was to be—starve, or else. "You cannot find the theory or purpose of UNRRA in the revised statutes or in the treaties," LaGuardia told
the Senate committee, "but if you will go across the street to the library
and ask for a book called the New Testament, there you will find the spirit
of UNRRA, and you will find the purpose of it, and you will find the way
it was administered."

LaGuardia spoke to no purpose. It was a bitter spectacle for the dying
man to see, as he predicted, that the United Nations would begin to break

down once we abandoned international principles in the handling of the food problem. He died an unhappy man; in Washington the kind of men and policies he fought in the '20s were back in power; abroad he saw the old mistakes and a new war coming. The few who saw him toward the last knew that sorrow stood at his bedside. The peace death promised was unwelcome to one whose joy it had always been to war for the good.

Albert Einstein

Albert Einstein, the great physicist, peace advocate, socialist, and humanist, died on April 18, 1955. His friend I. F. Stone penned this warm and very personal tribute.

·   ·   ·

April 25, 1955

Professor Einstein would not have liked a stuffy tribute. My wife and I loved him. He was a charter subscriber to the *Weekly*, and often strained its primitive bookkeeping facilities by renewing when no renewal was due. We and our three children had the great pleasure on several occasions of having tea with him at his home. It was like going to tea with God, not the terrible old God of the Bible but the little child's father-in-heaven, very kind, very wise and yet himself very much a child, too. We feel that we have lost a friend.

If our dim understanding of his work has any validity, we thought of it as a lifelong search for a new and greater unity in physical phenomena, and the re-establishment of the possibility of law in the universe. A world made up only of statistical probabilities offended his profoundest instincts; he was like Bach or Beethoven, striving for new harmonies, but with the tools of mathematics and physics. There were times when one felt his infinite zest in the search that was his life, though he sadly called himself a has-been last time we saw him, which was last August.

The man who sought a new harmony in the heavens and in the atom also sought for order and justice in the relations of men. As the greatest intellectual in the world of our time, he fought fascism everywhere and feared the signs of it in our own country. This was the spirit in which he advised American intellectuals to defy the Congressional inquisition and refuse to submit themselves to ideological interrogation. In that position he was in-terpreting the First Amendment as Jefferson would have done.

Professor Einstein—if I read him rightly—felt like a failure rather than a success: he died without quite achieving that unified theory he sought. But his was a beautiful and satisfying life, and nothing would have pleased him more than how many—and such diverse—people remember him with af-fection, especially the children of the neighborhood in Princeton who recall the cookies he gave them.

In that Olympus where he goes to dwell with his few peers, this is some-thing all his own. Newton and Copernicus and the misty Pythagoras, too, could sweep the heavens with their grasp—but none of them were remem-bered by so many humble friends, for so many simple human kindnesses. In this realm, far beyond politics and physics, Einstein reigns alone in warm human memory.

Goldwater and His Tribe

In July 1964, the Republican Party nominated Senator Barry Goldwater for president, then by far the most right-wing candidate in the party's history. Goldwater was overwhelmingly defeated that fall, but his candidacy made a national political figure out of Ronald Reagan and laid the groundwork for the conservative ascendancy of the 1980s. In this essay, I. F. Stone offers a portrait of Goldwater and his sunbelt conservative followers, the new breed of Republicans who would eventually come to dominate national politics.

.　　.　　.

July 27, 1964

THE PROCESS OF PICKING A PRESIDENTIAL CANDIDATE bears only a distant relation to sober discussion of political issues. To see one in action is to see first of all that politics is a form of sports; the atmosphere in the crowded lobbies of the St. Francis and the Mark Hopkins in San Francisco, where each candidate had his rooters and his pennants, was much like that before a football game. At some of the most exciting moments, the convention seemed to call for coverage by an anthropologist. To descend from the galleries into the depths on the Cow Palace floor during one of the many demonstrations was to dive into a brightly lit jungle, a high forest of banners, with the horns blaring and the drums beating, as if for tribal war. At duller moments, during the long stretches of venerable clichés in the nominating speeches, the convention seemed to provide a psychic massage through semantic manipulation; all those familiar phrases about free enterprise began to seem like incantations, handed down from the past as sure formulas for the ills of the body politic. The platform could be read as ritual, as a form of verbal magic, the reassuring recitation of a secular mass.

We are familiar with the politics of insecurity when it exploits the insecurities of the poor. At the Republican convention one could see in action the politics which plays on the insecurity of the rich. The Goldwaterites made their appeal to people who were afraid—rich, powerful, fortunate beyond any dominant class in history, yet afraid. Some of the fears were obvious: fear of losing their property and power, fear lest the value of their dollars be diminished by the inflation which accompanies the welfare state. Above all they did not want to lose the old familiar devil of their neatly Manichean universe, the need for a devil being as deep as the need for a God. Communism as the devil had long been one of the main pillars in the edifice of their simple faith. Now it, too, was threatened by more sophisticated and pragmatic attitudes.

Goldwater expressed their alarm when he told the platform committee, "I was surprised, and am concerned, that during these platform hearings, mention even of the word 'communism' has been the exception rather than the rule." He complained that "even in the keynote address" it seemed to be taboo. "This Administration," he protested, "pretends that communism has so changed that we can now accommodate it. Our party cannot go the final and fatal step and pretend that it doesn't even exist." They didn't want to hear about the differences between Russia and China or the deviationist tendencies in Rumania or to be told that some communists were better than others. They wanted their old comfortable picture of a monolithic communism restored. A pragmatism without a devil frightened them more than a communism without a God. To realize that even at Republican platform hearings people had stopped speaking of communism seemed to them almost impious, if not evidence of the subtlest communist plot of all.

The Goldwaterite picture of themselves, as of their hero, is as distant from reality as the rest of the private universe they are defending. The frontier virtues they claim to embody are as synthetic as the frontier they inhabit. Their desert is air-conditioned and landscaped; their covered wagons are Cadillacs; their chaps are from Abercrombie & Fitch; their money, like their candidate's, is mostly inherited from grandpappy, or acquired with their wives. In their favorite campaign photos, on that horse and under that ten-gallon Stetson, looking into the setting sun, is no cowboy or even rancher but a Phoenix storekeeper. The Western trade he caters to, in business as in politics, is dude ranch.

This he-man's claim to fame in business is the development of "antsy-pants," men's underdrawers decorated with ants, a cute specialty item he advertised some years back in the wide open spaces of Manhattan through *The New Yorker* magazine. He roughs it in a $150,000 gadget-filled showplace of a home, designed, his architect said, as "a rough-hewn house for a rough-hewn guy," a sort of de luxe model log cabin to give one that authentic latter-day Lincoln decor. Low education and low intelligence, Goldwater once declared to the delight of his equally well-upholstered followers, are the real causes of poverty. One wonders what he, who did not last out more than one year of college, would have done if a family fortune and a family business did not await him back home. What he preaches is the same "rugged individualism" with which Herbert Hoover sought to combat the New Deal thirty years ago. Its essential phoniness could not have found a more perfect embodiment. The crowning touch is that this half-Jewish grandson of a Polish Jewish peddler who won acceptance for himself and his family on the tolerant frontier should emerge into politics as the hero of the racist forces in our society. It's enough to make one anti-Episcopalian.

This Mr. Conservative of 1964 is quite different from Taft, the Mr. Conservative of 1952. In foreign policy Taft was an isolationist; he wanted to keep the country out of trouble. Goldwater, though not an internationalist, is an ultra-nationalist, who's ready to get into trouble anywhere. Taft fought NATO; Goldwater wants to strengthen it with nuclear weapons. Taft was what used to be called a Republican standpatter but with progressive fringes; Scranton was right when he declared several times in San Francisco that on such specific issues as labor education and housing, he was closer to Taft than was Goldwater. In the political spectrum Goldwater is half reactionary, half rightist European style. The same man who, in *The Conscience of a Conservative,* wrote that "our tendency to concentrate power in the hands of a few men deeply concerns me" could also say on ABC-TV's *Issues and Answers* (April 7, 1963), "I don't object to a dictatorship as violently as some people do because I realize that not all people in this world are ready for democratic processes. If they have to have a dictator in order to keep communism out, then I don't think we can object to that." It is no wonder that his nomination was regarded with dismay abroad everywhere but in Franco Spain and South Africa, and among the neo-fascists of Italy and

Germany. For this has been one of the principal alibis for fascism ever since the March on Rome. Il Duce, too, only acted to save Italy from communism, and there are rightists who would emulate him here if they could.

The menace of the Goldwater movement, however, is not that its ranks are full of "kooks" but that on the contrary most of those who showed up at the convention were upper middle class solid citizens, no more (or less) looney than their fathers were thirty years ago when the American Liberty League and the Un-American Activities Committee under Martin Dies readily led them to believe the New Deal was a communist plot, and that American workers then, like Mississippi Negroes today, would be wholly content were it not for foreign agitators and conspirators. Even the Southern delegation, whose headquarters at the Jack Tar Hotel I visited, in no way matched the dangerously delusive picture of this movement as made up of little old ladies in tennis shoes. The one Texan I talked to there said Johnson would probably carry Texas. Every one of the half dozen Southern delegates I talked with put "fiscal responsibility" not civil rights as the No. 1 issue. Whether this was how they really felt I have no way of knowing, but I believe it was an accurate reflection of a major concern. The retired bulk large in the ranks of the Goldwaterites; the perpetual inflation with which we have been accustomed to financing the welfare state taxes them, like all others (including workers) on fixed incomes, unfairly. The declining value of the dollar haunts them, and as one nice lady from North Carolina explained to me sweetly, "money is one of the most important things in the country." Significantly another reporter told me he found hostility to Wallace among these Southern Republicans; they saw eye-to-eye with him, of course, on race but regarded him on non-racial issues as too much of a "liberal," i.e. a social welfare spender.

Goldwater's support shades off toward the right into a wide variety of offbeat organizations and stray woozy millionaires. Most of them were loosely united under "Independent Americans for Goldwater," which opened a headquarters at 1175 Mission Street in San Francisco during the convention. The organizers were Kent and Phoebe Courtney, authors of such works as "Disarmament—a Blueprint for Surrender" and editors of *The Independent American.* Books by Goldwater and Welch of the Birch Society were on sale along with a wide selection of pamphlets proving that

Rockefeller was a tool of an international socialist conspiracy and that Nixon was soft on communism. The size of the movement may be indicated by the fact that a pre-convention rally drew only 700 people and the paid circulation Courtney claims for *The Independent American* is only 20,000. He turned out to be a blond, stout man with a high-powered salesman's manner. He said he was Minnesota born, but had lived in New Orleans since he was ten. He still has no trace of Southern accent. He said he was in marketing research before launching his publication and movement. He claimed to "pick up where the Birch Society leaves off." He said he was still a member of the Society but no longer an organizer for it. Courtney is also affiliated with the Citizens' Councils in Louisiana and told me that if the U.S. cut off relations with the Soviet Union "the whole civil rights movement would die on the vine." He claims to have sponsored the first Goldwater for President meeting in 1960 and thinks Goldwater will win unless, he hinted darkly, "we run into a contrived international crisis." He boasts of defeating Judd for re-election in Minnesota as "soft on communism," and regards the Council on Foreign Relations, a high-collar group which includes Allen Dulles and publishes *Foreign Affairs* quarterly, as the center of the Communist conspiracy in America. This is the kind of character Goldwater was asked to disavow by those who wanted a strong platform plank against extremists.

Several times Goldwater challenged his critics to define "extremism." I am convinced that in his mind the difficulty was a real one. The common denominator of these right-wing crackpot groups is that America is menaced by a worldwide communist conspiracy. But this is also a common article of belief in America. In Germany the way to Hitlerism was prepared by several generations of paranoid inculcation in the existence of a Jewish-Marxist conspiracy. So the emergence of rightists in control of the Republican Party was prepared by more than thirty years in which, first as part of the fight against the New Deal and then as part of the cold war, Americans have been led to believe in a communist conspiracy. The differences are in degree, but the effect is to push all of American politics rightward, so that groups which in any other country would be recognized as hopeless reactionaries or crypto-fascists can parade here as conservatives. While the left in this country has shriveled since 1948, rightism has flowered; it is almost impossible to tune in a car radio at any hour without hearing rightist speakers financed in part at public expense via some tax-exempt foundation or some oil millionaire grown rich on depletion allowances.

Interlocking with these civilian extremists is a broad band of military extremists to which Goldwater belongs. His affinity for the German militarists is instinctive; he belongs to the same breed as the right-wing German generals who thought they could use the Nazi riff-raff for their own purposes. Goldwater told *Der Spiegel* the German generals could have won the war but for interference by Hitler; the war itself might have been avoided if they, by interfering in politics, had not helped bring Hitler to power.* Goldwater's simple-minded ideas are precisely the kind the military has been spreading in this country through those "strategy for survival" conferences Fulbright attacked in 1961 and Goldwater and Strom Thurmond, both Air Force Reserve generals, defended. These reserve generals make up by the ferocity of their politics for the paucity of their combat records. They may not be as wacky as General Walker but they buy ideas from the same sources. Goldwater's speech writer, Karl Hess, the man who wrote those phrases about extremism in the defense of liberty never being a vice, is an example. He was a former editor of *Counterattack,* the vehicle of the entertainment blacklist; a contributing editor of the *American Mercury* during its worst years under the anti-Semitic Russell Maguire; a member of the anti-communist liaison set up by the evangelist Billy James Hargis in 1963 which included Birch Society members. Yet he was also made a consultant to the Advisory Committee to the Secretary of Defense on Non-Military Instruction set up in the wake of the famous Fulbright memorandum. From such sources does Goldwater obtain support, ideas and phrases. For him to condemn "extremism" would be to undercut his main political stock in trade.

The Goldwater candidacy gives the nation a clear choice but it is not a choice between conservatism and liberalism. The Goldwaterites who shrieked like a lynch mob at Nelson Rockefeller and responded with the wildest enthusiasm of the convention when Eisenhower attacked "columnists" are in no real sense of the word conservatives. The true conservative is their pet hate; he disturbs their most cherished dreams and nightmares by

---

*One reporter after hearing Goldwater's remark suggested a plank in the Republican platform condemning Hitler for having lost the war.

insisting as Rockefeller and Lippmann do, that the Republicans must adapt themselves to the real world. The Goldwater movement is a merger of the worst Southern racists, the right wing military and the obsessed inveterate anti-Communists, with those elements which have never reconciled themselves to the New Deal. Their candidate is ready to dabble in any irresponsible demagogy if it promises votes. The man who is so strong for states' rights when it comes to civil rights spoke as if the federal government had police power to protect Northern cities from maurauders—(Negro, that is)—but not Mississippi Negroes from mobsters. I don't think he can win but to assume from the polls that his defeat is a foregone conclusion would be criminal folly especially after the Wallace withdrawal; popular majorities are in no event the same as electoral college majorities. The Harlem riots are a foretaste of what could happen elsewhere to magnify that "white backlash" on which Goldwater and the white supremacists count. We are fortunate that, as in the final censure and political destruction of McCarthy, the forces opposing Goldwater are headed by a conservative and represent a coalition of civilized forces, conservative and liberal. The anti-McCarthyites found a leader in the Midwestern conservative Watkins. The anti-Goldwater forces are lucky to be led by a moderate conservative Democrat from Texas. But the victory will not be easy, and no one should stand aside from the struggle for it. The peace of the country and of the world may be decided by the outcome.

Curtis LeMay:
Cave Man in a Jet Bomber

Curtis E. LeMay was a general in the U.S. Air Force, an architect of the successful bombing campaign in the Pacific during World War II, and George Wallace's
vice-presidential running mate in 1968. He was also a vocal advocate of the aggressive use of military force, for example urging that the U.S. bomb the North
Vietnamese "into the Stone Age." In this essay, a review of LeMay's 1965 autobiography *Mission With LeMay,* Stone eviscerates LeMay and the jingoist, mili-
tarist philosophy he represented.

.   .   .

January 20, 1966

ONE OF GENERAL CURTIS LeMay's earliest memories*—he thinks it
must have been at four or five in the winter of 1910–11 or the next—was the
sight of his first plane. He ran as fast as he could to try to catch it. He felt
when it vanished that "I had lost something unique and in a way Divine."
At least this is the recollection, after a lifetime of bomber command, as he
told it to the writer of his story, MacKinlay Kantor. The general is not a religious man; this early feeling for the plane is the one note of piety in the
account he helped prepare of his life. Nor is he a man ordinarily moved by
beauty. It is the memory of the first plane he saw close-up on the ground
that evokes the one moment of aesthetic enthusiasm in the book; what he
remembers is "the appealing gush of its engine—the energy and beauty of
the brute." He went from Ohio State with an engineering degree to the old
Army Air Corps in 1928. In 1937 at Langley Field, he met the plane which
was to be linked with the most heroic episodes of his life—the B-17. There
he saw "seven of the Flying Fortresses squatting on the ramp." Of these he

---

*In *Mission with LeMay.*

326

writes "I fell in love with the 17 at first sight." Six years later he led an entire
Air Division of these bombers over the European continent. It was not until 1944, when he began the first fire raids over Japan, that he switched to
the bigger B-29. He can remember the smell of the B-17 as different from
the smell of any other plane. This ability to differentiate these mighty
metallic monsters by his animal sense of smell is even more impressive than
the love and worship that so closely linked this man to his machines. He
emerges in this story as much their instrument as they were his. LeMay's
later, long and stubborn rear-guard action to keep the bombers flying in the
age of the missile begins to seem touching, like any attempt to maintain the
vanishing familiar in a world of change without pity. So, unexpectedly, on
the bomber, too, Vergil's *lacrimae rerum* fall.

   Unlike Mao Tse-tung and Ho Chi Minh, the targets of whom LeMay
has dreamed voluptuously in recent years, our bomber general was of im-
peccably proletarian origin. His father began as a railroad worker but was
soon reduced to all kinds of handyman jobs to support his family of seven
children, a task at which he never fully succeeded. LeMay as the eldest began selling papers during high school to help the family budget, and sent
money home while he worked his way through college. Poverty and insecurity no more led him to question the economic system than the weather. Indeed he speaks of his father's struggles as if they were a meteorological
phenomenon. "Like many men in his category [not—let us notice—class]
and time, he was subject," LeMay relates, "to whims and pressures of regional and national economy." The Depression years, when he was a fledgling aviator, were hard for him and his family, but his only reference to
them is "Depression or no Depression, they were opening up airports all
over the country." Neither these early struggles nor his later experience in
military service with plane manufacturers notorious for overcharges, led
him to take a critical view of free enterprise. His nearest approach to an un-
friendly remark about the capitalist system is an angry comment in his account of how the Air Corps flew the mails in 1934 under Roosevelt. "The
public bought the idea (and still retains it)," he comments sourly, "that
scores of Air Corps pilots lost their lives in an heroic but absurd attempt to
emulate the superb performance of the commercial airlines." It is only in
the bitterness of his feud with McNamara, that he allows himself to reflect

by implication on the Business Man. "I hadn't spent the bulk of the years since World War II," he says, "in reorganizing any vast business for the purpose of pulling it from the red side of the ledger to the black. . . . I had reorganized and built up a vast business, the Strategic Air Command, but its mission was not to make a profit for stockholders. . . . I had not been in the financial and organizational side of the automobile business. . . . Thus it may be believed that Secretary McNamara and I would hold different views on the matter of manned aircraft."

This might be described as a *non sequitur de profundis,* since it is difficult to see why McNamara's experience in the (manned) automobile business should predispose him against the manned plane. LeMay's record otherwise is spotless. Though he did a tour of duty in Research and Development, the experience did not lead him (as it did General Gavin) to protest big business practices in dealing with the armed services, nor (like Admiral Rickover) to acid comment on performance and profits. The military-industrial complex never had an officer more loyally blinkered.

His reflexes were already exemplary when he joined the ROTC his first week at Ohio State. He recounts with relish being part of an ROTC mob on its way to "clean out" a bunch of campus pacifists until stopped by a First Lieutenant with more sense. He reveals that in those days on the same campus Milt Caniff, whose Steve Canyon is the Air Force's pride and joy, was then painting anti-military posters. No such ideological wild oats were sown by LeMay. Even in his youth he was no deviator.

LeMay's own story, as told by himself and prettied up by MacKinlay Kantor, is hardly a candid portrait. It reads like the glossy fiction at which Kantor is so adept. To separate the truth from the treacle is a sticky task. But the ferocious prejudices which brought LeMay and Goldwater together in a mutual admiration society break through: ". . . in a day when labor unions howl for a twenty-four-hour week, and God knows what fringe benefits besides" . . . "some newly emergent so-called Republic in darkest Africa" . . . "the Whiz Kid liberal of today" . . . "the intellectuals, the inveterate pacifists, the dreamers and idealists . . . who believed firmly that the soft answer turned away wrath." In recalling the San Francisco Fair of 1915 to celebrate the opening of the Panama Canal, the prose turns apoplectic at the thought that if any man had said then that some day we would agree not to fly the U.S. flag over the Canal "unless the Panamanian flag floated beside it, on the same level" we would have "suspected that man to be a traitor." Since it was LBJ who agreed to this traitorous concession, it is not hard to believe that the President was glad to "press the flesh" with LeMay in farewell last January 31 after the shortest extension of service ever given a Chief of Staff—ten months from the previous April, or just long enough to keep LeMay from campaigning for Goldwater.

LeMay's attitude toward his bomber command exploits are of a piece with these ripe reflections. He says defensively in his Foreword that his bombings were of "military targets" on which attack was "justified morally." But he can't resist adding a sneer, "I've tried to stay away from hospitals, prison camps, orphan asylums, nunneries and dog kennels." He says, "I have sought to slaughter as few civilians as possible." But a few pages later he is boasting that in the great fire raids on Japan, "We burned up nearly sixteen square miles of Tokyo." He quotes with relish General Power, who led that raid and later succeeded him as head of the Strategic Air Command, as saying that this one attack on Tokyo produced "more casualties than in any other military action in the history of the world, greater than those of Hiroshima and Nagasaki put together.

These were civilian casualties. For all his businesslike attitude toward bombings, a touch of unseemly zest colors LeMay's jubilant description, "Enemy cities were pulverized or fried to a crisp." Secretary of War Stimson, we now know, was horrified by these fire raids, and called in General Arnold to protest that the Air Force had promised there would be only precision bombing in Japan. In the autobiography Stimson wrote after the war with McGeorge Bundy, he admitted that "in the conflagration bombings by massed B-29s" he had found himself permitting "the kind of war he had always hated." Stimson later told Robert Oppenheimer* he was appalled by the lack of public protest and thought "there was something wrong with a country where no one questioned" such raids. Even more appalling is the inability of men in the highest offices to control their instruments once war breaks out. This is a lesson to be ignored at our peril.

*This and the two previous references are from Giovannitti and Freed's fascinating recent account, *The Decision to Drop the Bomb.*

The excuse General Arnold gave Secretary Stimson is the same excuse LeMay offers at a later point in his story, that the wide dispersion of Japanese industry made the fire raids necessary. He claimed with what seems obvious and characteristic exaggeration that in the ruins one could see "a drill press sticking up through the wreckage of every home." "We knew we were going to kill a lot of women and kids when we burned that town," he now says. "Had to be done." But there were other reasons for indiscriminate urban bombing. As so often happens, the Air Force changed doctrine to suit its weapons. The b-29s, as Giovannitti and Freed explain, "had been designed for daylight precision bombing" but the effects had proven disappointing. The Air Force then decided that incendiary bombing against the cities of Japan, with their crowded quarters and wooden construction "would be more effective." LeMay in a message to Norstad, then Chief of Staff of the 20th Air Force, felt the air war against Japan presented "the AAF for the first time with an opportunity of proving the power of the strategic air arm" (Giovannitti-Freed). The fire raids were the greatest advertisement yet for strategic air power. But they were only made possible because naval blockade had strangled the Japanese economy. The Japanese air force in the homeland had become almost non-existent so that low-level fire raids could be staged with little resistance and few losses. These raids were dramatic but were they necessary? A passage in the U.S. Strategic Bombing Survey study of the effects on Japan's war economy (p. 38) indicates that LeMay does not tell the whole story when he claims that widespread killing of women and children was unavoidable. "Although an effort was made," this report says of the fire raids, "to direct these attacks toward targets the destruction of which would do damage to industrial production, *the preponderant purpose appears to have been to secure the heaviest possible morale and shock effect by widespread attack upon the Japanese civilian population.*"

No matter how you choose to disguise it, the essence of the victory-by-airpower thesis is victory by terror against the civilian population. The ideas of the Italian Douhet and of the American Billy Mitchell grew out of the doctrine of the Prussian military writers of the nineteenth century. "The moment a national war breaks out," General Julius von Hartman wrote in 1877, "terrorism becomes a necessary military principle." This was the origin of *Schrecklichkeit,* the doctrine of frightfulness applied by the Germans in the First World War. Military airpower, as Douhet and Mitchell envisaged it, was to give the doctrine a new dimension. The rationalization they offered is that all-out bombardment would shorten the war and be more humane in the long run.

Hindenburg once wrote in the same spirit during World War I while he was commander in Poland, "Lodz is starving. That is deplorable, but it ought to be so. The more pitiless the conduct of the war the more humane it is in reality, for it will run its course all the sooner." The date of the utterance is enough to demonstrate the fallacy of the proposition. It was November 20, 1914, and the war was to last four years more despite these frightful beginnings.* Yet men like LeMay, Nixon, and Goldwater peddle the same fallacies when they urge us to "save lives" and "shorten the war" by mass bombings of North Vietnam and, if necessary, of China.

Just as the First World War proved that frightfulness would not bring victory, so the Second World War proved that Douhet and Mitchell were wrong about aerial bombardment. "The result of warfare by air," Mitchell wrote in 1930 (*Skyways,* p. 256), "will be to bring about quick decisions. Superior air power will cause such havoc, or the threat of such havoc, in the opposing country that a long drawn-out campaign will be impossible." But the Second World War lasted two years longer than the First despite aerial bombardment of unparalleled weight and horror. Strategic bombing failed to break Britain's will to resist. Germany's war production rose steadily until the summer of 1944; the Nazis did not capitulate until Allied and Russian ground armies met on the Elbe. Japan was defeated by blockade. "World War II proved in every instance," Marshall Andrews wrote in his incisive little book, *Disaster Through Air Power,* a decade ago, "that strategic bombing was costly all out of proportion to whatever results it obtained."

LeMay regards terror from the skies as the one sure remedy for all political ills. He reveals that for three years—that is since 1962—he had been urging in the Joint Chiefs of Staff that the way to end the war in Vietnam was to let them know that "we're going to bomb them back into the Stone Age." This is one of his favorite phrases; in World War II he boasted that

*Marshall Andrews, *Disaster Through Air Power,* p. 39.

the Japanese air raids "were driving them back to the Stone Age."* The Stone Age is a metaphor for the days when brute force reigned supreme; instinctively LeMay harks back to it. He is as simple minded in prescribing strategic bombing for small wars with underdeveloped peoples as in big wars with industrialized societies. He reminds us that in the Korean war his "immediate suggestion" was to "go up north and burn the principal cities." But he does not frankly admit how ineffective airpower proved in the Korean war. One has only to compare his account with that in the Air Force's own official history of the Korean war,[†] to see how dubious his advice was. Strategic bombing, aerial reconnaissance, and interdiction bombing all failed in the Korean war. LeMay does not tell us how quickly his advice about going north and burning down its cities was taken. Between August 10, 1950, one month after the war began, and September 25, the Far East Air Forces Bomber Command leveled every urban and industrial target above the 38th parallel except some naval oil storage tanks too close to the Russian border to be bombed without risk. But the war went on for three more years. Aerial reconnaissance also failed to detect the Chinese intervention that followed this massive devastation on their border. "According to Chinese Communist records captured much later," the official AF history reveals (p. 16), "the Chinese had begun to slip troops across the Yalu as early as 14 October" or just four days before MacArthur announced that the Korean war was "definitely" coming to an end. By then major portions of the Chinese Fourth Field Army were in North Korea. Interdiction was no more successful. Though "Operation Strangle" and "Operation Saturate" made sensational headlines in the U.S. press, as do current "interdiction raids" on North Vietnam, they no more succeeded then than now in interdicting supply lines. Our troops were pushed back to the 38th parallel. Despite bombardment so lavish that one Air Force officer said "we were trading b-26s for trucks," the communists were able to fire 102,000 rounds against Allied positions in May, 1952 as compared with 8000 the previous July and they soon built up enough anti-aircraft, as the official Air Force history admits, "to take an unacceptable toll" of our bomber planes.

---

*Gar Alperovitz's *Atomic Diplomacy: Hiroshima and Potsdam,* p. 106.
[†] *The U.S. Air Force in Korea, 1950–53,* by Futrell, Moseley, and Simpson.

One explanation lamely offered by LeMay in his autobiography is that bombardment failed because of an "undying Oriental philosophy and fanaticism." He says, "Human attrition means nothing to such people," that their lives are so miserable on earth that they look forward with delight to a death which promises them "everything from tea-parties with long dead grandfathers down to their pick of all the golden little dancing girls in Paradise." Anyone capable of such silliness is a poor guide to Asian military policy. Neither Buddhism nor Confucianism nor communism offers life after death of any kind, much less "golden little dancing girls in Paradise"—he has them mixed up with Mohammedanism. The notion that poor people care less for their own lives and those of their children belongs to Kipling-era colonialism. Was it Oriental fatalism that maintained London's spirits during the blitz?

LeMay's other explanation, of course, is the MacArthurite complaint that the communists were allowed to have a bomb-free sanctuary in Manchuria. One answer to this is that we had a bomb-free sanctuary ourselves in Japan which we used as the Reds did Manchuria for rest and supply. There is also another answer. LeMay concedes the little-known fact that the communists also allowed us a bomb-free sanctuary in Korea itself. LeMay says we learned later that the Migs in Manchuria had the range to reach the front lines in Korea. "If I had been working for the other side," he writes, "and had all those Migs in Manchuria that the Chinese had, I would have run General MacArthur right out of Korea. . . . With that Mig force, any energetic commander could have cleaned out all the airfields we had in Korea, and mighty soon . . . then they could have started working on the troops. Why they didn't do it I'll never know." In this revealing conjecture LeMay unwittingly provides his own explanation for the restriction against bombing Manchuria of which he so bitterly complains.

Despite this experience, LeMay nowhere soberly discusses the question of what to do if the Chinese react to the devastation of North Vietnam as they did to that of North Korea. The early predictions of the victory-by-air-power people have proven ludicrously wrong in the Vietnamese war. General Thomas S. Power, retired, who was LeMay's successor as Chief of the Strategic Air Command, wrote two years ago in his book *Design for Survival* that an aerial ultimatum and selected bombing of military depots would force the North to surrender "within a few days." Almost a year has now passed since Johnson adopted the LeMay-Goldwater-Power-Nixon thesis and began to bomb the North, but the only visible result has been increased infiltration. Instead of a slow trickle of Southerners heading home for guerrilla war, full North Vietnamese regiments now appear in the South. Blackmail by bombardment—the new euphemism for it, in the words of our current U. S. Air Force Chief of Staff General McConnell, is "strategic persuasion"*—has failed. Instead of giving the President "a heavily flexible tool," as General McConnell blandly phrases it, "in inducing North Vietnam eventually to accept his offer of unconditional discussions," strategic bombardment has galvanized North Vietnam into greater and more open aid to the Southern insurgents. Strategic bombing in the South—the use of sledgehammers against gnats—has also proved a failure, as shown by the mounting number and size of Vietcong attacks. Though General McConnell is still calling these B-52 saturation bombings "highly effective" they run counter to anti-guerrilla experience in the Philippines, Malaya, and Algeria. The Air Force's own most experienced anti-guerrilla expert, General Lansdale—reputedly the Quiet American of Graham Greene's novel about Indochina, and now an advisor to Ambassador Lodge—has protested in vain that indiscriminate area bombing only increases a civilian bitterness which facilitates Vietcong recruitment. The reader of LeMay's story would never guess such vital problems are raised by his brutal quickie proposals.

What if our escalating military action against North Vietnam, like invasion of North Korea, is followed by Chinese intervention? Will LeMay, Nixon, and Goldwater then advocate the bombing of China—and of Russia if it aids China—in a giddy logical progression that Herblock, in a recent cartoon, brilliantly called "Total Peace Through Total Victory Through Total World Blowup"? Here again *Mission with LeMay* is far from candid. No one would guess from it how basic to Air Force thinking is the idea of the first strike and of preventive war. The first explicit though hitherto almost unnoticed formulation of these strategies may be found as early as 1947 in *Air Campaigns of the Pacific War,* a book the Air Force published because it did not like the U. S. Strategic Bombing Survey with its

*Speech to the Detroit Economics Club, December 6, 1965.

downgrading of airpower.* A section of this book is called "Keeping the American Public Informed With Respect to the Danger of Accepting the First Blow in a Future War." This sets forth a new definition of what constitutes an act of war:

> We must recognize [it says] that an overt act of war has been committed by an enemy when that enemy builds a military force intended for our eventual destruction, and that the destruction of that force before it can be launched or employed is defensive action and not aggression. . . . As a nation we must understand that an overt act of war has been committed long before the delivery of that first blow and that the earlier such an overt act is recognized the more effective the defense can be.

Then U. S. Army Infantry Major, now Colonel Lawrence J. Legere, Jr., to whose unpublished 1950 Ph.D. thesis we owe this revealing quotation, comments, "Whatever this unique concept is, it is not international law. It may be an example of the kind of reasoning Hitler used to justify his wars of aggression." It is also the rationale for the kind of "preventive" blow at China and its nuclear installations LeMay and the Air Force favor. McNamara's warnings to last December's meeting of the NATO Council about China's coming nuclear power may give them new support. McNamara, like Stimson, could find his military instruments running away with him.

The pages in *Mission with LeMay* which discuss preventive war against Russia verge on self-caricature in their light-minded shallowness. LeMay says that there was a time in the period before the Russians got the Bomb and their achievement of a stockpile, when we could have destroyed all of Russia "without losing a man to their defenses. The only losses incurred would have been the normal accident rate for the number of flying hours which would have been flown to do the job." This assurance that we would not have lost a *single* plane begins to sound like something out of *Doctor Strangelove*. So does LeMay's idea that America could then have said to Russia, "'Here's a blueprint for your immediate future. We'll give

---

*The U.S. Strategic Bombing Survey was established by Stimson in 1944. Franklin D'Olier was the chairman; George Ball, J. K. Galbraith and Paul Nitze served as officers.

you a deadline of five or six months'—something like that—'to pull out of the satellite countries, and effect a complete change of conduct. You will behave your damn selves from this moment forth.'" It is hard to believe that this is not satirical fiction: General Turgidson at work and play.

All through the years to which LeMay refers, he was sounding the alarms on Capitol Hill; we were in danger of being overrun by Russian hordes; we were woefully short of bombers and later of missiles. He and his supporters were the ultimate source of the imaginary bomber gap and the equally imaginary missile gap. Now he tells us we could have smashed all Russia even before the missile age without losing a single plane. He even says one "might argue whether it would be desirable to present such a challenge to the Russians, even at this [1965] stage." Obviously he thinks we have enough now to put Russia in the reformatory by ultimatum.

The strangest aspect of LeMay's story is his detachment. While he is ready to bomb almost anybody, he really seems to hate almost nobody— nobody, that is, among America's national enemies, past, present, or future. Their destruction is his job, the occasion for demonstrating his abilities. This is no winged warrior, with blood-lust in his veins, as in the ancient Sagas; no young Mussolini thrilling to the red flowers that spring from the Ethiopian earth as the bombs fall from his plane. He even has words of praise for Mao Tse-tung and his ready cooperation in helping U.S. fliers downed over Chinese Communist territory during World War II. If he ever gets his chance to blow Mao to Kingdom Come, it will be with no hard feelings whatsoever.

What LeMay really hates, with an abiding and never slaked passion, is first and above all the U. S. Navy. If war were the product only of hate and not of institutional patterns, it is the Navy the Strategic Air Command would strike some black night in swift preventive action before those "web-footed" (a favorite phrase of LeMay's) so-and-so's could get more money out of Congress for contraptions the Air Force regards as useless and competitive. Russia is a necessary anti-hero in the Air Force's dramaturgy, but the Navy is Enemy No. 1 from of old. This sibling feud began with the bomber vs. battleship controversy; one of its earliest episodes was the trial "bombing" of the battleship *Utah* three years before World War II. LeMay's account hints darkly at "perfidious tactics" in the War Department through which enemy spies, naval spies that is, obtained advance information on the Air Force's plans in that test. Hate and suspicion of the Navy appear and reappear as the darkest thread in his story. This is because, short of abolishing the Navy altogether, it has to have its own aircraft in support of its traditional functions. Planes must protect surface ships, provide them with reconnaissance, supply them with firepower in battles against other ships, hunt out submarines and lay mines. The Army, too, could use its own tactical air forces; both the Russians and the Germans, in different ways, effectively provided close support planes under the direction of the ground commander. But the U.S. Army gave up its fight to control its own tactical arm long ago and clings only to its helicopters. The Navy, on the other hand, not only refused to throw in the sponge but hit the Air Force an unforgivable blow in developing the carrier, a floating air base with its own planes. This ended the Air Force dream of controlling all military aviation, and made peaceful coexistence between Air Force and Navy unthinkable.

LeMay's other unforgivable enemy is McNamara. For LeMay no ideological difference could be deeper than their dispute over the manned bomber. But the inexorable logic of industrial society and the airpower it spawned are against LeMay. The rise of airpower has from the beginning injected the idea into warfare that the machine was more important than the man. And the supersonic speed and enormous complexity of modern combat airplanes have reduced the pilot to a relatively minor cog in a machine. As McNamara said in giving the death blow three years ago to LeMay's last great bomber project, the B-70, the bomber has become a manned missile with "none of the advantages or flexibility generally attributed to manned bombers." Their flight has to be directed from the ground in "pre-planned attack against previously known targets," a mission better performed by the swifter and simpler unmanned missile. LeMay, by the strange reversal of events, has come to seem a Don Quixote in his old age, as he has seen more and more of his airmen go underground like moles to tend missiles. Billy Mitchell envisaged pilots as a new chivalric order of the air; they have instead become sitters for panels of pushbuttons. Yet while LeMay despises McNamara as a factory manager, he himself reveals throughout his story the attitudes not so much of a warrior as of a great industrial expert, albeit in demolition. The machine molded him and the machine threatens to replace him—and the machine, like the policies he advocates, lacks mind and heart.

But this tough old troglodyte is not through yet. The whole Air Force drive in Vietnam is to transform the war we can't win to a war we might; from a war for the loyalties of the Vietnamese people into a war to destroy them; this is giving the obsolete B-52 its last murderous gasp over South Vietnam's jungles and rice paddies. There is also China, weak and with only a few atom bombs. The Air Force recognizes the mutual stand-off in its relations with the Soviet Union, but its Strategic Air Command hungers for a last chance against China. LeMay in retirement, unmuzzled, could be more dangerous than when he was Air Force Chief of Staff. The delusion of an easy victory-by-airpower may yet bog us down like the Japanese in endless land war with mankind's most numerous and enduring people. This is the danger.

Epilogue:
For a Universal Day of Atonement

The final word: a reflection on the tragic nature of twentieth-century history, occasioned by the guilty verdict pronounced on December 11, 1961, on Adolf Eichmann, the Nazi mass murderer sometimes called the "Chief Executioner" of the Third Reich.

.   .   .

December 18, 1961

WALKING AROUND EAST BERLIN IN 1959, I wandered into a theatre where a movie was playing called *Sterne* (Stars). The stars were the stars of David the Jews wore in the Hitler period. It was a Bulgarian–East German film about a Jewish concentration camp girl with whom a Wehrmacht officer falls in love. Later he joins the Partisans after she is packed into the freight cars for Auschwitz. When I heard that the Eichmann verdict had finally been handed down in Jerusalem, I remembered a scene in that film when the concentration camp inmates first heard rumors that the Germans were burning up people in crematoriums. They went to their leader, an old Jewish doctor, and he reassured them saying, *"Aber die Deutschen sind auch Menschen,"* i.e., "The Germans are also human." He feels no human being could possibly do anything so wicked; the rumors couldn't be true.

In that darkened movie house, amid all those Germans, I cried, remembering the survivors with whom I travelled as a reporter from Poland to Palestine in the spring of 1946, and the stories they told me. I haven't had the heart to follow the Eichmann trial. This one man in the dock is too trivial beside the mountainous toll of humiliation and death he symbolized. Whether sincerely or not, the picture he drew of himself was a picture likely to appeal to many Germans as guilty as he—the picture of the fussy bureaucrat who only did his duty, a cog in a machine. How easily the Germans excuse themselves.

But we learn nothing by blaming them. Events since the war have prepared greater crematoriums. Everywhere men excuse themselves the same way. We dropped "little" bombs on the innocent in Hiroshima and Nagasaki. Now we and the Russians together are prepared to drop bigger ones. The issues have become blurred. And these dreadful truths have become stale and futile commonplaces we all ignore.

I don't know what the verdict will be on Eichmann. I don't care. But it would honor world Jewry if the judges were to refuse even in his case, with all it implies, to impose the death penalty Israel abolished. It would be a noble rebuke to an un-Christian Christian world and to a still brutal Russian communist world of death sentences for minor offenses—to two worlds which share the poison of anti-Semitism still despite the Gospels they respectively proclaim and the horror to which Hitler showed it could lead. Let Eichmann live on like Cain, with the Mark upon him.

It is more important to recognize that the Mark is on all of us. What good is it for Moscow to accuse Heusinger of war crime when Khrushchev himself threatens it on a greater scale, and we do likewise? Would an extraterrestrial tribunal after a new war distinguish between Russians and Americans and Germans? Is mass murder justified for any reason whatsoever? Is not every national leader a war criminal if he does not recognize that no dispute justifies risking the future of our common human species?

I would proclaim a day of meditation on the crematoriums a universal Day of Atonement. I would remember that we all marched with Eichmann to the prison or the gallows. Whether it was the human incinerator or the H-bomb, we built it. To be human is to be guilty. No other message has the dimensions to match what Eichmann's trial recalled.

INDEX

PublicAffairs is a publishing house founded in 1997. It is a tribute to the standards, values, and flair of three persons who have served as mentors to countless reporters, writers, editors, and book people of all kinds, including me.

I.F. STONE, proprietor of *I. F. Stone's Weekly*, combined a commitment to the First Amendment with entrepreneurial zeal and reporting skill and became one of the great independent journalists in American history. At the age of eighty, Izzy published *The Trial of Socrates*, which was a national bestseller. He wrote the book after he taught himself ancient Greek.

BENJAMIN C. BRADLEE was for nearly thirty years the charismatic editorial leader of *The Washington Post*. It was Ben who gave the *Post* the range and courage to pursue such historic issues as Watergate. He supported his reporters with a tenacity that made them fearless and it is no accident that so many became authors of influential, best-selling books.

ROBERT L. BERNSTEIN, the chief executive of Random House for more than a quarter century, guided one of the nation's premier publishing houses. Bob was personally responsible for many books of political dissent and argument that challenged tyranny around the globe. He is also the founder and longtime chair of Human Rights Watch, one of the most respected human rights organizations in the world.

For fifty years, the banner of Public Affairs Press was carried by its owner Morris B. Schnapper, who published Gandhi, Nasser, Toynbee, Truman, and about 1,500 other authors. In 1983, Schnapper was described by *The Washington Post* as "a redoubtable gadfly." His legacy will endure in the books to come.

Peter Osnos, *Founder and Editor-at-Large*